A Dash . . .

A Pinch . . .

A Smidgen . . .

More Than A Cookbook

A Collection of
Recipes and Remembrances
presented by the
Grady County Historical Society

A Dash... A Pinch... A Smidgen . . .
More Than A Cookbook

Published by
Grady County Historical Society
P. O. Box 586
Cairo, Georgia   39828

ISBN: 0-9748935-0-1

First Printing, October, 2003
Second Printing, February, 2004

Table of Contents

Cookbook Committee

Carolyn Herring Chason
Shirley Maxwell Gale
Annette Carter Harrell
Betty Nowell Hester
Alice Courtney McCorkle

Donna Cooper Powell
Lyn Richardson Robinson
Gloria Robinson Searcy
Barbara Chapman Williams

Acknowledgements

Mary Chason
Chason and Willett
Elizabeth L. Cline
W. L. Duke
Kenneth Gale
Bobby Harden
Karen Harrison
Betty Hester

Debbie Jenkins
Miss Myrt's
Richard A. Powell
Rockdale Transport Services
Roddenbery Memorial Library
The Cairo Messenger
John W. Walker
Judy Walsh

The Grady County Historical Society wishes to express our sincere appreciation to the many people who took the time to share favorite recipes and remembrances to make this more than a cookbook. Some of the recipes are treasured family keepsakes. We hope you enjoy the treasured memories on the pages that follow.

Poppy China

"Poppy China", the 'Olivia' pattern by Homer Laughlin, featured on the covers, served as a common denominator in the rural south during depression times. The richer people used it for their everyday dishes, while the poorer used it on Sunday--or if you only had a few pieces, you used it all the time!

These dishes were available at redemption centers in most towns. Many families saved the coupons from Octagon Soap wrappers and Silver Cow Evaporated Milk labels to get these premiums.

The glass tumblers were received for purchasing Standard coffee from the route man who visited the homes on a regular basis.

These dishes and glasses are now much sought after collectibles.

Carolyn H. Chason

A Dash... = 1/8 Teaspoon
A Pinch... = 1/16 Teaspoon
A Smidgen... = 1/32 Teaspoon

In The Beginning . . .

Grady County, A Background Sketch

Grady County is considerably younger than most of Georgia's other 159 counties, only seventeen being younger. It, along with seven other counties, was created in 1905, and named for Henry Woodfin Grady, the famous Georgia journalist and orator who championed the "New South" movement for the southern states during the decade of the 1800s.

The geographic area from which it was created, however, was Creek Indian territory until 1814, and belonged neither to the United States nor the State of Georgia. During the War of 1812, Georgia became involved in fighting both Great Britain and the Creek Indians. The Lower Creeks, who lived mostly in Georgia, were sympathetic to the United States, but the

Upper Creeks, living mostly in Alabama, aligned themselves with Great Britain and were the source of many barbaric massacres and unrelenting depredations. To quell the threat of the marauding Upper Creeks, Andrew Jackson and his Tennessee Militia were sent to help subdue them. In March 1814, Jackson was successful in defeating the Creeks in the famous battle of Horseshoe Bend on the Alabama River. Five months later, he forced them to sign the Treaty of Fort Jackson, by which the Creeks gave up nearly all their lands in Alabama and a strip across the southernmost part of Georgia, which included the territory that would eventually become Grady County.

The provisions of the Treaty, however, permitted the Lower Creeks to remain on the ceded territory east of the Chattahoochee River, supposedly to serve as a buffer between the angry Upper Creeks and the Spaniards and Seminoles in Florida. Georgians were greatly displeased with this provision, for in a very short time the region became a thoroughfare for the renegade Upper Creeks to move southward to join the Seminoles in Florida. This caused another vexing situation and it was not until 1818, near the end of the First Seminole War, that the ceded strip of land in Georgia passed from federal ownership to the State of Georgia. The legislature in Milledgeville acted promptly, and on December 15, 1818, passed an act dividing the newly ceded territory into the three large counties of Early on the west, Irwin in the middle, and Appling on the east, and authorized it to be surveyed into land lots and districts. To provide for a rudimentary Inferior Court system of government to conduct business and to hold elections, the three counties were formally organized in 1819. In the same year, Spain ceded Florida to the United States, thereby removing another deterrent to settlement of Georgia's newest frontier.

Before the creation of the counties, a few white Indian traders had moved into the area, but they were located adjacent to the Creek villages, which were mostly concentrated along the Flint and Chattahoochee Rivers. To encourage settlement, Georgia made land ownership in Early, Irwin, and Appling counties available to its citizens by the 1820 Land Lottery Act. Most of the "fortunate" drawers did not want to move into the desolate pine and wiregrass barrens, and willingly sold their newly acquired land at prices considerably lower than land value elsewhere in the state. Eager for land, pioneer settlers mostly from the Carolinas, with a fewer number from Virginia and elsewhere, were willing to relocate, many of them having already migrated to middle Georgia. They purchased large tracts of the cheap land and, by the early 1820s, settlement was well underway.

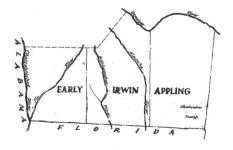

The Land Lottery of 1820 distributed the land in Early, Irwin, and Appling counties. (This territory had been ceded by the Creeks in 1814-1815).

The only roads in the wiregrass-pine barrens were primitive three-notch wagon trails where Indian paths had previously existed, and most of its streams were not navigable, except by canoe or small flatboat. Deprived of accessible transportation, the pioneers were forced into a self-reliant way of life, one of subsistence farming and herding, even though they were large landowners. Lack of any efficient transportation also played a role in subdividing the three large border counties into smaller ones to better accommodate county business and government. In 1823, Decatur County was created from the southern portion of Early, and in 1825, Thomas County was formed from the eastern part of Decatur and a part of Irwin. It was eighty years later before an eastern strip of Decatur and a western strip of Thomas were used to create Grady County.

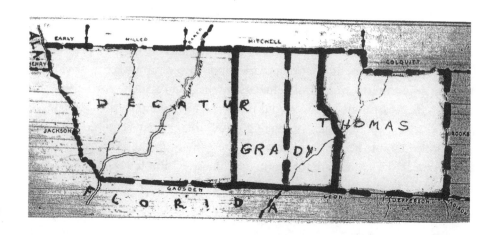

The act creating Grady County from portions of Decatur and Thomas Counties was signed in 1905 with the new county to be established on January 1, 1906.

Proposals for a new county, to possibly be named Maxwell, originated as early as 1904. This spawned much wrangling and heated debate between the local proponents who wanted to be a separate county and others who were opposed. As momentum for a new county gained wider acceptance, the major issue of contention became the location of the county seat. Both Whigham and Cairo were intensely desirous of that distinction. After bitter infighting and considerable influential political maneuvering, Cairo was finally chosen. The official signing of the Act to create Grady County occurred on August 17, 1905. Later in October of that year, an election for the citizens to choose county officials was held, and on January 1, 1906, the newly created county began operating as a separate unit of Georgia's state government organization.

The dreary pine and wiregrass barrens to which the original settlers came proved to be most beneficial, with bountiful supplies of timber, an abundance of streams, and soils that produced fertile, prime farmland. It has been characteristic that persons who came to the area have tended to remain, and family names of the earliest inhabitants are still commonplace in Grady and the surrounding counties. Only after the two World Wars and a shift from subsistence to commercial based farming, has there been any significant change in the make up of the area's population. Even so, Grady County can still be promoted as being included in "The Greatest Diversified Farming Area of America."

Wayne Faircloth

Wiregrass and pine trees

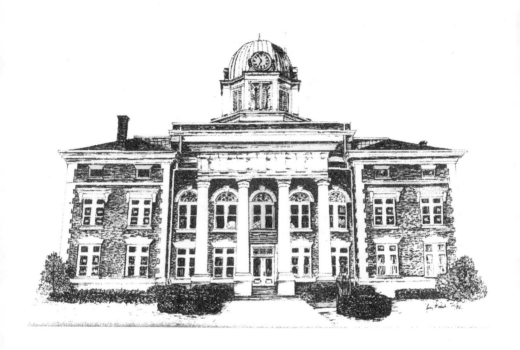

Grady County Courthouse

The Grady County Courthouse was built in 1908 for $60,000. It had three stories, an attic, and a cupola with a clock and was considered one of the prettiest public buildings in Georgia. It was destroyed by fire on February 18, 1980.

The Grady County Museum and History Center
(Cairoga Club Building)

Just north of the railroad on the west side of Broad Street stands a structure that was built by W. B. Roddenbery in 1920. It replaced an old wooden building that at the time of its demolition was, probably, the oldest in Cairo. The new business house had three stores on the ground level—the gents' furnishing store, owned by J. W. Britt, the Sanitary Barber Shop, B.J. Lumley, proprietor, in the middle section, and the end store (south) occupied by Tony Mike. The second floor was used by a social, athletic club, which also acted somewhat like a Chamber of Commerce. Later the second floor was used as offices for the Roddenbery enterprises.

In 1993, the building was donated to the Grady County Historical Society for use as a museum. The Board of Commissioners of Grady County assumed ownership in 1994 and leases the structure to the society for as long as it remains in use as a museum or depository for the historical or other items of interest to the citizens of Grady County.

Funds for repairs, renovations, and improvements have come from Society fundraisers, an insurance claim, Governor's Discretionary Fund Grants, a Pioneer Hibred International grant, and a $50,000.00 matching grant from an anonymous donor.

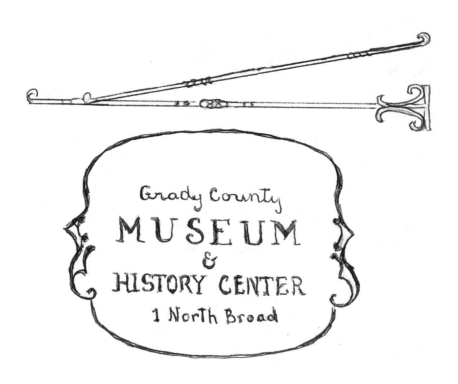

Appetizers . . .

Ballad-Faulkner-Faulk House

The Miller Brothers built this one story frame house with a hip roof and gable for Mrs. Phate (Fannie) Ballad in 1907. It was sold to George Faulkner in 1929 and about twenty years later to Jack Key. Other owners were Hudson Rossi, Ernest Faulk, and Grace Merritt. It is located on Broad Street in Pine Park.

Cheese Ball with Black Olive and Onion

2   8-ounce packages cream cheese
1   stick of butter or margarine
¼   cup spring onion, chopped
¼   cup black olives, chopped
½   cup chopped toasted pecans

Cream margarine and cream cheese. Add onions and black olives. Mix well form ball, roll in chopped toasted pecans. Refrigerate until ready to serve with crackers. Can be frozen.

Lyn Robinson

Given to me by a friend from Conyers about 1980.

Cheese Ball

2   8-ounce packages cream cheese
¼   cup of chopped celery
¼   cup chopped onions
¼   cup chopped bell pepper
1   8-ounce can crushed pineapple, well drained
1   tablespoon seasoned salt
1   cup chopped nuts

Mix all ingredients except nuts. Form ball, roll in chopped nuts. Cheese ball is best if made and refrigerated a couple of days ahead of serving.

Fay Brannon

Chili Cheese Log

2   8-ounce packages cream cheese
3   tablespoons salsa
1   1.25-ounce package chili seasoning mix
Grated Monterey Jack cheese

Blend chili seasoning mix, cream cheese, and salsa. Shape into log or desired shape. Garnish with Monterey Jack cheese and nuts if desired.

Donna Cooper Powell

Almond Chicken Ball

2   8-ounce packages cream cheese, softened
2   tablespoons steak sauce
1½   cups minced cooked chicken
⅓   cup minced celery
¼   cup minced green onions
¼   cup chopped pimento
¼   cup fresh parsley, divided
¼   cup chopped toasted almonds
Wheat crackers

Combine cream cheese, steak sauce, and chicken; blend well. Add celery, onions, pimento, and 2 tablespoons parsley; mix well. Shape chicken mixture into a ball. Wrap in wax paper and chill 4 hours or overnight. Toss reserved parsley with almonds. Roll ball into parsley mixture until well covered. Serve with wheat crackers.

Nancy C. Clark

Egg Rolls

Meat, cut in small pieces (Chicken, pork, or shrimp)
½   cup dry sherry
2   tablespoons cornstarch
3   tablespoons soy sauce
1   medium cabbage, shredded
3   medium carrots, shredded
2   stalks celery, shredded
1   large Spanish onion, sliced
5   tablespoons oil, divided
1   can sliced water chestnuts
1   can sliced and pieces mushrooms
Egg roll wrappers

Mix sherry, cornstarch, and soy sauce. Add meat and marinate for 30 to 45 minutes. Heat 3 tablespoons oil in large wok, frying pan, or boiler; add meat and stir constantly until is cooked (will turn white). Remove meat from pan. In 2 tablespoons oil, add vegetables and cook, stirring occasionally until cabbage and onions are transparent. Add meat, chestnuts, mushrooms, and stir well. Heat thoroughly. Cool; wrap in egg roll wrappers, seal with a (little) cornstarch in water. Fry in wok or frying pan in deep fat until golden brown.

Dot Dalton

Bacon Wrapped Water Chestnuts

2   cans whole water chestnuts
1   pound bacon, cut in thirds
1   12-ounce bottle cocktail sauce
1   cup sugar

Wrap each chestnut in bacon piece. Secure with toothpick. Place in baking pan in single layer. Bake at 400 degrees for about 30 minutes or until brown. Heat cocktail sauce mixed with sugar until dissolved. Place cooked bacon wrapped chestnuts in serving dish and cover with sauce.

Ruth Sims

Tortilla Roll Ups

1   8-ounce package cream cheese
1   small can green chiles
1   bunch green scallions, chopped
6   ounces grated Monterey Jack cheese
6   ounces grated cheddar cheese
1   package flour tortillas

Mix filling ingredients in food processor. Spread mixture evenly on tortillas and roll up. Refrigerate to chill. Cut into bite size pieces. Serve with salsa.

Pam Mason

Cheese Krispies

2   cups all-purpose flour
2   cups Rice Krispies
8   ounces sharp cheese, grated
2   sticks margarine
¼   teaspoon cayenne pepper

Sift flour and cayenne pepper together; cut in margarine and add cheese. Mix well. Drop by ½ teaspoons on cookie sheet and flatten with fork. Bake at 350 degrees for 12 to 15 minutes.

Agnes Williams

Monterey Jack Cheese Crisps

1   pound package KRAFT Monterey Jack cheese (Must be Kraft)
Cayenne pepper

Cut cheese into ¼-inch thick slices, then cut into 1-inch squares. Place squares 3 inches apart on parchment lined cookie sheet. Bake in preheated 400 degrees oven for 8 to 10 minutes or until golden brown. Sprinkle with cayenne pepper after cooking. Remove, cool, and store in airtight container. Yield 35 to 42 crisps.

Andrea Powell Webb

Cheese Straws I

2   8-ounce packages sharp Kraft cheese
3½   cups sifted flour
2   sticks Blue Bonnet oleo
1   tablespoon Tabasco sauce
½   teaspoon salt
¼   teaspoon red pepper

(Grate cheese and leave out overnight with oleo). Mix and beat well until very creamy. Sift all dry ingredients and add to cheese mixture, small amounts at the time. Mix well. Add Tabasco and mix well. Put through cookie press. (I use long flat strips and cut before baking). Bake at 325 degrees for 10 to 15 minutes. Do not brown.

Edith M. Prevatte

Recipe given to me by the late Mrs. E. A. Rogers, Pelham, GA. (She stressed using Kraft cheese and Blue Bonnet oleo). She baked wedding cakes, tea cakes, cheese straws until well into her nineties. Many from Grady and Mitchell Counties experienced her baking at one time or another.

Cheese Straws II

1   pound sharp Cracker Barrel cheese, grated
1   stick margarine, softened
2¼   cups flour
1½   teaspoons baking powder
3   teaspoons cold water
¼   teaspoon cayenne pepper

Cream cheese and margarine. Add dry ingredients. Mix well. Bake at 325 degrees for 10 to 15 minutes or until done.

Lucy Singleton

Recipe given to me by Helen Sellers, received from her mother- in-law, Mrs. Leon Sellers.

Olive Puffs

1   10-count can biscuits
1   small jar stuffed olives
Parmesan cheese

Cut each biscuit into quarters. Shape quarter around well drained olive. Roll into ball and roll in cheese. Bake on ungreased baking sheet in 375 to 400 degrees oven for 6 to 9 minutes. Can bake ahead and freeze. Yield 40 puffs.

Cheryl Hunziker

Salsa Shrimp in Papaya

12   ounces cooked shrimp, rinsed and drained
¾   cup salsa
½   teaspoon lemon pepper seasoning
3   ripe papayas, halved, peeled, and seeded
Lettuce leaves
Fresh parsley, chopped
Lemon slices and juice

Sprinkle lemon juice over shrimp. Add salsa and seasonings, cover and marinate for 1 hour or overnight. Arrange papaya on lettuce leaves, fill with shrimp. Garnish with parsley and lemon slices. Good with chilled white wine and bread sticks. Yield 6 servings.

Nancy Baker Beasley

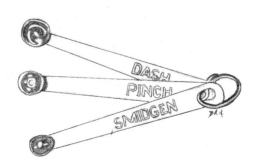

Sugared Peanuts

2   cups sugar
1   cup water
5   cups peanuts

Melt sugar in water in heavy boiler and pour in peanuts. Cook on high heat until thick and nuts are coated. Pour and spread evenly on greased cookie sheet. Bake at 300 degrees about 45 minutes, turning every 15 minutes with wooden spoon. Let cool before eating or bagging.

Linda Hopkins Perry

Sugared Nuts

2   cups pecan halves
½   cup water
1   cup sugar

Mix all ingredients and cook over medium heat until crystallized about 10 minutes. Spread on buttered pan and salt lightly. Bake at 300 degrees for 15 minutes. Turn nuts and continue baking for 15 minutes. Do not over bake. Other nuts may be used.

Louise Anderson

Parching Peanuts
Conventional Oven Roasting
Place raw peanuts, in shell or shelled, one layer deep in a shallow baking pan. Roast in a 350 degrees oven for 15 to 20 minutes for shelled and 20 to 25 minutes for in-shell peanuts. Remove from heat just short of doneness desired as peanuts continue to cook as they cool.
Microwave Oven Roasting
Place 2 cups raw shelled peanuts in a 10 x 6-inch glass dish. Dot with butter or margarine. Microwave on high for 2 minutes. Stir. Continue to cook 2 minutes at a time--followed by stirring until peanuts have been microwaved 10 to 12 minutes. Remove from microwave to cool. Season to taste.

White Trash

1	12-ounce box Golden Graham cereal
1	12-ounce box raisins
3	cups roasted peanuts (24-ounce jar)
2	cups peanut butter
1	12-ounce package semi-sweet chocolate morsels
1	stick margarine
1	16-ounce box confectioners sugar

Mix cereal, raisins, and peanuts in large container. Melt over low heat, butter, peanut butter, and chocolate morsels; stirring well. Let cool and pour over cereal mixture and mix well. After cooling, place mixture in large paper bag. Pour in box of sugar and shake until mixture is coated. Keep in airtight container. Makes enough for a crowd.

Mary Robertson

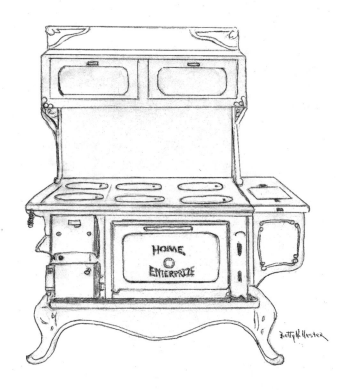

Dipper's Delight

Pineapple Sauce
1   12-ounce jar pineapple preserves
¼   cup prepared mustard
¼   cup horseradish

Combine all ingredients in saucepan. Cook over low heat, stirring for 5 minutes until thoroughly blended.

Dill Sauce
½   cup sour cream
½   cup mayonnaise
2   tablespoons finely chopped dill pickle
1   teaspoon dill weed

Combine all ingredients. Let stand at room temperature 1 hour to allow flavors to blend.

Royalty Sauce
1   cup catsup
6   tablespoons margarine
2   tablespoons vinegar
1   tablespoon brown sugar
½   teaspoon dry mustard

Combine all ingredients in saucepan. Cook over low heat for 5 minutes, stirring constantly. Serve any of above sauces with fried chicken tenders.

Nancy C. Clark

Kathy Lindgren's Summer Dip

1   16-ounce container large curd cottage cheese
1   large tomato, diced
1   small can green chiles, chopped
Green onions, chopped
Lawry's seasoning, to taste

Combine all ingredients. If made too soon, tomato juices will settle. Make and serve same day.

Jamie Lindgren Porter

Sonya's Dip for Kielbasa or Smoked Sausage

Grape or Apple Jelly
Mustard

Mix to taste. Beat with a mixer to give smooth consistency.

Jamie Lindgren Porter

Mexican Dip

1   pound ground beef
1   pound ground hot sausage
1   large onion, chopped
1   can cream of mushroom
1   8-ounce jar picante sauce
1   pound Velveeta cheese

Brown ground beef, sausage, and onion; drain. Pour in crock pot or large thick boiler. Add soup, cheese, and sauce. Cook on low heat. Serve with dip chips. Makes a large quantity.

Joy Hickey

I make this recipe for church get-togethers. It is easy to make and is always a hit.

Shrimp Dip

1   cup boiled shrimp, peeled, and chopped
1   .7-ounce Good Seasons Italian salad dressing mix
1   16-ounce carton sour cream

Mix all ingredients and refrigerate until ready to serve. Best if made a day ahead. Best served with Fritos Scoops.

Shirley Gale

I just threw the ingredients together for a party several years ago and it was very simple and so good. I have made it many, many times.

Onion Dip

2   cups Vidalia onions, chopped
2   cups mayonnaise
2   cups Swiss cheese, grated

Mix, heat, and serve as dip. Wheat thins are good with this dip.

Emelynn Carlisle Odom

Mississippi Sin

1   loaf French bread
1½   cups sour cream
2   cups shredded cheddar cheese
1   8-ounce package cream cheese, softened
⅓   cup chopped green onion
½   cup chopped ham
⅓   cup chopped green chiles
1   teaspoon Worcestershire sauce
Dash of Tabasco sauce
Salt and pepper to taste

Hollow out bread, reserve for dipping. Mix all ingredients; pour inside, replace top and wrap in foil. Bake at 350 degrees for 1 hour. Can mix ingredients up ahead. Good with dip style Fritos.

Nancy Baker Beasley

Artichoke Spinach Dip

1   14-ounce can artichoke hearts, drained and chopped
1   10-ounce package spinach, thawed and drained
1   large onion, chopped
1   4.5-ounce can chopped green chiles, drained
1   2-ounce jar pimento, drained
¾   cup mayonnaise
¾   cup grated Parmesan cheese
¾   cup grated Italian style cheese
¾   cup grated cheddar cheese
2   tablespoons sour cream
¼   cup green onions, sliced
Dash garlic powder and black pepper

Combine all ingredients, reserving portion of cheddar cheese and green onions for garnish. Spread evenly in baking dish. Sprinkle with remaining cheese and onion. Bake at 350 degrees for 30 minutes. Garnish with cherry tomatoes.

Andrea Powell Webb

Mexican Cheese Dip

1   16-ounce carton sour cream
1   envelope ranch dressing mix
1   package Kraft Mexican cheddar cheese
1   3-ounce package bacon bits

Mix sour cream and ranch dressing. Add cheese and bacon bits until the consistency to dip with chips. Great with Fritos Scoops or Torengos Tortilla chips.

Julie W. Stewart

Hot Crab Dip

1   8-ounce package cream cheese, softened
2   6½-ounce cans crab meat (or frozen)
4   ounces sour cream
1   tablespoon mayonnaise
3   teaspoons Worcestershire sauce
1   teaspoon prepared mustard
3   dashes of garlic salt (optional)
½   cup grated cheddar cheese, divided

Beat cream cheese until smooth; add remaining ingredients. Put in a 1½ quart baking dish, add remaining cheese. Bake at 350 degrees for 30 minutes. Serve with Fritos Scoops.

Karen (Mrs. Embree) Robinson

Hot Broccoli Dip

1	10-ounce package chopped broccoli, drained
½	cup chopped onion
½	cup chopped celery
½	cup chopped mushrooms
3	tablespoons margarine
¼	cup chopped pimento
1	10¾-ounce can cream of mushroom soup
1	6-ounce tube garlic cheese or Cheez Whiz with dash of garlic powder
¼	teaspoon lemon juice
⅛	teaspoon seasoned salt

Dash of Tabasco sauce
Can of crabmeat (optional)

Sauté onion, celery, and mushrooms in margarine. Combine broccoli, soup, and cheese; cook on low heat until cheese melts. Add sautéed vegetables to mixture, stirring well. (Add crabmeat, if desired.) Serve hot with crackers or toast points--remove crust from bread and cut bread into 4 triangles; spread with margarine and toast for 30 minutes at 350 degrees until golden brown.

Andrea P. Webb

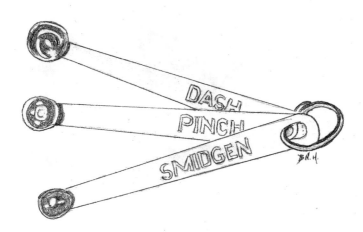

Pepperoni Pizza Dip

½   cup mayonnaise
1   8-ounce carton chives and onion cream cheese
1   3-ounce package pepperoni, chopped
¾   cup grated Parmesan cheese
2   tablespoons chopped ripe olives
⅓   cup pizza sauce
¼   cup minced green pepper
⅓   cup sliced green onion
½   teaspoon Italian seasonings

Combine all ingredients; spoon into 1 quart baking dish. Bake at 350 degrees for 20 minutes. Sprinkle extra Parmesan cheese and broil 1 to 2 minutes. Garnish with extra green onion and ripe olives. Serve warm with crackers and chips.

Andrea P. Webb

Smoked Mullet Dip

1   cup mullet flakes, boneless, baked or smoked
8   ounces cream cheese
2   tablespoons grated onion
½   teaspoon Spanish paprika
1   tablespoon lemon juice
2   celery stalks, chopped fine
Seabreeze salt to taste

Mix mullet with other ingredients; serve with favorite crackers.

Seabreeze Salt
1   cup salt
1   heaping tablespoon black pepper
1   heaping tablespoon white pepper
1   heaping tablespoon garlic powder

Mix ingredients well.

Hazel Logue

I had never eaten mullet until I came to South Georgia. It is so good. These recipes are from my daughter as mullet is her favorite fish to eat.

Dried Beef Dip

1   large jar Armour Dried Beef, chopped fine
1   pint sour cream
¾   cup chopped pecans
2   tablespoons Hidden Valley Ranch dressing mix (optional)

Mix well. Chill and serve.

Sharon Whitfield

Alabama Caviar

2	15½-ounce cans black-eyed peas, drained
½	cup chopped onion
½	cup chopped green pepper
½	clove garlic
¼	cup sugar
¼	cup vinegar
1½	teaspoons salt

Black pepper and hot sauce to taste

Place toothpick in garlic clove. Mix peas, onion, green pepper, and garlic. Dissolve sugar, vinegar, and salt over low heat; add to peas mixture. Refrigerate 12 hours. Remove garlic clove. Serve with Fritos Corn chips. Great for New Year's parties, picnics, and football gatherings.

Dot Dalton

Chili Con Queso Dip

2	pound box Velveeta
2	small cans taco Sauce
2	small cans green chiles

Jalapeno pepper, chopped fine
Dashes of hot sauce

Melt all together in double boiler.

Frances McNaughton

This dip is an excellent appetizer and was served many times during the years in the military in the many places where we were stationed--France, India, and in the U.S.

Beverages . . .

Broome House

In the late 1800s, Elisha and Sophie R. Broome built their home in the Reno Community.

Berry Wine

1   quart blackberries
3   pounds sugar (6 cups)
1   cup hot water

Mix in a plastic or glass container. Stir with a wooden spoon. To test for sweetness, place a clean raw egg in mixture (if egg floats, sugar is ok--if egg sinks add more sugar until egg stays afloat). Remove egg after test. Let mixture set for 14 days then strain and bottle up. Store in cool dark place.

Annette P. Blackmon

Recipe was passed down by Ethel Gainous Gringer (born 1879). Her family's remedy for upset stomach was a ¼ to ½ cup dose of this berry wine.

Blackberry Shrub

Use ripe blackberries. Wash. Cover with apple vinegar (2 years old) and cook until soft. Strain and sweeten juice to taste; boil down until it is the consistency of thick syrup. Bottle and put in a cool dark place. When serving, use 3 or 4 tablespoons to a glass of cold water.

Carolyn H. Chason

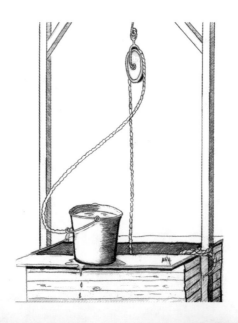

Eggnog

2½   dozen eggs
1¾   pounds sugar
¼   gallon whiskey
½   gallon cream, whipped

Separate eggs, beating yolks very well for ½ hour. Add sugar slowly, beating for another ½ hour. Add whiskey (this amount makes nog very strong, use less if you wish or to taste), and continue beating, taking an hour to complete whiskey, small amount at a time; add whipped cream and white of eggs beaten stiff. This recipe makes 2½ gallons. Shake or stir before serving.

Joyce Van Landingham

This recipe was from my Uncle R.T. McManeus (1935).

My Eggnog

1 egg per person (separate yolks and whites). Beat whites until real stiff, adding 1 teaspoon of sugar for each white. Beat yolks until light; add 1 tablespoon sugar for each egg yolk. Add 1 tablespoon whiskey for each egg yolk. Mixture should be thick. Fold in the stiff whites. Fold in a small container of whipping cream, whipped until stiff. Fold gently into other mixture. Serve with a dash of nutmeg atop each cup.

Nancy Baker Beasley

Recipe is from Newell Thornton Baker from her father Rufe Newell Thornton. I still remember Mother and Daddy mixing this up on New Year's Eve. We usually had several other couples from our street in for this. After the "nog" we all went out onto the street and burned our Christmas trees. A nice memory.

Nellie's Eggnog

6   eggs
1   cup sugar
1   pint whipping cream
1   tub Cool Whip
3   ounces Bacardi Rum
1   pint bourbon

Separate the eggs, putting the yolks in large mixing bowl and the whites in smaller bowl. Beat the yolks at medium speed and slowly add the cup of sugar until the mixture is a light, creamy texture. Add rum and bourbon at a slower speed until everything is well mixed. Set bowl aside. Beat the egg whites until stiff and fold into the yolk mixture. Next, beat the whipping cream until stiff and fold this into the mixture. Fold in a tub of Cool Whip. Continue folding the mixture until most of the lumps are gone. Chill the eggnog for 1 hour. Serve in coffee cups, sprinkle with nutmeg and enjoy spoonfuls of this delicious holiday concoction. Serves 8 to 10 people.

John L. Mason

Hot Chocolate Mix

1   box powdered milk (5 or 6 quarts)
½   cup powdered sugar
1   cup Nestle's Quik
½   cup Cremora

Mix powdered milk, sugar, Nestle's Quik, and Cremora. Store in airtight container. Use ¹/₃ cup mix to 1 cup hot water.

Deborah Phillips

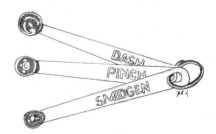

Julius' Orange Drink

1   6-ounce can frozen orange juice concentrate
1   cup milk
1   cup water
1   teaspoon vanilla flavoring
10 to 12 ice cubes

Put all in blender. Blend. Serve and enjoy! Serves 4 to 6.

Austin Tyler

Quick Coffee Punch

½   cup instant coffee
2   cups hot water
1   cup sugar
1   gallon milk
½   gallon chocolate ice cream
½   gallon vanilla ice cream

In saucepan combine coffee, water, and sugar. Bring to boil, stirring frequently. Remove from heat and cool. Pour into punch bowl; stir in milk and add ice creams. Stir to mix.

Nancy Clark

Russian Tea

1	gallon water
2	sticks cinnamon
30	whole cloves
2	cups sugar
5	tea bags
1	6-ounce frozen orange juice
2	tablespoons lemon juice

Boil water, cinnamon, cloves, and sugar for 5 minutes. Add tea bags. Steep 5 minutes. Strain and add juices.

Kathryn Miller Jones

This recipe was given to me by Louise Roberts.

Wassail

2	quarts apple juice
1	pint cranberry juice
¾	cup sugar
2	sticks cinnamon
1	teaspoon whole allspice
1	small orange studded with cloves
1	teaspoon rum flavoring

Mix apple and cranberry juice together in crock pot. Add sugar, cinnamon sticks, allspice, orange with cloves, and flavoring. Cook on high for 1 hour or on low for 4 to 8 hours.

Deborah Phillips

Jell-O Punch

1   3-ounce package Jell-O (any flavor, choose by desired color)
1   46-ounce can pineapple juice
1   46-ounce can grapefruit juice (or equivalent frozen juice)
1   cup boiling water
1   tablespoon almond extract
1   cup sugar
2   cups cold water
1   quart bottle ginger ale

Dissolve gelatin in hot water, add sugar and other ingredients except ginger ale. Mix well. Chill. Pour over ice and slowly add ginger ale, just before serving. May thicken after 24 hours. Serves 25.

Carolyn J. Hopkins

This recipe is from Jean Jones of Camilla, Georgia.

Cranberry Punch

¾   cup packed brown sugar
1   cup water
¼   teaspoon salt
¼   teaspoon nutmeg
½   teaspoon cinnamon
½   teaspoon ground cloves
2   16-ounce cans jellied cranberry sauce
3   cups water
1   quart pineapple juice

Day before make syrup. Bring to boil sugar, water, salt, and spices. In kettle crush cranberry sauce with fork, add 3 cups water. Beat until smooth with whisk or mixer. Add pineapple juice to the hot syrup. Simmer about 5 minutes. Serve cold or serve hot with dots of butter and cinnamon sticks. Makes 2½ quarts.

Laurie Carlisle Conradi

This recipe came from Mrs. Edwin Carlisle.

Gwen's Punch

25 packages Kool-Aid
12 pounds or 22½ cups sugar
2   large frozen orange juice
1   small frozen orange juice
3   small frozen lemon juice or lemonade
2   quarts pineapple juice plus 1 pint
5   quarts ginger ale
6¼ gallons water

Mix all of the above except ginger ale. Add ginger ale just before serving.
250 punch cup servings.

Carolyn J. Hopkins

Peach Punch

48   (12-ounce) cans peach concentrate
3½   gallons water
2   quarts champagne (optional)
4½   quarts ginger ale
3   pints orange juice
1½   cups pineapple juice
1½   cups lemon juice
3   quarts fresh peach halves and slices

(If peach concentrate is not available, prepare a puree of fresh, ripe peaches, using your blender to achieve the desired smoothness.) Mix all liquid ingredients. Add peach halves and slices into the punch just before serving. Serves 200.

Carolyn H. Chason

This punch was introduced at the Georgia Executive Mansion and is served on many state occasions. Recipe was given to me by Georgia's first lady in 1965.

Punch for any occasion

Juice of 1 dozen lemons (No bottled stuff, Please)
1   46-ounce can pineapple juice
1   46-ounce can orange juice
2   cups sugar
½   gallon water
1   tablespoon almond flavoring
1   teaspoon vanilla flavoring
1   quart ginger ale

Combine all ingredients except ginger ale and allow to meld. Chill and add ginger ale when ready to serve.

Shirley Gale

Recipe was given to me by a friend many years ago. It is easy, economical, and delicious.

Similar recipe submitted by Helen C. Bishop.

Sherbet Punch

2   liter bottle of ginger ale
1   46-ounce can pineapple juice
½   gallon raspberry sherbet

Combine the ginger ale and juice in a punch bowl. Add scoops of sherbet just before serving. Throw in some fresh and/or frozen fruit for a final touch.

Claire C. Willett

Vacation Bible School Punch

Tea
Pineapple juice
Grape juice

Mix all ingredients together and serve over ice.

Annette C. Harrell

Recipe was my grandmother Sarah Palmer Harrison's (born 1880) greatest joy. It was her "mission" to make and take this punch to Vacation Bible School at Pine Level Baptist Church each year and serve to all the boys and girls. It was usually served in a #3 washtub with a dipper. This was one of my fondest memories of my VBS years.

Sassafras Tea

To make sassafras tea we would go to the woods and find a sassafras bush. We would get the roots and wash until clean. We would boil the roots and make the tea. Syrup was used as our sweetener.

Margaret P. Courtney (1912-2003)

I remember helping my mother gather the roots from the woods.

DIPPER GOURD

Salads . . .

Cannon House

In 1889, this house was built for Francis and Augusta Wight Brannon. It was considered one of Cairo's prettiest homes. It was bought by the Hugh G. Cannons and owned by them for over sixty years. It is now owned and being restored by the Wilkes Nicholsons.

Cranberry Salad

2   3-ounce packages cream cheese
2   tablespoons mayonnaise
2   tablespoons sugar
1   16-ounce can whole cranberry sauce
1   8-ounce can crushed pineapple
½   cup nuts, chopped
1   8-ounce carton whipped topping

Soften cream cheese; blend in mayonnaise and sugar. Add fruit and nuts. Fold in whipped topping. Pour into flat pan or foil lined muffin cups. Freeze until firm.

Agnes Williams

Cranberry Waldorf Salad

1½   cups cranberries, chopped
1   apple, chopped
1   cup celery, chopped
1   cup seedless grapes, halved
⅓   cup raisins
¼   cup walnuts, chopped
1   tablespoon sugar
¼   teaspoon cinnamon
1   8-ounce carton vanilla yogurt, nonfat

Mix all ingredients together and toss. Cover and chill for at least two hours.

Pearl Thomas

Creamy Fruit Salad

1   8¾-ounce can fruit cocktail
1   3-ounce package apricot gelatin
1   cup boiling water
1   3-ounce package cream cheese
¹/₃   cup mayonnaise

Drain fruit, reserving syrup. Add water to syrup to make ½ cup. Combine gelatin and boiling water in blender, low speed until dissolved. Add measured liquid, cream cheese and mayonnaise. Blend on high speed. Pour in a 9 x 13-inch dish. Chill until firm. Garnish, if desired. 6 to 8 servings

Laurie Carlisle Conradi

This is the recipe of Oze Carlise Mixon.

Divinity Fruit Salad

3   egg yolks
3   tablespoons sugar
3   tablespoons vinegar
2½   cups marshmallows
1   #2 can crushed pineapple, drained
1   cup nuts, chopped
1   pint whipping cream, whipped

Mix first three ingredients together and slowly heat in a double boiler. Add marshmallows and stir until dissolved. Remove from heat. Add pineapple and nuts. Fold in whipped cream. Chill.

Carolyn H. Chason

This recipe was a favorite family Christmas dinner dish of the late Sarah C. Thursby (Mrs. Howard), who shared it with me in the late 1950s.

Lime Jell-O Salad

1   3-ounce package lime Jell-O
1   cup hot water
½   cup sweet milk
½   cup mayonnaise
½   cup cottage cheese
1   8-ounce can crushed pineapple, drained
1   cup pecans, chopped

Mix gelatin with hot water. Add milk, mayonnaise, and cottage cheese. Let stand until almost congealed and add pineapple and pecans.

Mary Ellen Schafer

Our Favorite Mandarin Salad

1   large orange gelatin
1½   cups boiling water
1   large can crushed pineapple
1   can mandarin oranges
1   6-ounce can frozen orange concentrate
1   small package instant lemon pudding
1   cup cold milk
1   cup whipped topping

Dissolve gelatin in boiling water. Add pineapple, mandarin oranges, and orange concentrate. Stir well. Put into oblong dish and congeal. When congealed; mix lemon pudding and milk. Fold in whipped topping. Spread mixture over salad.

Nancy C. Clark

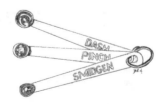

Pineapple Salad

1   cup chopped pretzels
1   stick margarine, melted
½   cup sugar
1   8-ounce cream cheese, softened
1   8-ounce carton whipped topping
⅓   cup sugar
1   large can pineapple tidbits
½   cup pecans, chopped

Mix pretzels, margarine, and ¼ cup sugar together. Spread on cookie sheet and bake at 350 degrees for 7 minutes. Set aside. Mix cheese, sugar, pineapple; add nuts, mix well. Fold in whipped topping. Refrigerate until ready to serve. Before serving, stir pretzel mixture and salad mixture together. Use as a salad or light dessert.

Betty Ragan

Recipe from my nephew's wife, Martha Massey of Tifton, Georgia. It is very good.

Pink Salad

1   3-ounce package strawberry gelatin
1   cup whipped cream or cool whip
½   cup pecans, chopped
1   8-ounce can crushed pineapple, undrained
1   cup cottage cheese

Combine gelatin and pineapple in saucepan. Bring to a boil for 3 minutes, stirring occasionally to prevent sticking. Cool. Fold in cottage cheese, cream or cool whip and pecans. Refrigerate until firm.

Pearl Thomas

This was a recipe that my aunt, Virginia Thomas Rosser, used. It is easy and good!

Stir and Go Salad

1   3-ounce package gelatin (any flavor)
1   8-ounce can crushed pineapple
1   cup cottage cheese
1   cup cherries
1   cup whipped topping, thawed

Empty dry gelatin in a bowl. Stir in other ingredients. Chill and go.

Sue Askew

Mama's Frozen Salad

2   small containers Cool Whip (59 cents size)
1   cup sour cream
1½   cups sugar
1   large can crushed pineapple, drained
1½   cups pecans, chopped
5   mashed bananas
½   cup chopped cherries

Combine ingredients in order listed. Put in large Pyrex dish and freeze.

Sonya Porter

Bean Salad

1   can green limas
1   can Blue Lake string beans
1   can garbanzo chick peas
1   can yellow wax beans
1   bell pepper, cut fine
¾   cup sugar
1   teaspoon pepper
1   teaspoon salt
¾   cup vinegar
¼   cup Mazola oil

Drain all the vegetables. Mix sugar, pepper, salt, vinegar, and oil. Heat until sugar melts. Pour over vegetables and marinate overnight in the refrigerator. Note: Keeps for several days and gets better and better.

Alice Shores Dodson

Bloody Mary Salad

1   envelope unflavored gelatin
½   cup water
1   cup Bloody Mary cocktail mix
¼   cup chopped onion
¼   cup chopped celery
Lettuce leaves
¼   cup mayonnaise

Sprinkle gelatin in water and heat slowly until gelatin is dissolved. Stir in cocktail mix. Chill until consistency of unbeaten egg white. Stir in onions and celery; pour into individual molds and chill until firm. Serve on a lettuce leaf with a dab of mayonnaise.

Nancy Baker Beasley

Great with egg casserole as brunch dish or late night dinner. We used to serve this at midnight on New Year's Eve.

Broccoli Salad

Bunch of Broccoli flowerettes, cut in small pieces
4 to 5 strips cooked bacon, crumbled
1 cup white raisins
1 Vidalia onion or purple onion, cut up
1 cup mayonnaise
1 tablespoon white vinegar
1 to 2 teaspoons sugar

Mix all ingredients together and marinate a few hours or overnight in the refrigerator.

Louisa Perkins

Crunchy Broccoli Slaw

1 bag broccoli slaw
¼ cup vinegar
½ cup sugar
½ cup oil
1 package Ramen noodles (any flavor, don't use the seasonings)
½ cup sunflower seeds
¼ cup sliced almonds

Mix first 4 ingredients and marinate for several hours or overnight. Add nuts and seeds. Break noodles into small pieces and add. Mix together and serve.

Betty Ragan

This recipe was given to me by my daughter, Peggy McAuley Ford, who received it from a friend, Susan Griffith, in Dallas.

Cabbage Salad

½   cup oil
¼   cup sugar
¼   cup white vinegar
1   package chicken flavored Ramen noodles, broken
2   dashes of pepper
1   bag shredded cabbage
4   green onions, chopped
2   tablespoons sunflower seeds
1   small package slivered almonds

Mix oil, sugar, vinegar, chicken flavored Ramen noodles ,dash of pepper. Mix and set aside. Shortly before eating, mix in cabbage, onions, sunflower seeds, and almonds. Mix well and serve.

Celeste C. Tyler

Carrot and Pineapple Salad

1   3-ounce package orange gelatin
1   cup hot water
1   small can crushed pineapple
½   cup diced celery
1   tablespoon vinegar
½   cup grated carrots

Blend the gelatin and hot water. Add remaining ingredients. Chill in salad mold.

Ann Robertson

Corn Salad

2	12-ounce cans of shoepeg corn, drained
2	tomatoes, seeded, drained, chopped (do not peel)
1	bell pepper, seeded and chopped
1	purple onion, chopped
1	cucumber, peeled, seeded, and chopped
½	cup sour cream
4	tablespoons mayonnaise
2	tablespoons white vinegar
½	teaspoon celery seed
½	teaspoon dry mustard
½	teaspoon black pepper; salt to taste

Mix all together. Refrigerate overnight. Good with barbecue, burgers, and stuffed tomatoes.

Pam Mason

Cornbread Salad

1	8½-ounce box Jiffy Corn Muffin Mix
1	package Ranch Salad Dressing Mix
1	cup sour cream
1	cup mayonnaise
2	16-ounce cans pinto beans, drained
½	cup onions, chopped
½	cup green bell pepper, chopped
3	large tomatoes, chopped
2	cups shredded cheddar cheese
1	16-ounce can whole kernel corn, drained

Prepare corn muffin mix according to directions. Cool and crumble. Combine ranch mix, sour cream, and mayonnaise; set aside. Place ½ of the crumbled cornbread in the bottom of a large serving bowl or dish. Top with ½ of pinto beans, onion, bell pepper, tomatoes, cheese, and corn (in layers). Spread ½ of the salad dressing mixture over the top. Repeat all layers using the other ½ of all ingredients. Garnish top as desired (tomatoes, cheese, etc.) Cover and chill for 2 hours.

Betty W. Harrison

Georgia Cornbread Salad

1   box Jiffy cornbread mix
1   12-ounce package bacon
1   cup sweet pickle relish with juice
3   large tomatoes, chopped
1   large bell pepper, chopped
1   large Vidalia onion, chopped
1   cup mayonnaise

Prepare cornbread according to directions. Cool and crumble into small pieces. Cook bacon, drain, and crumble. In a large glass bowl, layer half of cornbread, relish and juice, tomatoes, onion, peppers, bacon and ½ cup mayonnaise. Repeat. Serve chilled. This is best made with really good tomatoes. Don't be afraid to use more mayonnaise, if you need to.

Mary H. Chason

Freezer Cucumber Salad

6   cucumbers, peeled and sliced thinly
2   teaspoons salt
1   2-ounce jar chopped or sliced pimentos
½   cup sugar
½   cup white vinegar
¼   cup vegetable/olive oil
1   teaspoon dried dill weed

Mix salt and cucumbers and let stand for 2 hours. Drain. Mix sugar, vinegar, and oil in a small saucepan. Bring to boil. Let cool. Add pimentos and dill to cucumbers. Toss cucumbers with cool dressing. Do not drain. Package in freezer containers. Maybe frozen up to 2 months. Makes about 3 pints.

Betty W. Harrison

Our Favorite Chicken Salad

3   cups chopped meat (use leftover chicken or turkey breast)
½   cup salad dressing (Miracle Whip)
½   cup sliced almonds
½   cup chopped celery
½   cup pickle cubes, sweet
¼   cup chopped red apple
½   teaspoon salt
Pepper to taste (white or black)

Mix all of above together, refrigerate at least 3 hours--serve on bed of lettuce or as a sandwich filling. Leave meat very chunky when using for a salad. White tuna can be used.

Wynell Mitchell

Pasta Salad

1   8-ounce package pasta shells
½   cucumber, diced
½   green bell pepper, diced
½   red/yellow bell pepper, diced
16   ounce bag four cheese, shredded
1   package Italian dressing season mix
½   cup sugar
½   cup mayonnaise
¼   cup vegetable oil
¼   cup white vinegar

Cook pasta according to directions and cool. Mix pasta, cucumber, bell peppers, and cheese together. In a different bowl, mix sugar, mayonnaise, vegetable oil, vinegar, and Italian dressing. Pour over pasta mixture and stir. (Best served cold)

Allison M. Bass

This recipe from my Aunt Deb was served at my wedding reception.

Macaroni Salad

1   can condensed milk
¼   cup sugar
½   cup vinegar
2   cups mayonnaise
1   teaspoon salt

Combine all ingredients for dressing.

1   package (14 to 16 oz) macaroni, cooked, drained, and cooled
1   cup green pepper, cut up
Diced onion, to taste
4   carrots, shredded
½ to ¾ cup cheddar cheese, shredded

Combine all ingredients in salad bowl; mix well and pour dressing over the mixture. Mix. Store in tightly covered container and refrigerate. This makes a big batch and keeps for several days.

Celeste Chason Tyler

Recipe shared by a sister-in-law; it is a favorite at "potlucks" here in the Mid-West.

Mama's Potato Salad

3½	pounds potatoes (10 medium), cubed
6	hard-boiled eggs
1	medium onion, finely chopped (use Vidalia onions if in season)
½	cup mayonnaise
½	cup evaporated milk
1	tablespoon Dijon mustard
3	tablespoons balsamic vinegar
¼	cup sugar
¼	cup homemade pickles, finely chopped
1	teaspoon salt
½	teaspoon pepper

Paprika (optional)

Cook potatoes in boiling, salted water until tender. Drain and cool. Separate hard-cooked egg yolks from whites. Set yolks aside. Chop whites and add to potatoes in bowl. Add onion to potatoes. In small bowl, mash yolks. Stir in mayonnaise, milk, vinegar, mustard, sugar, salt, and pepper. Pour over potato salad and mix well. Taste and adjust seasonings, if needed. Garnish with egg slices and paprika. Chill until serving time. Serves 12 to 15.

Julie W. Stewart

My family enjoys this recipe at family dinners, reunions, and church fellowships.

Greek Salad

One head lettuce
1   large or two small tomatoes
1   medium yellow onion
Juice from 1½ lemons
8   Greek olives (calamata)
6   ounces block of feta cheese
½   teaspoon Cavender's Greek Seasoning
Salt, black pepper, dried oregano to taste
1   teaspoon Tabasco sauce
3   ounces light olive oil

Tear lettuce into bite size. Slice tomatoes bite size. Dice onion fine. Add lemon juice, olives, feta, Cavender's, salt, pepper, and oregano. Note: Do not add Tabasco sauce and olive oil until ready to serve. Mix well and serve.

Chuck Thomas

Peas and Tomato Aspic

1   3-ounce box lemon gelatin
2   cups tomato juice
Salt and pepper to taste
1   tablespoon sugar
1   tablespoon vinegar
1   cup canned English peas
1   cup diced celery

Prepare gelatin as directed using tomato juice instead of water. Stir well. Add salt, pepper, sugar, and vinegar. Stir well and let cool. Add drained peas and celery. Pour into mold to congeal. Serve on lettuce. Use mayonnaise to garnish if desired.

Pearl Thomas

Strawberry Aspic

1   can stewed tomatoes
2   tablespoons grated onion
3   tablespoons tarragon vinegar
2   shakes of Tabasco sauce
½   teaspoon salt
1   small package strawberry gelatin

Blend tomatoes and onion in blender; add vinegar, Tabasco, and salt. Bring to a full boil and stir in gelatin. Chill in mold or glass dish.

Danielle Lewis Jones

Poppy Seed Dressing

¾   cup sugar
⅓   cup cider vinegar
1   teaspoon salt
1   teaspoon dry mustard
1   teaspoon onion, finely grated
1   cup vegetable oil
1   tablespoon poppy seed

Combine sugar, vinegar, salt, mustard, and onion in a small mixing bowl; beat with electric mixer until sugar dissolves. Continue to beat slowly adding oil. Stir in poppy seeds. Cover and chill thoroughly; stir before serving. Yield 1¾ cups.

Emelynn Carlisle Odum

Raspberry Vinaigrette Dressing

1   tablespoon Dijon mustard
1   tablespoon sour cream
1   teaspoon sugar
½   cup of **Raspberry vinegar**
¼ to ½ cup olive oil

Whisk together to the consistency you like (some people like a more vinegary dressing). Pour over salad greens.

Pam Mason

J.R. White House

Built during 1912 by a local building crew, this house was the home of Mr. and Mrs. J.R. White. Mr. White died during World War II and his wife continued to live in the home until her death in 1972. Nan and Arley Fisher purchased the home in 1984 and began restoration, renovation, and a split level addition.

Breads . . .

Clower-Southall-Kelly-Brown House

This beautiful home was built circa 1911 for Dr. and Mrs. Eugene Clower. It was sold to the Southall family who lived here for many years. Dr. and Mrs. Lumis Brown and boys are now the owners.

Hushpuppies

1   cup plain cornmeal
½   cup plain flour
1   teaspoon baking powder
1   teaspoon salt
1   teaspoon sugar
½   cup onions, chopped
1   16-ounce can creamed corn
Water

Mix dry ingredients. Add onions and corn. If too stiff, add a little water.
Drop by heaping teaspoons into hot oil. Cook until brown.

W.H. (Billy) Hester

Southern Fried Cornbread

1   cup fine Sholar's Cornmeal
2   cups water
Cooking oil
Salt

Mix and let sit for 5 minutes. Add more water if needed. Pour into hot,
heavily greased flat wrought iron baker or frying pan and cook on medium
heat.

Betty Hester

Mama Mitchell's Muffin Bread

3 to 4 tablespoons fat (shortening)
1   cup plain cornmeal
½   cup plain flour
1   teaspoon baking powder
¼   teaspoon salt
½   teaspoon sugar
2   eggs
Buttermilk (enough to make cake batter consistency)

Heat fat in baking pan or iron skillet. Sift dry ingredients together 3 times. Put into mixing bowl. In separate bowl, mix eggs and buttermilk--DO NOT BEAT--stir just enough to break yolks. Briefly stir—do not beat--liquid into dry ingredients. Add 1 tablespoon of fat to batter. Pour into hot skillet. You should hear sizzling sound. Spread if necessary using a minimum of touching. Bake at 375 to 400 degrees for about 12 to14 minutes (until top is pleasingly brown.)

Frances Mitchell

Mama Mitchell (Mrs. Nora) said, "The batter 'sposed' to look holey (bubbly) and light." None of my mother's 3 daughters have been totally successful in making it taste and smell "just like Mutha's." Cook a batch and call me to come and taste it. Recipe submitted in memory of Nora Dalton Mitchell by her "knee-baby".

Cornbread I

1   cup plain white cornmeal (medium grind)
1   tablespoon flour
2   teaspoons baking powder
½   teaspoon salt
¼   teaspoon baking soda
1   cup buttermilk
1   egg, slightly beaten
3   tablespoons melted shortening, oil, or bacon drippings

Preheat oven to 450 degrees. Generously grease 6 or 7-inch round iron skillet with shortening and heat in oven until very hot. Place meal, flour, baking powder, soda, and salt in mixing bowl. Mix buttermilk and egg; add to dry ingredients. Pour melted shortening or bacon grease into mixture and mix well. Pour batter into hot skillet. Place in oven and bake about 20 minutes or until brown on top. Cool somewhat, then remove bread by turning it upside down onto serving plate. Slice like a pie. (Pointed ends make it easier to "sop syrup".)

Mrs. Ben F. Brinkley, Jr.

Recipe found in a very old cookbook after desperately seeking a cornbread recipe that would please my father-in-law after his precious wife died and I became his main cook. It's the only thing I cooked that he asked for again, and again, and again! B.F. loved to eat it with a glass of cold buttermilk

Corn Sticks

2	eggs, well beaten
1½	cups buttermilk (or 1 cup buttermilk and ½ cup water)
½	teaspoon baking soda (add little more if the milk is real sour)
¼	teaspoon salt
2	teaspoons baking powder
1½	cups cornmeal (approximately)
1	tablespoon sugar
2	tablespoons oil

Preheat oven to 400 degrees. Grease corn stick pan well and put in the oven until it gets hot. Add milk, shortening, and salt to the beaten eggs. Add meal, being careful while adding as meal varies and the batter should be a medium batter. Beat smooth. Dissolve soda in a spoonful of cold water. Stir in baking powder and soda. Add to mixture, stir well, and pour into hot corn stick pan. Bake until the corn sticks are light brown and crusty. (Approximately 15 to 20 minutes).

Claire Chason Willett

My grandmother (Elizabeth J. Herring) made these corn sticks often, for they were favorites of her grandchildren when we were growing up.

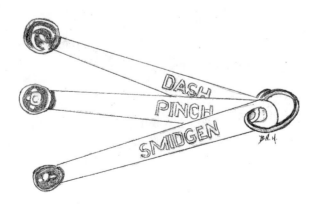

Cornbread Muffins

1   cup all-purpose flour
¾   cup cornmeal
1   tablespoon sugar
1   tablespoon baking powder
¾   teaspoon salt
2   eggs
1   cup milk
¼   cup oil

Mix dry ingredients together. Mix milk, eggs, and oil; add to dry ingredients and mix. Bake at 400 degrees for 20 minutes. Yields 12 muffins. Makes good cornbread dressing.

Doris Harrison

Recipe given to me by Laura Lee of Cairo.

Similar recipes submitted by Christine Cooper and Esther H. Carter.

Cornbread II

1   cup cornmeal
1   teaspoon salt
½   teaspoon baking soda
2   teaspoons baking powder
1   egg
1   cup buttermilk
2   tablespoons bacon drippings

Preheat oven to 450 degrees. Sift dry ingredients. Beat egg into buttermilk. Combine dry ingredients with egg and buttermilk mixture until just blended. Pour bacon drippings in a cast iron pan; pour batter into pan. Bake for 15 to 20 minutes. Slice and serve.

Gladys Ponder

David's Cornbread

2   parts cornmeal (I use Alabama white fine ground)
1   part self-rising flour
Milk to make consistency
Salt to taste
Grease (bacon drippings)

Mix ingredients to a thick mixture and spoon into a well-greased cast iron griddle. Bake at 400 degrees until brown, about 20 to 25 minutes. Butter while warm and eat with vegetables, especially greens. Cornbread is good when eaten warm or cold with a glass of iced tea.

David L. Stewart

I use an antique cast iron griddle to cook this recipe that belonged to my grandmother, Minnie Spearman Owens Bryant, mother of Lucy Belle Owens Stewart.

Pone Bread

2   cups corn meal
2   tablespoons cooking oil
1   teaspoon salt
2   teaspoons baking powder
2   teaspoons sugar
1½   cups milk

Preheat oven to 400 degrees. Mix all ingredients. If too stiff, add more milk. Heavily grease baking pan; heat pan in oven before making the little pones (patties). Dough should be just stiff enough to hold shape. Bake about 20 minutes. If bottoms are brown but tops are not, turn on broiler unit--but keep watch!

Sarah Chason

This is one of my dad's favorite breads.

Cracklin' Bread

2   cups cornmeal
1½   cups finely broken cracklin's
1½   cups milk or water
1½   teaspoons salt
¼   cup grease (bacon drippings)

Soak cracklin's in hot water, enough to cover. Mix all ingredients. Make into small patties and place in large greased skillet. Grease top of patties. Bake in hot oven, 450 degrees about 20 minutes or until golden brown.

Wynell Mitchell

Crackling Bread

2   cups cornmeal
1½   cups milk or water
1½   cups finely broken cracklings
1   egg
1½   teaspoons salt

Mix all ingredients thoroughly and pour into greased pan. Top of bread should be greased before baking. Bake for 1 hour at 325 degrees..

Winnie Prince

Cush

2   tablespoons meat drippings
2   tablespoons butter
3   cups cornbread and biscuits
Salt and pepper to taste
1   chopped onion
2   eggs, well beaten
1   teaspoon ground sage
Sweet milk

Heat meat drippings and butter in a heavy skillet. Break up cold cornbread and biscuits. (Use more cornbread than biscuits.) Add to hot fat, salt, pepper, onions, and eggs. Stir and cook until light brown. Add sage and butter. Add milk to make a soft, mushy batter and cook until fairly dry. (Note: The mushy batter can be baked at 350 degrees for 15 minutes.)

Kathryn Miller Jones

What is the origin of "CUSH"? Whoever or whatever, this economy dish is well known in various Southern states as bread.

Georgia Breadcrumb Pancakes

1   tablespoon butter or margarine
1½ cups sour milk
1   cup dry breadcrumbs
2   eggs, well beaten
½   cup flour
½   teaspoon salt
1   teaspoon baking soda
½   cup blueberries or strawberries

Melt butter or margarine, add to milk; pour over crumbs. Add eggs and dry ingredients sifted together. Mix well. Add berries. Drop by tablespoonfuls on hot greased griddle. Small cakes are easier to manage.

Kathryn Miller Jones

Whole Wheat Bread

1   package yeast
¼   cup shortening
½   cup brown sugar
1   teaspoon salt
2¾   cups warm water
3½   cups whole-wheat flour
4   cups white flour

Add yeast, salt, sugar, and shortening to warm water and mix well. Add whole wheat flour and 1 cup white flour; stir. Add enough white flour to make dough that leaves the side of the bowl. Turn out onto floured board and knead enough to make smooth dough, adding flour as necessary. Put dough into greased bowl, cover, and let rise until double in size. Punch down and turn on board. Divide in half and let dough rest 10 to 15 minutes. Form 2 loaves and put into greased loaf pans. Allow to rise until dough is level with top of pan. Bake at 375 degrees for 45 minutes. Cover with foil for last 20 minutes if necessary to prevent crust from becoming brown.

Kathryn Miller Jones

Recipe given by Dorothy Jones.

Buttermilk Biscuits

2   cups self-rising flour
⅓   cup Crisco shortening
1   cup buttermilk

Mix flour and Crisco until crumbs form. Add buttermilk--maybe a little less than cup. Form into a soft ball of sticky dough. Dump on a floured board and knead until smooth. Roll to ½-inch thickness and cut with a water glass. Cook in pre-heated 450 degrees oven for 20 minutes, until brown. Serve with fried apples and country ham.

Susan Yancy Perkins

David's Homemade Biscuits

Self-rising flour
Buttermilk
Salt to taste

Pour the amount of buttermilk you want into a bowl and whip with spoon the amount of flour you want to add until it is thick. NO grease in the biscuit mixture. Spoon dough into a heavy cast iron griddle. Pat the top of biscuit with grease to have a golden color on top. Bake at 425 degrees for 15 to 18 minutes. Butter as desired.

David L. Stewart

These are called syrup-sopping biscuits. The key to having a great biscuit is whipping with a spoon. I use my grandmother's antique cast iron griddle and also use the same recipe to cook biscuits on the old wood stove. Our wood stove is old and still in excellent condition and I prepare old fashioned meals when we get together with friends. My recipes are fond memories of the meals served at home with our family of thirteen children.

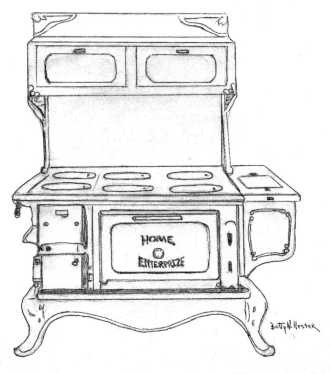

Mexican Cornbread

1¾   cups cornmeal
1   tablespoon baking powder
½   teaspoon baking soda
⅓   cup cooking oil
1   teaspoon salt
½   teaspoon sugar
1   cup buttermilk
1   cup cheddar cheese, grated
2   jalapeno peppers, chopped
2   eggs
½   cup onion, chopped
½   cup bell pepper, chopped
1   can creamed corn

Mix all ingredients together and put in greased 9 x 13-inch pan. Bake at 350 degrees for 25 to 30 minutes.

Carolyn Trawick

Recipe from my mother and a family favorite.

Julie's Oatmeal Bread

1¼   cups water
1   cup quick oatmeal
½   cup soft butter
1   cup sugar
1   cup brown sugar
2   eggs
1   teaspoon vanilla extract
1½   cups plain flour
¾   teaspoon cinnamon
½   teaspoon salt
1   teaspoon baking soda
¼   teaspoon nutmeg

Boil water and take off stove, add oatmeal and let sit covered with lid for 20 minutes. Beat butter until creamy. Add sugars and beat until fluffy. Add eggs and vanilla, beat until fluffy. (Beating is key to having moist bread.) Mixture will be thick at this point. Add oatmeal and blend. Mixture will get creamier at this point. While everything is beating, in another bowl, combine and sift flour, cinnamon, soda, and nutmeg. Stir into creamed mixture. Pour into greased and floured pans. Bake at 350 degrees for 40 to 45 minutes. (Check for doneness after 35 minutes.) Recipe makes 4 loaves. Freezes well.

Carolyn Fulton

Sour Milk Griddle Cakes

2   cups flour
1   teaspoon salt
1   teaspoon baking soda
2   cups sour milk
1   egg, beaten
1   tablespoon melted shortening

Sift flour and salt. Dissolve soda in the milk and add to the flour mixture.
Add egg and shortening. Mix well. Drop by tablespoon on a hot, well-
greased griddle and brown on both sides. Serve hot with syrup or jam.

Pearl Thomas

Recipe of my mother, Pearl Maxwell (Mrs. George G., Jr.) Thomas.

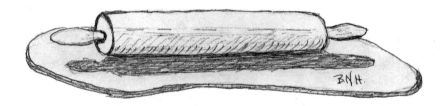

Georgia Bread

1½	cups plain meal
1	tablespoon flour
1	teaspoon baking powder
1	teaspoon salt
½	cup syrup
2	eggs
½	stick butter, melted
1	tablespoon grated orange rind
¼	cup milk

Mix together with wire whisk. Pour into greased pan. Bake at 375 degrees until done.

Yvonne Childs

This recipe was used almost daily when my Mom (Zelda Sanders Hiers) and her sisters, Ruby Sanders Faircloth and Lillian Sanders Durham, were growing up in the Nicholville community. After doing some experimenting, my Mom, Aunt Zelda, Aunt Lillian and I came up with what we think is almost a duplicate recipe. They had no sugar, so they used syrup extensively as sweetener. Georgia Bread and Syrup Pies were favorites of my great grandmother, Zanobia White Miller (1853-1920) and my grandmother, Maggie Belle Miller Sanders. Zanobia made them for many years prior to 1900.

Sally Lunn (Williamsburg)

½   cup butter
½   cup sugar
4   eggs, beaten
1   cup milk
1   yeast cake dissolved in ¼ cup lukewarm water
4   cups flour
½   teaspoon salt
1   teaspoon baking powder

Cream butter and sugar, add eggs. Add milk and yeast with water. Sift flour and salt, add to mixture. Set to rise for 2 hours. After mixture rises, beat in baking powder. Pour into a shallow pan and let it rise for 1 hour. Bake at 450 degrees for 15 minutes. Cut into squares and serve hot.

Mabel Van Landingham Kral

This bread was a specialty of Lillian and Gladys Paulk. They grew up in Cairo and their home was where Jenkins IGA Grocery is now located. They taught in Columbia, S.C., and came home for the holidays, summers and retirement. They were first cousins to Roscoe Van Landingham. They delighted in seeing that the stockings of the five Van Landingham children were bountifully filled.

Sweet Potato Pone

3   cups grated raw sweet potatoes
½   cup brown sugar
1   cup cane syrup
3   eggs
2   cups sweet milk
½   cup melted butter
½   teaspoon cinnamon
½   teaspoon allspice
Dash salt

Combine all ingredients. Place mixture in greased baking dish and bake at 350 degrees for about 1½ hours.

Winnie Prince

Recipe handed down to my sisters and me from our mother.

Ham and Cheese Muffins

2   cups self-rising flour
½   teaspoon baking soda
1   cup milk
½   cup mayonnaise
½   cup finely chopped, cooked ham
½   cup shredded cheddar cheese

Combine flour and soda in large bowl. Combine milk and mayonnaise; stir in ham and cheese. Add this mixture to dry ingredients. Stir just until moistened (batter will be similar to biscuit dough). Fill greased muffin pans ²/₃ full. Bake at 425 degrees for 16 to 18 minutes. Yield 12 muffins. Great for brunch or Sunday dinner.

Julie W. Stewart

Recipe given to me by Belinda Smith.

Ever-Ready Muffins

1   15-ounce box Raisin Bran
5   cups all purpose flour
3   cups sugar
5   teaspoons baking soda
2   teaspoons salt
4   eggs, beaten
1   quart buttermilk
1   cup corn oil

Combine first 5 ingredients in a very large bowl. Make a well in center of mixture; add eggs, buttermilk, and oil. Stir just enough to moisten dry ingredients. Cover and store in refrigerator until ready to bake. (Batter can be kept in refrigerator as long as 6 weeks.) When ready to bake, spoon batter into greased muffin tins, filling ²/₃ full. Bake at 400 degrees for 12 to 15 minutes. Yield 5½ dozen.

Eleanor Lee

Yeast Rolls

1   cup scalded milk, cooled
½   cup sugar
1½   teaspoons salt
1   stick margarine, melted
3   eggs, beaten
1   cup warm water
1   teaspoon sugar
2   packages yeast
6   cups flour (4 white and 2 wheat)

Dissolve yeast in warm water and 1 teaspoon sugar; set aside. Combine eggs, milk, sugar, margarine, and salt. Add yeast mixture and flour; stir well. Batter will be soft. Refrigerate overnight. Knead on floured board (you can roll out or pinch off in balls). Place on greased baking sheet or muffin pan Let rise 1½ hours. Bake at 375 degrees until brown. Yield 3 dozen.

Patsy (Pat) Bentley

Amy Brown's Hot Rolls

1	package dry yeast
¼	cup warm water
1	cup milk, scalded
2	teaspoons shortening
2	tablespoons sugar
1	teaspoon salt
1	egg, well beaten
2¾	cups enriched flour

Soften yeast in water at 110 degrees. Combine milk, shortening, sugar, and salt. Cool to lukewarm. Add yeast; add egg, gradually stir in flour to form soft dough. Cover, let rise in warm place until double in size. Turn out on floured board, roll and cut into 3 x 4-inch pieces. Fold into about 3 x 2-inch roll. Place on grease baking sheet. Let rise to double in size. Bake at 400 degrees about 15 minutes.

Thomas William Brown, son of late Perry Glenn and Aleyne Williamson Brown

Recipe, probably, from Amy Brown's mother, Mrs. William B. Brown (nee Claude Catherine Maxwell (1872-1942).

Celia's Spoon Bread

Combine 2 beaten eggs with 1 cup of sifted cornmeal, 2 tablespoons shortening, 1 teaspoon salt, 2 teaspoons of baking powder, and 1 cup of sweet milk. Mix all together. Stir in 1 cup of cold cooked grits. Put in baking dish. Place dish in a pan of water. Bake 40 minutes in 350 degrees oven.

Maggie Roddenbery

My mother's recipe, possibly, brought with her from Virginia in early 1900s.

Doughnuts

4   cups sifted flour
1   teaspoon salt
2   teaspoons baking powder
1   teaspoon nutmeg (optional)
1   cup sugar
1   egg, beaten
2   cups milk
2   tablespoons melted shortening
1   teaspoon vanilla

Sift together flour, salt, baking powder, and nutmeg. Add sugar and mix to a light, soft dough with egg, milk, shortening, and vanilla. Turn onto well-floured board, roll to ½-inch thick, cut with doughnut cutter. Cook about 3 minutes in deep, hot fat--360 to 375 degrees turning as they rise to the top of hot oil. Drain on paper towel and sprinkle with powdered sugar.

Patsy (Pat) Bentley

My mom used this recipe from the Rumford Complete Cookbook (1944) to make these when I was a child.

Fried Syrup Biscuits

Slice 4 cold biscuits (left over from previous meal) into 3 slices for each biscuit. Fry on medium heat in grease and/or butter until lightly browned. Pour into cast iron frying pan enough cane syrup to cover biscuits, adding butter during cooking stage. Let cook until syrup is of medium consistency (making sure it does not candy).

Esther H. Carter

My Cheese Biscuits

8   cups self-rising flour
1   teaspoon salt
8   rounded tablespoons Crisco (about the size of an egg)
2   cups milk
6   cups grated cheddar cheese (approximately)

Chop shortening into flour and salt. (I use my food chopper.) Add milk. This should be a very "gooey" mixture. Work by hand the cheese into the flour mixture well. Keep the mixture soft (not too much flour worked in). Take ½ of mixture and place on floured wax paper or pastry sheet. Roll out to about ¼-inch thickness. Cut with biscuit cutter. Place on 2 large, greased, thick baking pans. Bake at 400 degrees for 10 minutes.

Laurie Carlisle Conradi

Recipe of Annie Laurie Carlisle. A favorite of young and old, we enjoyed these all our lives.

Hidden Valley Ranch Cheese Puffs

2   cups shredded sharp Cheddar cheese
¾   cup mayonnaise
1   tablespoon Hidden Valley Original Ranch Salad Dressing Mix
10   1-inch slices French bread (fresh or frozen)

Mix the first 3 ingredients. Spread mixture on bread slices. Broil until puffed and golden for 3 or 4 minutes. Good with grilled steak and chicken.

Julie W. Stewart

Banana Nut Bread

½   cup butter
1¼   cups sugar
2   eggs, separated
3   large ripe bananas, mashed
2   cups flour
½   teaspoon salt
1   teaspoon baking soda
½   cup pecans, chopped

Cream butter and sugar, add egg yolks and beat well. Add bananas; add flour that has been sifted with salt and soda. Stir in nuts. Beat egg whites until stiff and fold into the mixture. Bake in well greased loaf pan with paper in bottom and greased. Bake at 350 degrees for 1 hour. Cool in pan for about 20 minutes before removing.

Louise Richter

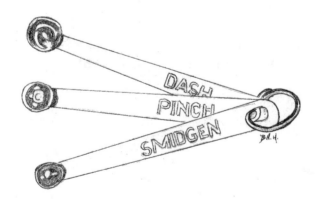

Coffee Cake

1   box white cake mix
1   small package instant vanilla pudding
1   cup water
1   cup oil
4   eggs
1   teaspoon vanilla
1   tablespoon butter
¾   cup sugar
3   teaspoons cinnamon

Mix cake mix, pudding mix, water, and oil. Add eggs one at a time. Add vanilla and butter. Grease and flour a 9 x 13-inch pan. Mix cinnamon and sugar, set aside. Pour half of batter into the pan and top with half of sugar/ cinnamon mixture. Pour remaining batter and sprinkle remainder of sugar/ cinnamon mixture. Swirl with knife and let set for 15 minutes. (Very important.) Bake at 350 degrees for 40 minutes.

Glaze
1   cup 10X powdered sugar
1   tablespoon milk
1   teaspoon vanilla extract

Mix and pour over cake while still warm.

Susan Chastain

This recipe is from a dear 87 year old neighbor, Lucille McKoon, who lives beside our lake house. She always brings coffee cake over while we are at the lake.

Pecan Pie Muffins

1   cup light brown sugar
½   cup all-purpose flour
1   cup chopped pecans
2   eggs
1 to 1¼ sticks butter, melted
1   teaspoon vanilla extract (optional)

Mix brown sugar, flour, and pecans; add eggs, butter, and vanilla. Mix well. Pour into a greased muffin pan. Bake in preheated 350 degrees oven for 20 minutes. Yield 12 muffins.

Alice Robinson

Griddlecakes with Fried Syrup

2   cups sifted all-purpose flour
3   teaspoons baking powder
½   teaspoon salt
1   tablespoon sugar (optional)
2   eggs, well beaten
1½   cups milk (scant)
2   tablespoons shortening, melted

Mix and sift dry ingredients. Combine eggs and milk; add flour mixture and beat only until smooth. Add shortening. Bake on a greased hot griddle. For a thick cake, reduce amount of milk. Do not over beat batter. Makes about 24 small cakes. Serve with butter. My family always serves them with Fried Syrup for a nice supper meal.

Fried Syrup

In an iron skillet, pour the amount of cane syrup needed for the number of people. Add butter accordingly. Bring to a boil and reduce heat. Let simmer until syrup thickens to desired consistency. Serve in a gravy boat with the griddlecakes.

Iris Harvey Smith

Soon after I married, my grandmother gave me a copy of the griddlecake recipe to go in my file. She noted that it came out in the Atlanta Journal Sunday paper. There was no date on clipping. I have never seen a recipe for fried syrup, but it was a favorite at our house.

Keepsake Biscuits

1   quart milk or cream
2   tablespoons white sugar
Enough flour to make dough stiff
1½   cups butter or lard
1   teaspoon cream of tartar
1   teaspoon salt

Knead well and mold into neat small biscuits with your hands. Bake well and you will have a good sweet biscuit that will last for weeks in a very dry place. They are great for traveling. (Bake at 425 degrees for 15 to 20 minutes.)

Sheila Barnes Thornton

This recipe was written down by my grandmother, Thelma Chastain Crew, given to her by her mother, Lela Collier Chastain. Original date of recipe was 1890.

Mayonnaise Rolls

1   cup self-rising flour
3   tablespoons mayonnaise
½   cup milk
¾   teaspoon sugar

Combine all ingredients just until dry ingredients are moistened. Spoon into greased muffin pan. Bake at 425 degrees for 15 minutes.

Joyce M. Pickens

Raisin Nut Sandwiches

1   15-ounce box raisins
Pecans
1   8-ounce package cream cheese, softened
Mayonnaise

Grind raisins and nuts together. Add cream cheese and enough mayonnaise to make mixture easy to spread. Best on whole wheat bread.

Marion Walker

Party Ham Sandwiches

1   stick margarine, melted
1 to 3 tablespoons mustard
1   tablespoon Worcestershire sauce
1   tablespoon poppy seed
2   packages dinner rolls
2   5-ounce cans chunk ham
4   ounces shredded Mozzarella cheese

Heat margarine, mustard, Worcestershire sauce, and poppy seed. Cut rolls in half and brush butter mixture on both sides. Sprinkle ham on bottom of rolls, sprinkle cheese over ham and place top of rolls on cheese. Place back in tray and cover with foil. Bake at 325 degrees for 15 minutes or until cheese is melted.

Karen Moltz

Recipe used for Senior Citizens meeting at Capel Baptist Church where my husband was pastor. He passed away in 2002.

Pimento Cheese Sandwich Filling

1   pound cheese, grated
½   small can pimento
Onion, size of egg, grated
3   shakes of celery salt
Salt and pepper to taste
Salad dressing, enough to spread easily

Mix all ingredients together and let sit 6 to 8 hours before making sandwiches.

Winnie Jean Hester

Recipe of Mrs. A. J. Miller from Spring Hill Church's Cookbook from many years ago.

Cream Cheese Sandwiches

8   ounces cream cheese, softened
1   ripe banana, mashed
½   teaspoon fresh lemon juice
½   cup raisins
½   cup toasted nuts, any kind
4   slices fresh or canned pineapple, chopped
Chopped dates, pears, apples, strawberries (optional)

Combine all ingredients and any optional ingredient. Spread on whole wheat, raisin bread or date nut bread.

Nancy C. Clark

Benedictine Cucumber Sandwiches

1   large cucumber
8   ounces cream cheese, softened
2   tablespoons onion, grated
¼   teaspoon salt
1   tablespoon mayonnaise
Dash of green food coloring

Pare, grate, and drain cucumber. Combine all ingredients in food processor. Serve as is for sandwich spread. Thin with sour cream to make a dip for vegetables.

Carolyn H. Chason

This was a popular recipe from Benedict's Restaurant, Louisville, KY, during the early 1900s, according to my friend who shared this.

Zucchini Nut Bread

3   eggs, beaten
2   cups sugar
1   cup oil (prefer Crisco or Wesson)
1½   teaspoons baking powder
2   teaspoons cinnamon
3   teaspoons vanilla flavoring
2   cups zucchini, peeled and grated
3   cups plain flour, sifted
1   teaspoon baking soda
1   teaspoon salt
1   cup nuts (pecans or walnuts)

Grease and lightly flour 3 loaf pans, set aside. Combine eggs, sugar, and oil; mix well. Add remaining ingredients and mix until well blended. Bake at 350 degrees for about 45 to 50 minutes. Cool on racks for about 5 minutes. Remove from pans and finish cooling on racks.

Pamela C. Forrester

I love to cook and bake and have been making this recipe for the last 20 years. At Christmastime, I bake to my heart's content and give the results to special friends and neighbors. Every year the requests for my Zucchini Bread gets longer! Enjoy with a good cup of coffee or a nice cold glass of milk.

English Tea Muffins

2   cups plain flour, sifted
4   teaspoons baking powder
2   teaspoons sugar
½   teaspoon salt
1   egg
3   tablespoons butter, melted
1   cup milk
½   cup raisins, chopped fine
2   teaspoons chopped citron
Cinnamon sugar

Mix ingredients as for biscuits. Roll ¼-inch thick. Brush with melted butter and sprinkle with cinnamon sugar and chopped fruit. Roll as for jelly roll. Cut with sharp knife about 2-inches thick. Bake at 425 degrees for 25 minutes.

Paulette Daughtry

Recipe from old Watkins Recipe Book belonging to my mother, Bessie Lawrence Robinson.

New Hope Primitive Baptist Church

Established in 1885, this church is located about twelve miles northeast of Cairo.

Dinner on the Grounds

Fence table for dinner on the grounds

Cheese, Eggs, And Pasta . . .

Herring House

A Greek Revival style home that was built in the "North Carolina Settlement" in the 1840s by Hanson William and Amy Caroline Anders Herring. It was a landmark of the Calvary community for over 130 years.

Ol' Time Macaroni and Cheese

1   8-ounce elbow macaroni, cooked ,and drained
½   cup finely chopped onions
¼   cup finely chopped pimentos
2 to 3 cups grated red rind cheese (also called Rat Cheese)
        reserve ¾ cup
1½   cups sweet milk
4   eggs
Salt and pepper to taste

Spray baking dish with non stick spray. Mix all ingredients except for milk, eggs, and reserved cheese in large bowl. Beat eggs and milk separately and add to other mixture. Stir well and pour into baking dish. Top with reserved cheese. Bake at 350 degrees for 15 to 20 minutes or until set and topping is melted.

Sheila Barnes Thornton

Given to me by my Granny (Louise Van Landingham Barnes) . It is my children's favorite.

Macaroni and Cheese I

1   small box macaroni (cooked according to directions)
1   can cream of mushroom soup
½   can of milk (above soup can)
½   cup chopped onion
1   small jar pimento
½   cup mayonnaise
1½   cups grated cheese
½   stick margarine
Cracker crumbs

Mix all ingredients together in casserole dish (save ½ of cheese, margarine, and cracker crumbs for topping). Bake at 325 degrees for 30 minutes.

Laura M. Brinkley

I love my Aunt Sarah Courtney's mac and cheese.

Macaroni and Cheese II

8 ounces macaroni
2 cups cottage cheese
1 egg, beaten
²/₃ teaspoon salt
Dash of pepper
2 cups shredded cheddar cheese
Paprika

Cook macaroni; rinse and drain. Combine next six ingredients; add macaroni and stir well. Spoon mixture into lightly greased 2-quart casserole. Sprinkle with paprika. Serves 6 to 8. Bake at 350 degrees for 45 minutes.

Hilda D. Weeks

Recipe was Elsie Weeks' recipe (Joe B. Weeks' mother).

Macaroni and Cheese III

1½ cups milk
2 eggs
2 cups cooked macaroni, drained
1 cup grated cheddar cheese
Salt and pepper

Mix milk and eggs; add to macaroni while stirring. Add cheese, reserving ¼ cup for topping. Season to taste. Place in buttered casserole and sprinkle with reserved cheese. Bake at 350 degrees approximately 45 minutes or until set and slightly brown. Yield 6 servings.

Claire C. Willett

Pimento Macaroni

2   cups macaroni
1   pound grated cheese
1   can cream of mushroom or celery soup
1   cup mayonnaise
1   small jar chopped pimento
¼   cup chopped green pepper
1   tablespoon grated onion

Cook macaroni as directed on package. Drain macaroni and mix all other ingredients in it. Put in casserole dish and bake at 350 degrees for 20 minutes.

Carolyn Trawick

Recipe from my grandmother and a favorite of the family.

Holiday Macaroni

2   cups uncooked macaroni
1   can cream of chicken soup
1   can cream of mushroom soup
½   cup chopped onion
1   4-ounce can pimento, chopped
¼   cup chopped bell pepper
¾   pound shredded cheddar cheese
½   cup mayonnaise

Cook macaroni according to directions; do not add salt. Mix remaining ingredients until well blended. Fold in cooked macaroni. Pour mixture into a 9 x 13-inch baking dish and bake for 45 minutes at 350 degrees.

Joyce Pickens

Margaret K. LeGette's Red Macaroni

8   ounces elbow macaroni
2   cans tomato soup
1   pound sharp cheddar cheese, grated
1   can mushrooms (pieces and stems), drained
WorcestershiresSauce

Cook macaroni per directions. Mix ingredients (reserve some cheese for top.) Season with Worcestershire Sauce to taste. Put in 2-quart casserole dish and top with cheese and paprika. Cook in 350 degrees oven for 30 minutes or until bubbly.

Margaret Tyson

Pineapple Casserole I

1   20-ounce can crushed pineapple, drained
1   20-ounce can tidbits pineapple, drained
6   tablespoons flour
1   cup sugar
1   cup crushed Ritz cracker crumbs (1 stack)
2   cups shredded cheddar cheese
½   cup melted margarine

Drain pineapple, reserving 6 tablespoons of juice. Combine sugar and flour, stir in the reserved juice. Add cheese and pineapple, mix well. Pour into a greased casserole dish. Combine melted margarine and cracker crumbs, stirring well. Sprinkle over pineapple mixture. Bake for 30 minutes at 350 degrees or until lightly browned.

Orine C. Bulloch

Similar recipe submitted by Betty Ragan.

Pineapple Casserole II

1   15¼-ounce can tidbit pineapple (juice and all)
1   egg
1   tablespoon cornstarch or 2 tablespoons flour
½   cup sugar
1   cup cheddar cheese

Topping
Ritz crackers (one stack)
1   stick margarine, melted

Mix all ingredients (except topping) and bake at 350 degrees for 25 minutes.
Crunch Ritz crackers and mix with margarine; pour on top and bake 10
minutes longer.

Carolyn Trawick

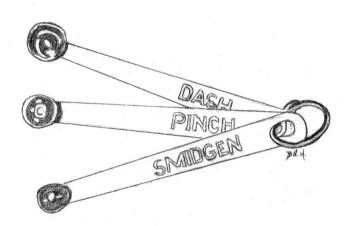

Savory Summer Pie

½   (15-ounce) package refrigerated piecrusts
1   small red bell pepper, chopped
½   purple onion, chopped
2   garlic cloves, minced
2   tablespoons olive oil
2   tablespoons chopped fresh basil
4   large eggs
1   cup half and half
1   teaspoon salt
½   teaspoon pepper
2   cups (8 ounces) shredded Monterey Jack cheese
⅓   cup shredded Parmesan cheese
3   plum tomatoes, cut into ¼-inch slices

Fit piecrust into a 9-inch deep dish tart pan; prick bottom and sides of piecrust with a fork. Bake at 425 degrees for 10 minutes. Remove from oven; set aside. Sauté bell pepper, onion, and garlic in hot oil in a large skillet 5 minutes or until tender; stir in basil. Whisk together eggs and next 3 ingredients in large bowl, stir in sautéed vegetables and cheeses. Pour into crust; top with tomato. Bake at 375 degrees for 45 to 50 minutes or until set, shielding edges with strips of aluminum foil after 30 minutes to prevent excessive browning. Yield 8 servings.

Hannah Rogers

Breakfast Soufflé

6	slices white bread, crust removed, cubed
4	eggs, beaten
2	cups milk
½	pound shredded cheese (cheddar or Colby)
½	pound ham, cooked, cubed
½	teaspoon dry mustard

Salt and pepper to taste

Mix, cover and chill overnight. Bake, covered, at 350 degrees for 1 hour.

Lyn Robinson

Cheese Strata

10	slices bread, with crusts removed
1	pound grated cheddar cheese
3	eggs
3	cups milk
1	teaspoon Worcestershire sauce
½	teaspoon cayenne pepper
½	teaspoon salt
2	teaspoons onion juice

Layer bread slices in baking dish and sprinkle with cheese. Beat remaining ingredients and pour over cheese and bread. Refrigerate several hours or overnight. Bake at 350 degrees until lightly browned.

Tommie Jean M. Cooper

Red Devil

1   pound sharp cheddar cheese
1   can tomato soup
2 or 3 eggs
2 or 3 tablespoons Worcestershire sauce
Dash of Tabasco (if desired)

Melt cheese in top of double boiler. When entirely melted add tomato soup and stir until well blended and smooth. Combine eggs and sauce; beat well. Add this mixture to melted cheese and soup, stirring constantly until mixture thickens. Serve on toast. Good served with green salad. (Can be used as an appetizer served with crackers.)

Margaret W. Magahee

Recipe was one that my mother, Augusta C. Wight (1892-1993) used often.

Country Grits and Sausage

2   cups water
½   teaspoon salt
½   cup uncooked quick grits
4   cups shredded extra sharp cheddar cheese
4   eggs, beaten
1   cup milk
2   pounds mild bulk pork sausage, cooked, crumbled, and drained

Bring water and salt to a boil; stir in grits. Return to boil and reduce heat; Cook 4 minutes. Combine grits and cheese in large bowl until cheese is melted. Beat eggs and milk together. Add small amount of hot grits mixture to egg mixture, stirring well. Combine the two mixtures. Add sausage; stir well. Pour into 8 x 12 x 2-inch pan or 2 (8-inch) square pans. Cover and refrigerate overnight. Remove from refrigerator; let stand 15 minutes. Bake at 350 degrees for an hour. Perfect dish for Christmas morning. It is easy to make the night before and in the morning there is no fuss and it is delicious!

Mary H. Chason

Brown Rice

1   cup rice
1   can French Onion soup
1   can beef Consommé
1   stick margarine
1   small can mushrooms (optional)

Brown the rice in margarine in microwave for about 5 minutes, stirring occasionally. Add remaining ingredients. Cover. Cook for 1 hour in 350 degrees oven.

Pat Bell

My sister, Carolyn Adams, fixed this for my son, Chad, when he visited her in Decatur, Georgia, and he loves it!

Kevin Chason's Favorite Brown Rice

1   can French Onion soup, undiluted
1   can Golden Mushroom soup, undiluted
1   can Consommé, undiluted
1   stick butter or margarine
1½   cups rice, uncooked, long grain

Put all ingredients in a pot. Heat until butter is melted and all soups are well blended. Stir. Pour into a greased casserole dish; cover with foil. Bake at 350 degrees for about an hour or until liquid is absorbed.

Mary H. Chason

There are a lot of recipes out there for brown rice, but this one is the absolute best.

Brains and Scrambled Eggs

1   set or 16-ounces hog brains
1   tablespoon oil
4   eggs, beaten
1   teaspoon salt
½   teaspoon pepper

Cook brains in oil in fry pan; add salt and pepper; stir in eggs. Continue to cook until eggs are done; serve hot.

Myrt McCorkle

First time I cooked this recipe, I boiled brains in water for 30 minutes not knowing how to cook them with no recipe. I scrambled them together and my husband, Earl, ate the whole recipe. When we returned home from a hog killing, I learned the right way from his mother, Etta McCorkle.

Deviled Eggs

6   hard-boiled eggs, peeled
2   tablespoons Miracle Whip salad dressing
½   teaspoon prepared mustard
1½   teaspoons sweet pickle relish
1½   teaspoons dill pickle relish
Salt and pepper to taste

Cut the eggs in half lengthwise and remove the yolks. In a medium size mixing bowl, mash the yolks and add the salad dressing, mustard, relishes, salt, and pepper. Blend well. Fill the egg white cavities with yolk mixture. Sprinkle lightly with paprika, if desired. Put in a deviled egg dish with olives or pickles in the middle.

Sarah and Phillip Chason

We eat lunch at Granddaddy and Grandma Chason's house every Sunday. We have been helping to make Deviled Eggs since we were little.

Broome Mule Barn

A mule barn with the hay loft, located on the Broome's farm.

Meats . . .

Hawthorn House

William Bryant Hawthorn, Jr. (grandson of William Hawthorn) built this edifice for his parents on land that had been owned by the family since they came to the area. It was a popular style of the period and is said to be haunted.

Chicken Biscuit Stew

¼　cup margarine
⅓　cup flour
½　teaspoon salt
Dash of pepper
1 ⅓　cups chicken broth
¾　cup milk
2　cups cooked chicken, cubed
⅓　cup onion, diced
1　cup cooked peas
1　cup cooked carrots, small pieces
1　10-count can biscuits
Poppy seed

In 10-inch ovenproof skillet, melt margarine; blend in flour, salt and pepper. Add broth and milk; stirring until thickened. Add chicken, onion, peas, and carrots; simmer until bubbly. Arrange biscuits over chicken mixture. Sprinkle with poppy seeds. Bake at 375 degrees for 20 to 25 minutes. Yield 5 to 6 servings.

Mary Allegood

My mother (Ruby Cooper) enjoyed making this dish.

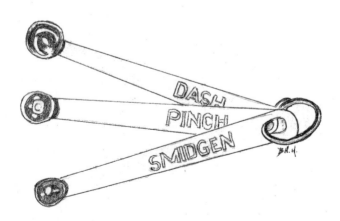

Southern Fried Chicken

2   3-pound chicken fryers or favorite parts
2   cups all-purpose flour
Salt and pepper to taste
1   cup milk or buttermilk
Vegetable shortening
1   tablespoon bacon grease

Cut the chicken into serving pieces, do not remove the skin; rinse under running water. Combine flour, salt, and pepper in a bag and shake until well blended. Pour the milk into a bowl. Heat skillet to about 375 degrees, fill the skillet half full of shortening and add the bacon grease. Dip the chicken into the milk; then place in the bag. Shake to coat evenly and place chicken in the preheated skillet. Fry the chicken until golden brown and crisp, 15 to 20 minutes. Turn chicken and fry an additional 15 minutes or until golden brown. (Turn the chicken only once.) Drain on paper bag or paper towels. Repeat procedure with the remaining chicken. Serve warm or room temperature. Serves 8.

Celeste Chason Tyler

Glopy Chicken

1   chicken fryer, cut into parts
1   package dry onion soup mix
1   8-ounce jar Wishbone Red Russian salad dressing
1   18-ounce jar apricot preserves

Put chicken in baking dish. Mix soup, dressing, and preserves and pour over chicken. Bake at 350 degrees for 30 to 40 minutes. Serve on bed of rice.

Kelly Scott

A high school teacher gave me this easy recipe--really delicious!

Honey Hough's Smother Fried Chicken

1   frying sized chicken, cut up
Salt and pepper
Oil/fat/butter
Milk and water

Salt and pepper chicken. Brown in oil in skillet. Add milk and water. Cover. Simmer 15 to 20 minutes.

Jean Hough

Like most people, Honey raised her own chickens. They were white and she kept them clean and white by washing them in lye soap wash water every week. They never had mites (lice).

J. T.'s Fried Chicken

Use salt and pepper to season the chicken and flour with Martha White flour. Fry in a deep pan with Sessions Peanut Oil after it has reached 350 degrees. Do not remove chicken until it has browned and floats on top of oil.

Crystal Cook

This was my grandfather's (J.T. Sumner, Jr.) recipe that he used at all functions of the First United Methodist Church and other organizations.

Chicken and Scampi

3	pounds fryer breast, deboned and cut into chunks
1	tablespoon salt
½	teaspoon pepper
¼	cup butter
3	small onions, chopped
1	clove garlic, crushed
3	tablespoons parsley
½	cup port wine
8	ounces tomato sauce
1	teaspoon dried basil
1	pound raw shrimp, cleaned

Sauté chicken in salt, pepper, and butter until golden. Add all ingredients except shrimp and simmer, covered, for 30 minutes. Add shrimp to simmering chicken and cook, uncovered, for 3 to 4 minutes, until shrimp are tender.

Nancy C. Clark

Chicken and Dressing with Giblet Gravy I

Boil 1 hen that has been seasoned with salt and pepper, using 2 or 3 quarts of water. When tender , remove from broth and set aside. Boil 4 eggs, chop and set aside--2 for the dressing and 2 for the gravy.

Dressing

2	cups cornmeal
1	cup plain flour
2	cups buttermilk
4	eggs
4	tablespoons shortening
1	teaspoon baking soda
1	teaspoon salt
2	teaspoons sugar

Mix well and pour into greased baking pan. Cook about 25 minutes at 350 degrees. Cool and crumble.

1	cup chopped onion
1	cup chopped celery
1	cup water or broth

Boil onions and celery in water/broth for 5 minutes. Mix with crumbled bread and 2 chopped eggs and broth (a little at a time). Continue adding broth until it is the right consistency. (If you do not have enough broth, milk or canned broth can be added.) Pour into greased baking dish. Bake at 375 degrees or until golden brown.

Giblet Gravy

3	cups chicken broth
1	cup chicken giblets, chopped
2	tablespoons flour
2	tablespoons butter

Salt and pepper to taste

Melt butter in skillet; add flour and mix well. Add remaining ingredients and 2 chopped eggs. Cook 3 to 4 minutes on medium heat, stirring often.

Helen C. Bishop

My mother, Maggie H. Chason, used this recipe.

Chicken and Dressing with Giblet Gravy II

1   fat hen (5 to 6 pounds)

Cook until tender, about 1½ or 2 hours. Boil the giblets along with the hen about 15 minutes before it is done. Add salt and pepper to taste.

Muffin Bread for Dressing
3   cups sifted cornmeal
½   cup bacon drippings or other fat
2½ to 3 cups buttermilk
2   eggs
1   teaspoon salt
1   teaspoon baking soda
1   teaspoon sugar

Mix all ingredients thoroughly. Pour into greased baking pan and cook 15 minutes in preheated oven at 450 degrees or until done. Makes better dressing not too brown. Turn muffin bread into roaster or pan to be baked in and add crust from ½ loaf white bread. Pour stock from hen over bread (leave 1½ cups for gravy) and add:

1   pint chopped celery
1   pint chopped onions
6   eggs, boiled and chopped
1   teaspoon black pepper or to taste
1   dash red pepper

Chip up bony pieces of hen, leaving ½ to go in gravy. Add ½ chipped meat and mix. There should be at least 1½ quarts stock. If you do not have rich stock, decrease bread and be sure mixture is not too thick. Cut hen in pieces and place on dressing. If using whole hen, use pint of oysters instead of chipped meat. Bake in preheated oven for 20 to 30 minutes at 400 degrees or until light brown (not dried out).

Giblet Gravy
Add remainder of chipped chicken and chipped up liver and gizzard and 2 to 4 boiled eggs (chopped) to 1 cup sweet milk, 5 tablespoons of dressing, dash of salt and pepper, and remainder of chicken stock. Bring to boiling point and serve on dressing. Serves 12.

Mrs. Evelyn Hester

Spanish Chicken

1   5 to 7 pound hen or fryers
1   large green pepper, chopped
1   large onion, chopped
1   tablespoon Worcestershire sauce
1   can garden peas
1   can Mexicorn
1   can tomatoes
1   16-ounce package noodles
Garlic salt to taste

Boil hen until tender and debone. Reserve at least 2 quarts of broth. Sauté the onion and pepper. Put the chicken and broth in large saucepan. Add Worcestershire sauce, onion and pepper. Bring to boil and add peas, corn, tomatoes and noodles. Add extra broth if needed. Cook until tender. Sprinkle with garlic salt as desired when served.

Betty W. Harrison

Chicken Parmesan

6   chicken breasts, skinless and boneless
Italian breadcrumbs
1   egg, beaten
Olive oil
1   small jar spaghetti sauce
1   cup mozzarella cheese, grated

Dip chicken in bread crumbs, then in beaten egg, then back in bread crumbs. Put olive oil in skillet ¼ inch deep and fry chicken until brown. Arrange chicken in shallow baking dish. Top with spaghetti sauce and bake 30 minutes in oven preheated to 350 degrees. Sprinkle cheese over last 5 minutes.

Deborah Phillips

Chicken Rotel

4   chicken breasts,
2   medium onions, chopped
1   bell pepper, chopped
1   stick margarine
1   medium jar or can mushrooms
2   cans diced Rotel Tomatoes
1   can cream of mushroom soup
1   pound Velveeta cheese, cut into squares
1   8-ounce box vermicelli spaghetti, cooked per directions

Cook chicken breast and pull apart. Sauté onions and peppers in margarine until clear. Mix all ingredients, adding vermicelli last. Mix all and put in casserole dish. Bake at 350 degrees for 30 minutes. Freezes well. Great one-meal dish with salad.

Betty Ragan

Recipe of Mattie Murphy.

Chicken Roll Ups

1   package crescent rolls
2   cups chopped chicken
1   cup shredded cheddar cheese
1   can cream of chicken soup
1   soup can of milk
1   2-ounce jar diced pimento

Mix together chopped chicken and cheese. Unroll crescent rolls. Place heaping tablespoon of chicken-cheese mixture on crescent roll and roll from large end to small end. Place in lightly greased 11 x 14-inch dish. Add soup, milk and pimento to remaining chicken mixture and pour over chicken rolls. Bake at 350 degrees for 30 to 45 minutes or until rolls are golden brown. Serves 8.

Ann Robertson

Chicken and Dumplings

1　　large fryer or hen
$^2/_3$　cup milk
¼　　cup shortening
2 or more cups self-rising flour

Boil fryer until tender, cool and debone. Mix other ingredients, adding flour as necessary. Roll out thin, cut and drop in boiling chicken broth. Add salt and pepper to taste. Boil 10 to 20 minutes.

Edith H. Sanders

Company Casserole

1　　can cream of chicken soup (Low sodium soup is best.)
1　　can cream of mushroom soup
1　　can cream of celery soup
1　　soup can of milk
1　　cup rice, uncooked
2　　cups chicken, cooked, deboned, shredded
¼　　cup butter or margarine, melted

Combine all soups and milk in large bowl; mix well. Add rice and chicken; mix well. Pour into casserole dish and pour melted butter/margarine evenly on top. Bake in preheated 300 degrees oven for one hour. Serves 6 to 8. Easy to double. Great for Sunday dinner.

Julie W. Stewart

Mamie Carlisle's Chicken Pie

Cut up one 2½ to 3 pound fryer. Salt and boil until tender. Have plenty of stock. Take chicken out of stock, debone. To make dumplings, use plain flour. Take 1 cup of stock and add 3 tablespoons of cooking oil; fix flour as you would for biscuits in bowl. Mix your pastry and knead until very smooth and it will not stick when rolled out. Cut pastry in strips 2 inches wide and long. Have your stock seasoned and boiling real fast. Drop in cut pastry one at a time. It will be done when you put all dumplings in. Place chicken and dumplings in 9 x 13-inch casserole dish. Sprinkle with boiled egg. Lattice top of casserole with 1-inch strips of same pastry. Brush with butter and brown in oven.

Laurie Carlisle Conradi

Mamma Carlisle made this for Sunday lunches, covered dish, "dinner-on-the-ground", and when any of us requested it. It was a favorite of all the grandchildren and even the great grandchildren.

Paella

6 to 8 pieces chicken
¾   cup butter or vegetable oil
1   medium onion, chopped
2   garlic buds, chopped
1   large tomato, chopped
1   small green pepper, chopped
3   medium carrots, sliced
1   teaspoon salt
Black pepper to taste
2   bay leaves
6   cups water
6   drops yellow food coloring
2   cups Spanish rice
1   package frozen peas
1   dozen stuffed olives
1   can shrimp
3   eggs, boiled and quartered

In large skillet or shallow granite boiler, melt butter and fry chicken on both sides until golden. Add onion, garlic, tomato, and green pepper; reduce high to medium; simmer 5 to 8 minutes uncovered. Add carrots, salt, pepper, and bay leaves. Add 1 cup water; cover and simmer on low heat about 1 to 1¼ hours until chicken is tender. Add 5 cups water, food coloring; stir lightly until coloring is mixed well. Add rice, sprinkling by hand all around the chicken. Do not stir at this point. Add peas and olives. Cover and cook on low heat until rice is tender. Do not overcook rice! When rice is tender, it should be moist. Excess liquid should be drained at this point. Add shrimp and eggs evenly over rice. Turn off heat and let stand, covered, 5 to 8 minutes. Very good served with garlic bread. (Note: Different seafood can be used. Calamari(squid), clean and slice as onion rings and fry with chicken. Mussels, clean and place in boiling water for 10 minutes. When shell opens, remove meat, add when rice is added. Baby crabs, clean and place in boiling water for ¾ to 1 hour, add when rice is added.)

Janice Tillis

I received this recipe from a beautiful neighbor, Nichole Busby, originally from France. Our husbands were stationed at Oxnard AFB, Camillo, California, in the mid-sixties.

Chicken Salad Casserole

2 to 4 cups cooked chicken, chopped
1   cup chopped celery
1   small onion, chopped
1   cup mayonnaise
1   can cream of mushroom soup
2   tablespoons lemon juice
1   small jar pimento
½   cups toasted almonds
2   eggs, boiled and chopped
2   cups crushed potato chips

Mix all ingredients except potato chips. Pour ½ chicken mixture in baking dish; add layer of chips; repeat layers. Bake at 350 degrees for 25 minutes. Serves 6.

Nancy Baker Beasley

Mother (Newell T. Baker) got this recipe from Grace Herring (Mrs. Ernest), who lived "down in the country", Calvary. They were good friends for years.

Easy Chicken Dumplings

2   cans cream of chicken soup
2   cans cream of celery soup
2   cans of chicken broth
2 to 3 cans of chicken (deboned)
1   12-ounce package flour tortillas
Black pepper and salt to taste

Mix soup and broth in a large boiler. Cook on low heat until all dissolved, stirring often. Bring to good boil about 3 to 5 minutes. Add pepper. Rinse out all soup cans and add water to mixture. Add salt. Cut or tear tortillas into small pieces. Stir into mixture. Cook on very low heat for about 10 minutes. Stir often to prevent sticking to bottom of boiler and scorching.

Carolyn J. Hopkins

Recipe of Marianna First United Methodist Church.

White Chili

1	tablespoon vegetable oil
2	medium onions, chopped
2	garlic cloves, minced
2	4-ounce cans chopped green chiles
1	tablespoon plus 1 teaspoon ground cumin
1½	teaspoons dried oregano leaves, crumbled
½	teaspoon cloves
¼	teaspoon cayenne pepper or to taste

4 to 6 cups chicken stock or broth
4   cups diced cooked chicken
1   pound great northern beans, cooked or 3 cans white beans
Salt and pepper to taste
Grated Monterey Jack or cheddar cheese, salsa, and sour cream for
    garnish

Heat oil in large saucepan over medium high heat, add onion and garlic and cook until tender, about 5 minutes. Add the chiles and spices and cook about 1 minute longer. Add 4 cups of stock, beans and chicken and cook over low heat for 1 hour; add more stock if necessary. Cook only 40 minutes if using canned beans. Season with salt and pepper. Serve garnished, if desired. Makes 8 servings.

La Vonne Childers

Chicken Tetrazzini

½   stick butter, melted
½   teaspoon salt
¼   teaspoon pepper
½   teaspoon nutmeg
3   tablespoons flour
1   cup heavy cream
½   cup sherry
2   cups chicken broth
2   chickens, cooked and deboned
½   pound cooked spaghetti, drained
1   small jar pimento
½   cup green pepper, chopped
1   small jar mushrooms
1   tablespoon lemon juice
½   teaspoon grated onion
½   cup Parmesan cheese

Mix butter, salt, pepper, nutmeg, flour, cream, and broth and cook over low heat until thickened to make a white sauce; stir often. Add remaining ingredients except cheese. Pour into baking dish and top with cheese. Bake at 375 degrees about 25 minutes.

Mary Thomas Ward

Bar-be-cued Chicken

Whole fryer or cut up fryer pieces, browned
3   cups tomato juice
1   tablespoon sugar
½   cup vinegar
3   tablespoons Worcestershire sauce
½   cup catsup
4   teaspoons mustard
1   teaspoon pepper
2   teaspoons salt
Chopped onion

Combine ingredients and pour over chicken in a baking dish. Bake at 350 degrees for 1 hour.

Sue Askew

Easy Chicken Pot Pie

3 to 4 cups chicken, boiled and deboned
1   can cream of chicken or celery soup
1   14-ounce can chicken broth
1   cup plain flour
3   teaspoons baking powder
1   cup milk
1   stick margarine, melted

Place chicken in bottom of a 9 x 13-inch baking dish. Mix soup and broth, pour over chicken. Mix flour, baking powder, and milk; pour over pie mixture to form crust. Drizzle margarine over top. Bake at 350 degrees about 45 minutes or until lightly browned. Serves 6 to 8. (1½ cups of Bisquick Mix and 1½ cups buttermilk can be substituted for flour, baking powder, and milk.)

Carolyn Trawick

Easy Company Chicken

3 to 4 chicken breasts, boneless and skinless
2   cans cream of mushroom soup
½   cup white wine
1   tablespoon minced garlic
Parsley
Salt and pepper to taste
4   slices Swiss cheese
Italian breadcrumbs

Preheat oven to 350 degrees. Mix soup, wine, garlic, salt, pepper, and parsley. In baking dish, place chicken and cover with Swiss cheese; cover with soup mixture. Sprinkle with breadcrumbs, covering soup mixture. Bake for 35 to 45 minutes.

Kelly Scott

Cornish Hens

2 or 3 Cornish hens
1   package herbed seasoned stuffing mix
Raisins, divided
Chopped walnuts
Butter, divided
Salt and pepper to taste
1   jar red currant jelly
1   teaspoon allspice

Combine stuffing mix, raisins, and walnuts and stuff hens. Place in baking dish with breast side up and season with melted butter, salt and pepper. Bake at 400 degrees for 45 minutes to 1½ hours. About 20 minutes before hens are finished, cook sauce of jelly, 4 tablespoons butter, allspice, and raisins over low heat. Drizzle over hens, reserving portion of sauce as accompaniment.

Kim Sowers

Turkey with Stroganoff Gravy

½   cup butter or margarine, melted
1   clove garlic, cut
1   cup minced onions
2   cans cream of chicken soup
2   chicken bouillon cubes, dissolved in ½ cup water
1   pint sour cream
1   8-ounce can sliced mushrooms, drained
Salt and pepper to taste
Sliced roast turkey

Sauté onion and garlic in butter until golden; remove garlic. Add soup and dissolved bouillon; heat thoroughly. Add sour cream, mushrooms, and seasonings. Serve with slices of roast turkey on steamed rice. Yields 12 servings. Good for party buffet.

Mrs. J. B. Roddenbery, Jr.

Recipe found in Grady County Farm Journal many years ago.

Wild Duck Casserole

3 or 4 wild ducks
1   onion
1   potato
1   bay leaf
1   8-ounce package herb seasoned stuffing mix
1½   cups sweet milk
2   eggs, beaten
1   stick margarine, melted
1   cup chopped onion
½   cup chopped celery
½   cup mayonnaise
1   can cream of mushroom soup, undiluted
1   cup grated cheese
1½   cups duck broth

Boil ducks in salted water with onion, potato, and bay leaf until tender (about 2 hours). Remove duck from bones and cut into pieces. Pour 1½ cups broth over stuffing mix. Combine other ingredients except soup and cheese. Place in a 9 x 13-inch baking dish, cover and let sit overnight in refrigerator. Before serving, spread soup over top. Bake at 350 degrees for about 1 hour or until set and brown. Sprinkle grated cheese over top and return casserole to oven until melted. Serves 10 to 12.

Iris H. Smith

Doves with Wild Rice

10 to 12 whole dove breasts
½   teaspoon seasoned salt
½   teaspoon salt
¼   teaspoon black pepper
1   cup water, divided
½   cup butter, melted
2   tablespoons lemon juice
1   tablespoon flour
Cooked wild rice

Place dove breasts in a large iron skillet. Sprinkle breasts with salt and pepper. Pour ½ cup water into skillet, cover tightly and steam over medium heat 20 minutes. Remove lid and continue cooking until all water is gone. Add butter and lemon juice to skillet. Continue cooking until breasts are brown on all sides. Remove breasts from skillet. Add flour to drippings in skillet, stirring until smooth. Add ½ cup water; cook until thickened, stirring constantly. Pour gravy over breasts. Serve over wild rice.

Carolyn H. Chason

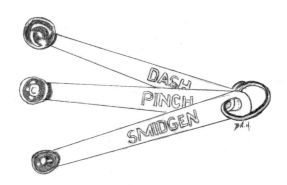

Deer Chili

2	pounds ground venison
1	pound ground beef
1	large onion, chopped
4	tablespoons chili powder
1	8-ounce can tomato sauce
1	cup water
1	tablespoon salt
¼	teaspoon black pepper
8	tablespoons Worcestershire sauce
4	15-ounce cans spiced chili beans

Brown meats in large covered pan. Add onion and 2 tablespoons chili powder and cook 10 minutes. Add tomato sauce, water, salt, pepper, and Worcestershire sauce. Cook over low heat for 15 minutes. Add beans and simmer, stirring occasionally for 30 to 40 minutes. Add more chili powder, if desired. Yield 4 quarts.

Brian Chason

Italian Chili

1	pound sweet Italian sausage
1	cup chopped onions
1	cup chopped green pepper
4	cups tomato juice
1	14½-ounce can stewed tomatoes
1	cup uncooked elbow macaroni
1	teaspoon chili powder
1	teaspoon salt
1	tablespoon sugar

Cut Italian sausage open and crumble. In a large skillet, cook sausage for 3 minutes; add onions and pepper and cook 3 minutes. Stir in the remaining ingredients. Cover and simmer until macaroni is done, about 15 minutes and stirring frequently. Serve hot.

Emogene S. Miller

Cherokee Casserole

1   pound ground beef
1   can cream of mushroom soup
1   can or pint stewed tomatoes
½   cup Minute Rice
½   cup chopped onion
½   cup chopped bell pepper
½   cup grated cheese

Brown meat, add onions and peppers and continue to brown. Add soup, tomatoes, and rice. Simmer 5 to 10 minutes. Put into baking dish, top with cheese and place in warm oven until cheese melts.

Eleanor Lee

This casserole is always enjoyed as one of our favorites to carry to potluck suppers.

Corned Beef Hash

½   can of corned beef
3   medium potatoes, diced
1   medium onion, chopped
4   tablespoons cooking oil
¼   teaspoon salt
Pepper to taste

Heat cooking oil until hot in a skillet. Add potatoes and stir for 6 minutes; add onions and stir for 7 minutes. Add salt and pepper. Break up the meat and stir. Cover with lid and simmer about 25 minutes, stirring occasionally. Serves 6.

Mabel Land

Brisket Stew Gruel

2   pounds brisket (chicken or pork can be substituted)
1   quart water
1   cup plain cornmeal
1   small onion, diced
Salt and pepper to taste

Boil the brisket (cut in 2-inch cubes) until tender, add salt and pepper while it cooks. Add onion and boil about 10 minutes longer. Mix cornmeal with enough water to make a thick liquid. Pour slowly into the meat and broth, stirring constantly. Simmer about 15 minutes. Serve over rice or mashed potatoes.

Patsy C. Plant

My mother made this stew back in the forties and fifties when I as a little girl. It was handed down to her from her Native American(Muskogee) ancestors. Native Americans used deer, squirrel, rabbit, or other wild game to make this dish.

Boiled Fresh Tongue

3½   pounds beef tongue
1   medium onion, sliced
2   tablespoons salt
½   teaspoon mustard seed
½   teaspoon red pepper
5   whole cloves
1   bay leaf

In 8 quart Dutch oven, add all ingredients and enough water to cover; heat to boiling. Reduce heat to low; cover and simmer 3 hours or until meat is tender. Plunge tongue into cold water and remove skin, bones and gristle. Serve with cranberry sauce.

Alice A. Harrison

Beef Roast

2½ to 3 pounds beef roast
1   envelope Lipton's beefy onion soup mix
1   can golden mushroom soup
2   tablespoons flour
8   ounces water
Salt and pepper to taste

Salt and pepper meat and place in a baking dish. Sprinkle soup mix around meat. Mix soup with ½ can warm water and pour into dish. Mix flour and warm water and add to liquid in dish. Stir gently and spoon some liquid over roast. Cover with foil with air holes. Bake at 350 degrees for 2½ to 3 hours.

Deborah Phillips

Lodge's Beef Stew

1   sirloin or round steak cut into bite size pieces
1   can cream of mushroom soup
1   envelope Lipton onion soup mix
2   cups water
Potatoes, cubed
Carrots, sliced into bite size pieces
Green beans, snapped

Brown the steak in a frying pan, reserving drippings. Mix drippings, soup and water until smooth. Bring to a boil and cook about 5 to 6 minutes. Add the potatoes, carrots, beans, and any other vegetables desired. Cook until tender. Serve as stew or over rice.

Annette M. Lodge

Steak Mareno

1 to 2 pounds top sirloin or London broil, cut into strips
2 tablespoons oil
1 14½-ounce can peeled tomatoes
1 envelope onion soup mix
2 tablespoons wine vinegar
½ green pepper, sliced
1 3-ounce can sliced mushrooms
¼ teaspoon garlic powder
1 teaspoon oregano (optional)

Sauté steak and pepper in skillet in oil. Add other ingredients. Simmer for 1½ hours or until done. To reduce cooking time, cubed round steak may be used. Simmer 30 minutes. If more liquid is needed, add tomato juice.

Ruth Thomas (Mrs. J. B.) Davis

Annie Laura's Corned Beef and Cabbage

1 medium cabbage
1 medium onion, chopped
Salt and pepper to taste
1 can corned beef
¼ cup chopped pimento

Chop cabbage and soak in cool, salted water, drain. Drop into hot bacon drippings and add onion, salt, and pepper. Cook about 20 minutes. Add corned beef and pimento. If not moist enough, add little water. Serve with small "hoe cake" cornbread.

Laurie Carlisle Conradi

Smothered Sweet Potatoes

Bake sweet potatoes, peel and cut in half. Boil stew beef until all to pieces. Thicken beef and juice with flour, salt, and pepper. Pour beef on top of potatoes and if you want it sweeter, add a little syrup on top.

Alice Courtney McCorkle

I ate this at home when I was very young and now my children enjoy this meal. If the sweet potatoes are not naturally sweet, we would pour cane syrup over them.

Beef Casserole

2	cups twist macaroni, cooked and drained
1	pound beef, browned and drained
¾	cup green pepper, chopped
1	can cream of onion or mushroom soup
¾	cup grated cheese
1	14¾-ounce can tomatoes
¾	teaspoon seasoned salt

Salt and pepper to taste
Ritz crackers, crumbled and soaked in cooking oil

Mix all ingredients except crackers and pour into 9 x 13-inch baking dish. Cover and bake at 350 degrees for 30 minutes. Remove cover and add cracker topping; bake about 10 minutes.

Mary Thomas Ward

Cornbread Meat Casserole

2	eggs, beaten well
1	cup milk
1	large can cream style corn
1	cup yellow cornmeal
½	teaspoon baking soda
¾	teaspoon salt
1	large can Le Sueur Peas
½	pound ground beef, browned
½	pound cheddar cheese, grated
1	large onion, chopped
4	jalapeno peppers, chopped (optional)

Stir together first 7 ingredients. Pour half of batter into greased 9 x 13- inch pan. Layer meat, cheese, onion, and peppers evenly over batter. Pour remaining ingredients on top. Sprinkle remaining cheese over top. Bake at 350 degrees 45 to 50 minutes. Serve with salad. Excellent for lunch and tastes better the next day!

Carolyn J. Hopkins

This recipe is from Janelle Merritt, Hixon, Tennessee.

Italy La Strata

1   pound lean ground beef
¼   cup minced onion
1   8-ounce can tomato sauce
1   teaspoon basil
1   teaspoon oregano
1   teaspoon chopped parsley
1   teaspoon granulated garlic
1   teaspoon salt
½   teaspoon pepper
1   4-ounce jar sliced mushrooms, drained or ¼ pound fresh, sliced
1   10-ounce package frozen chopped spinach, thawed and drained
1   8-ounce cottage cheese, dry curd
4   ounces skim milk Mozzarella cheese, shredded

Preheat oven to 375 degrees. In medium fry pan, sauté beef and onion until onion is tender and beef is browned. If using fresh mushroom, sauté in a small fry pan with small amount margarine until dry. To beef, onion, and mushrooms, add the tomato sauce, basil, oregano, parsley, garlic, salt and pepper. In a small bowl, combine spinach and cottage cheese. In an 8-inch square baking dish, arrange layers: spinach mixture, meat mixture, cheese. Repeat layers, ending with cheese. Serves 4.

Hilda D. Weeks

Tater Tot Casserole

1½   pounds lean ground beef
2   tablespoons minced onions
1   can cream of chicken or celery soup
1   small package frozen tater tots

Put uncooked ground beef into a baking dish. Sprinkle minced onions on top of meat and smooth undiluted soup over all. Layer tater tots on top and bake at 350 degrees for 1 to 1½ hours or until done.

Catherine Lacy

A family recipe.

Tallarina

2	pounds ground round
1	large onion, chopped
1	large bell pepper, chopped
1	12-ounce package noodles, cooked and drained
1	small can cream style corn
1	12-ounce can tomato juice
1	tablespoon chili powder
1	tablespoon basil

Salt and garlic powder to taste
3   cups grated cheddar cheese

Brown beef, onion, and pepper, drain well. Add noodles, corn, tomato juice, spices, and ½ of grated cheese. Garlic powder is main ingredient; keep adding garlic powder to taste. Sprinkle remaining cheese on top before baking. Bake at 350 degrees for 30 to 35 minutes.

Betty Banister

Been in our family forever!

Blue Gable Chili

5	pounds ground beef
5	celery stalks, chopped fine
1	large onion, chopped fine
3	15-ounce cans kidney beans
1	1.12-ounce can chili powder
1	tablespoon Tabasco sauce
½	small bottle ketchup
3	16-ounce cans tomatoes
1	teaspoon garlic juice
1	1.12-ounce can paprika

Salt and pepper to taste

In a large pot, brown meat and drain. Add onions and celery, sauté until transparent. Add remaining ingredients and simmer all day.

Marilyn W. Joyner

Recipe of the Blue Gable Drive-In given to me by the original cook and friend, Ed Bennett (now deceased).

Chili

2 pounds lean ground beef
1 large onion, chopped
2 cloves garlic, minced or 2 teaspoons garlic powder
1 can kidney beans
2 cans chili without beans
1 teaspoon salt
1 tablespoon chili powder
½ teaspoon cumin
½ can water, (rinse chili can)
Pepper and sugar to taste

Brown beef, onion, and garlic. Add remaining ingredients and simmer for 30 minutes on low; stir frequently.

Lequita LeGette and Margaret Tyson

A good recipe for beginner cooks. This core recipe has been handed down in the LeGette family for many years. I first remember Howard LeGette cooking it. Then sons, Jim, John, and Tom, and now the grandsons Ken and Bob. It changes from person to person. Some like it sweet and some like it spicy. You can season it to your taste. Double or triple the ingredients. Make a little or make a lot.

Easy Italian Spaghetti

1	pound ground beef
1	teaspoon salt
1	dash cayenne pepper
1	cup onions, thinly sliced
¾	cup green pepper, cut into thin strips
1½	cups beef broth (or hot water and 2 bouillon cubes)
1	cup thick tomato sauce or paste
1	teaspoon Worcestershire sauce
¼	cup grated Parmesan cheese
1½	teaspoons vinegar
5	cups cooked spaghetti

Separate meat into small pieces with fork and season with salt and pepper. Brown meat; remove meat, reserving drippings. Add onions and green pepper; cook gently for 10 minutes. Add remaining ingredients except spaghetti, simmer. Serve over cooked spaghetti.

Nancy Herring Stingley

This was a favorite recipe of my mother, Annie Lee McNair Herring, the first lunchroom supervisor of the Calvary School Lunchroom.

Ham and Broccoli Bake

1   20-ounce package frozen cut broccoli, cooked and drained
1   cup onion, chopped
¼   cup butter
1   can cream of mushroom soup
1   can cream of celery soup
2½   cups milk
2   cups shredded sharp American cheese
6   cups cooked ham, cubed
4   cups quick cooking rice

In saucepan, cook onion in butter until tender. In a large bowl, stir together soups, milk, and cheese. Add broccoli, onion, ham, and uncooked rice; mix well. Bake, covered, 45 to 50 minutes at 350 degrees.

Deborah Phillips

Brunswick Stew I

2	pork shoulders
6	large hens
6	pounds ground beef
9	cans of peas
18	cans of corn
24	cans tomatoes
1	large jar mustard
6	large bottles ketchup
2	bottles Worcestershire sauce
1	bottle hot sauce, to taste
2	boxes salt
1	large box black pepper
1	pound oleo
2	dozen lemons
1	small bottle vinegar
10	pounds onion
20	pounds potatoes
½	pound sugar

Season and cook hens and pork until meat falls from the bone. Tear into small bits with hands. Cook ground beef, add to meats. Use a portion of the meat stock for base of stew (may not need to use all of stock). Add oleo, onion, potatoes, and tomatoes. Begin to cook and add ½ of mustard, ketchup, Worcestershire sauce, and hot sauce. Add juice from lemons and add 6 rinds to stew. While cooking, use about 1 cup of vinegar, tasting it, as it needs to be tart. Add salt, pepper, and sugar to taste, add oleo as needed. Cook for 1 to 2 hours and add peas and corn, stir to prevent sticking. Serves 150 to 200 people.

Crystal Cook

This is a recipe used by my grandfather, J. T. Sumner, Jr., well-known cook in Cairo for many years.

Brunswick Stew II

1   hog head or Boston butt, cooked and chopped fine
5   pounds ground beef, browned
6   medium onions, chopped fine
3   15-ounce cans creamed corn
2   quarts or 4 cans stewed tomatoes
½   cup prepared mustard
2   24-ounce bottles ketchup
1   small bottle Crystal hot sauce
Salt and pepper to taste

In a large kettle, add meats and remaining ingredients. Bring to a boil and then simmer one hour or more, stirring often. Good served with potatoes.

Robert E. Lee

When I make Brunswick Stew, I usually double or triple the recipe. It freezes well and makes a quick meal.

Liver Pudding or Mush

1   fresh hog liver
1½   pounds fresh fat pork
2   cups cornmeal
Salt and pepper to taste
Red pepper and sage to taste

Cook liver and fat pork until tender. Remove from broth and mash liver with potato masher or grind well. Add cornmeal and spices. Add enough broth to soften the mixture. Cook in saucepan until meal is cooked, stirring constantly to keep from scorching. Put in sausage casings or in a mold. Press down until cold. Slice and serve cold. Delicious with baked sweet potatoes.

Alice A. Harrison

Liver pudding making usually followed the butchering of 8 to 10 hogs by my parents who had 10 children.

Edna Mae's Sausage Casserole

1	pound mild pan sausage
1	medium onion, chopped
2	tablespoons margarine
1	large egg
1½	cups shredded sharp cheese
¼	cup all-purpose flour
1	can cream of mushroom soup
4	medium potatoes, boiled and cubed

Brown sausage and crumble, drain fat. Cook onion in margarine. Mix onion, sausage, egg and cheese. Stir flour into soup and add to meat mixture. Fold in potatoes. Pour into baking dish. Bake at 400 degrees about 20 to 25 minutes. Good for brunch or supper. Serve with scrambled eggs and biscuits. Yields 4 servings.

Cathy Walden Moore

This is a recipe from Philadelphia, Mississippi, from a neighbor of my husband when he was a child. She said she "just made it up one day". She gave the recipe to us while my husband and I were on our honeymoon 35 years ago.

Barbecued Spareribs

3 to 4 pounds ribs, cut into pieces
1   lemon, thinly sliced
1   large onion, thinly sliced
1   cup catsup
$^1/_3$ cup Worcestershire sauce
1   teaspoon chili powder
1   teaspoon salt
2   dashes Tabasco sauce
2   cups water

Place ribs in shallow roasting pan, meaty side up. Place lemon and onion on each rib piece. Roast in very hot oven, 450 degrees for 30 minutes. Combine remaining ingredients, bring to a boil and pour over ribs. Continue baking at 350 degrees until tender; about 45 minutes to 1 hour. Baste ribs with sauce every 15 minutes. Add water if sauce gets too thick.

Janice Tillis

This recipe is from a close friend, Marcello Abbot, a military friend from Illinois.

Souse (Hog-head Cheese)

Take fresh neck bones, head, feet, and pork scraps and cover with water in a pot. Boil until meat falls from the bones. Remove bones from meat and discard. Chop meat fine or grind. Reserve stock. Add salt and pepper to taste. Add a pinch of sage (optional). Spread a clean cloth over a colander. Put meat in cloth, fold cloth closely over it and lay a weight on top so that it may press whole surface equally. When cold, take off weight, remove from cloth and colander. If you plan to serve the souse fresh, refrigerate. When congealed, slice and serve. If desired, dust with flour and fry in hot grease. Reserved stock may be substituted for water when cooking rice.

Helen C. Bishop

These directions for making souse came from my mother, Maggie H. Chason.

Mom's Pigtail Pilau

6 to 8 pigtails
Salt and pepper to taste
1   large onion, chopped
¼   teaspoon sugar
3   cups rice, uncooked

Place clean pigtails that have been salted and peppered in a pot , covered with water; add onions. Simmer slow until pigtails are tender. Add rice and bring to a rolling boil. If water does not cover rice by a ¼-inch, add more water. Cover pot and turn down to low. Cook 15 minutes, check seasonings and stir. If it is too dry, add little more water. If too wet, put tiny crack in cover and it will dry out.

Polly A. Kincaid

This recipe was used during hog killing time or shortly after by my mother. Even though I have to purchase high-priced pigtails, it is still delicious.

Mrs. Carson Bell's Brunswick Stew

Boil the head, feet and liver of one hog until tender enough to leave the bones. Remove from stock. Let cool and debone. Put through a food chopper or chip well. Put in a cooker or boiler and add:

2   quarts tomatoes (3 cans or more)
1   quart cooked corn
2   teaspoons black pepper
½   teaspoon red pepper
2   tablespoons prepared mustard or to taste
½   teaspoon Tabasco sauce
½   cup Worcestershire sauce
1   cup chopped onion
2   garlic buds

Add enough stock to make the desired consistency; boil a few minutes, stirring to prevent scorching. You may add a pinch of sage (optional).

Carolyn J. Hopkins

Chitterlings

To prepare chitterlings, empty and wash chitterlings (this sometimes was done in a nearby creek). Scald and soak. Turn and scrape; wash again in water containing soda. Wash again after taking from "soda water". Plait (similar to braiding)-- some "chitterlings cooks" do not plait or braid. Salt and pepper (using red pepper). Boil until tender. Now you are ready to cook them. Chop and stir fry in small amount of grease in a cast iron frying pan using a lid. Remove lid when chitterlings are done and brown.

Nellie M. Harrell

This is the manner in which my mother, Mrs. Ida Gray Murkerson, prepared chitterlings. (Some cooks choose to flour or meal chitterlings before placing in frying pan.)

Boiled Pig Feet

Wash 4 or 5 pigs feet until very clean. Place feet in boiling water for about 5 minutes, drain. Cover pig feet again with water and bring to boil. Reduce heat to medium. Salt and pepper to taste. Cook until very tender, about 1½ to 2 hours.

Ann Robinson Bracewell

This was one of Dad's (Bernard Gordye Robinson) favorite foods. When Mom became ill and was not able to cook for Daddy, he would ask me to cook the pig feet for him. When ready to eat, he would sit at the table, bless the food, and then say ,"Fit for a King".

Shirley's Washday Dinner

1   pound sausage meat, browned
1   quart canned tomatoes
3   ounces spaghetti, broken in half
¼   cup chopped onion
Salt and pepper to taste

Mix all ingredients in a large iron skillet and simmer until spaghetti is done.

Catherine Lacy

Handed down family recipe from Shirley Hudson, Tifton, GA .

Annette Harrell's Ham Pie

4   cups chopped ham
3 to 4 eggs, boiled and sliced
1   large bell pepper, chopped
2   stalks celery, chopped
1   onion, chopped
1   can cream of celery soup
1   can cream of mushroom soup
1   cup flour
¾   can evaporated milk

In a greased 9 x 13-inch baking dish, layer first 7 ingredients. Add flour and milk, mix thoroughly and pour on top. Bake at 375 degrees for 30 minutes. DO NOT add salt as the ham and soups have enough salt.

Robert Harrell

Low Country Boil

4	boxes crab boil
6	tablespoons salt
2	tablespoons Tabasco sauce
5	tablespoons Worcestershire sauce
¾	cup vinegar
5	small onions
2	pounds smoked beef sausage, sliced in 2-inch pieces
2	pounds Polish Kielbasa sausage, sliced in 2-inch pieces
10 to 12	ears corn on cob
6	pounds medium or large shrimp, shell on
20	small to medium whole red potatoes

Combine crab boil, salt, Tabasco, Worcestershire, and vinegar in large pot about ¹/₃ full of water. Boil 30 minutes at full boil. Add sausage, onions, and potatoes. Boil 15 minutes. Add corn and boil 5 minutes. Add shrimp last and cook only 5 minutes or less, just until pink. Drain well and eat. May be served with salad and bread. Serves 12 to 15 people.

Jimmy and Paulette Douglas

Flounder Francisie

1 pound flounder or sole (thin flat fish)
Flour
1 egg
Parsley
Salt and Pepper to taste
Parmesan cheese
Butter
4 ounces white wine
$^1/_3$ cup chicken broth
Lemon juice

Coat flounder with flour and then dip in mixture of egg, parsley, salt, pepper, and cheese. Place in pan with melted butter. Cook 5 minutes on each side or until brown. After cooking, put on paper towel. Drain pan. Add wine, broth, and lemon juice and cook down a little. Return fish to pan until sauce thickens. Serve with rice.

Kelly Scott

This is a family favorite that originated from a family friend, Donald McLean, of Connecticut.

Curried Shrimp

1   chicken bouillon cube dissolved in 1-cup hot water.
5   tablespoons butter, melted
6   tablespoons flour
2   cups milk
1½   tablespoons minced onion
1¼   teaspoons salt
1½   teaspoons sugar
¼   teaspoon ginger
2   teaspoons curry powder
2   pounds shrimp, peeled and deveined

Blend butter and flour. Slowly add milk and dissolved bouillon. Stir in spices and cook slowly until thickened. Add shrimp and cook 3 minutes. Serve on bed of rice with condiments such as pineapple, crumbled bacon, boiled egg slices, coconut, raisins, and chutney.

Jeanette L. Harrison

Crab Stew

2   pounds crabmeat
5   tall cans evaporated milk
5   cans cream of celery soup
1   quart half and half
2   sticks butter
1   quart milk
Salt and pepper to taste
Dashes of WorcestershiresSauce
Hot sauce

Pick through crabmeat to remove all shells. In a 10-quart pot, mix all ingredients. Simmer on low, stirring often until stew is very hot. Never let boil. Cool. Refrigerate. When ready to serve, heat until very hot remembering never to let stew boil. Serves 15 or more.

Jeanette L. Harrison

I serve this to my family on Christmas Eve before having the Family Christmas Tree.

Deviled Crab

1	pound crabmeat
2	hard cooked eggs, mashed
1	raw egg
4	tablespoons butter
½	cup crushed saltines
1	teaspoon Worcestershire sauce

Lemon juice to taste
Dashes of Tabasco sauce
Salt to taste
Evaporated milk

Mix the ingredients and season to taste. Use enough evaporated milk for a soupy consistency. Cook in a preheated 350 degree oven for about 30 minutes or until brown on top. This may be cooked in a baking dish or shells.

Margaret Tyson

This was one of my grandmother's (Margaret K. LeGette) recipes.

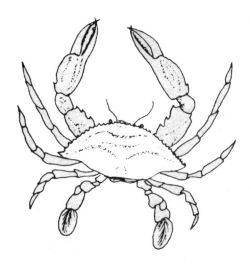

Salmon Stew

4   slices bacon
2   onions, chopped
3   carrots, diced
2   stalks celery, sliced
1 to 2 cans chicken broth
6   medium Irish potatoes, cubed
1   teaspoon salt
Black pepper and garlic powder to taste
1¼   pounds salmon filet, skinned, and cut into 1-inch pieces

Add all ingredients except salmon. Cook until done. Mash some of the potatoes against the side of the cooking pot to help thicken the stew. Add salmon and cook until it turns color. Do not overcook.

Annette C. Harrell

Each generation needs to have its own recipe to hand down and this is mine. Robert and I went to Alaska in 1990 to visit our youngest son. We ate Salmon Stew at a small restaurant in Juneau (their specialty which is served with cornbread) and enjoyed it so much. This is my version of that stew.

Charlie McNaughton's Famous Gumbo

Roux
¼   cup vegetable oil or bacon drippings
3   tablespoons flour

Make 'roux' using a heavy black iron pot or heavy skillet. Melt fat in skillet and stir in flour. Continue to stir over low heat until flour is dark brown. This takes time and patience, but it is worth it.

1   cup chopped celery and celery leaves
1   large onion, chopped
1   green pepper, chopped
1   16-ounce can tomatoes
2   cups sliced okra
3   cups chicken broth
1   bay leaf
¼   teaspoon thyme
2   tablespoons chopped parsley
Salt to taste
¼   teaspoon Tabasco sauce
3   cups cooked chicken, coarsely cut
1   pound shrimp
1   pint oysters

To roux, add celery, onions, and green peppers and continue stirring until tender. Add remaining ingredients except chicken, shrimp and oysters; simmer covered for about 45 minutes. Add chicken, shrimp, oysters; adjust seasonings. Simmer 10 minutes. Serve in large flat bowls over hot rice. Yield 6 to 8 servings.

Charlie McNaughton

Grady County was the "okra capitol" at one time in history. The word "gumbo" or "gombo" is West African for 'okra'. This popular meal is made of bits of either seafood, game or fowl and Creole seasonings cooked together and served over rice. Okra, a West African vegetable, came over with the slaves. The Choctaw Indians ground sassafras leaves to make the filé powder. Early settlers concocted the soups thickened with both ingredients. Born in New Orleans, now a Grady Countian, I received this recipe that had been handed down through generations and brought it to Calvary when I married Frances

McNair of Calvary in 1960. The folks around Calvary have been fortunate to have tasted my famous Gumbo for years.

Seafood Casserole

½   cup chopped green bell pepper
½   cup chopped onion
½   cup chopped celery
½   cup butter
²/₃   cup flour
½   teaspoon crushed fresh garlic
½   teaspoon salt
¼   teaspoon paprika
Red pepper to taste
1   can cream of shrimp soup
2   cups milk
8   ounces crabmeat, flaked
12 to 18 ounces shrimp cooked, peeled and deveined
1   8-ounce can water chestnuts, sliced and drained
4   ounces fresh mushrooms
2   tablespoons butter, softened
½   cup cheddar cheese
½   cup breadcrumbs

In skillet, sauté green pepper, onions, and celery in butter until tender. Stir in flour; cook 1 minute stirring constantly. Add garlic, paprika, red pepper, soup, and milk. Mix well. Cook until thickened, stirring constantly. Combine crabmeat, shrimp, water chestnuts, and mushrooms in a bowl. Mix well. Spoon mixture into a buttered 2-quart baking dish. Top with sauce. Sprinkle with mixture of butter, cheese, and breadcrumbs. Bake at 350 degrees for 30 to 35 minutes or until bubbly.

Sheila Barnes Thornton

This is a 4 generation recipe dating back to the 1920s. Recipe given to me by my great-aunt Thelma Van Landingham Crownover when I was 15 years old. This is a casserole even non-seafood lovers love. I handed it down to my daughter, Jamie Thornton Faircloth in 1999.

Broiled Mullet

2   fresh mullet, split down back with scales on
Lemon juice
Olive oil
Dried sweet basil
Seabreeze salt (See Smoked Mullet Dip, P. 29)
½   cup catsup
1   teaspoon mustard

Brush mullet with lemon juice. Coat with olive oil and sprinkle with basil. Add Seabreeze salt to taste. Broil on tray on heavy foil about 5 minutes or until lightly brown. Test with fork to see if done. Serve steaming hot. For optional topping, stir catsup and mustard on mullet; broil 1 minute.

Hazel Logue

Salmon Patties

1   large can pink salmon
1   egg
Salt and black pepper to taste
½   cup cornmeal
1   small onion, chopped fine

Mix egg and salmon, add salt and pepper. Add meal to mixture, enough to form rounded tablespoons of mixture to form balls or patties. Fry in hot oil until golden brown.

Mavis R. Zorn

Recipe used many times during our childhood by my mother, Bessie Lawrence Robinson.

Variation submitted by Alice C. McCorkle: May substitute flour for meal.
Variation submitted by Carolyn H. Chason: May add 2 tablespoons mayonnaise.
Variation submitted by Donna C. Powell: May substitute ¼ cup hushpuppy mix, dab of mayonnaise, pinch of dry mustard, and 2 to 3 dashes of Tabasco sauce.

Aunt Maggie Sholar's Weiner Stew

6   potatoes, cubed
1   can bean sprouts
1 to 2 onions, chopped
1   package wieners
Salt and pepper to taste
¼   cup oil

In stew pot, add potatoes, bean sprouts, and onions; cover with water. Salt and pepper to taste. Boil until potatoes are tender. Add cut wieners to mixture. Serves 4 people. Serve with very thin southern fried cornbread.

Betty Hester

This was made in Sholar's Grocery Store to feed employees.

Mason's Essential Spice Mix

2½   tablespoons paprika
2   tablespoons salt
2   tablespoons garlic powder
2   tablespoons black pepper
1   tablespoon onion powder
1   tablespoon cayenne pepper
1   tablespoon thyme
1   tablespoon dried oregano
1   teaspoon cumin
1   teaspoon crushed red pepper

Combine all ingredients in a bowl and mix thoroughly. Makes ½ cup. Keep sealed tightly. Use this to season meats, vegetables, and soups. Excellent, if I say so myself!

John L. Mason

Grady County Wash Pot Pilau

Equipment needed

1	8 to 12 gallon cast iron wash pot
1	4 foot wood stirring paddle
1	gallon glass or plastic pickle jar for measuring
1	flat shovel or rake for fire control
1	5 gallon bucket for measuring

Wash pot thoroughly, arrange Georgia light-wood (fat splinters) under small amount of dry pine wood split in 12 to15-inches in length. Add 7 gallons of clear water to pot. Light fire and add small amount of split oak wood after fire starts. Bring water to a boil. Add:

2	pounds of solid margarine
2	16-ounce containers chicken base (Tones brand) or
3	4.8 ounce containers chicken bouillon (Maggi brand)
10	pounds cooked, chopped chicken
2	large tablespoons black pepper
1	full gallon jar of converted rice (Uncle Ben's brand)

(No salt needed due to salt content of chicken base)

After pot boils again, add rice. Stir pot continually until rice begins to soften to taste, usually about 30 to 45 minutes. Pull fire from pot and cover with wood top. Check every 5 minutes for finished product. Add water, if necessary. Stir as needed. Rice should be ready to serve in 15 to 20 minutes. This cooking will serve at least 50 people.

Logan Lewis

Slaw, sweet pickles, bread or crackers added to a plate of the chicken and rice makes a nice meal. Plain pound cake adds the finishing touch.

Wash Pot

Chicken Pilau Suppers have been successful fund raisers for the Grady County Historical Society for several years. Logan Lewis serves as the "General of the Cooking Brigade". This dish is also known as pilaf, perlo, perloo, and purlou.

B.N.H.

Smokehouse

Every farmer had a smokehouse for curing meat products on his place. A fire would be built on the dirt floor to smoke the meat, which hung from the rafters.

Vegetables . . .

Old Log House on Bond Road

This log cabin increased in size as the family grew! The original structure was typical in this area in the 1800s.

Corn Chowder

Chop 1 small onion and cook on low heat in sauce pan in 2 tablespoons butter until clear. Bring 2 cans (14½-ounce) chicken broth, 3 medium potatoes (peeled and diced), 1 cup chopped smoked ham, 1 can (8¾-ounce) whole kernel corn, and ¼ teaspoon freshly ground pepper to boil in medium saucepan. Reduce heat, cover and simmer 15 to 20 minutes until tender. Whisk ¼ cup flour with 1 cup milk in bowl until smooth. Whisk into corn/potato mixture. Stir in ¼ cup butter and onions. Simmer, stirring for 2 to 3 minutes until butter melts and soup thickens. Sprinkle with parsley before serving. Makes 5 cups.

Deb Phillips

Quick Hamburger Soup

1 to 1½ pounds of hamburger meat (browned and drained)
1   medium onion, chopped
1   can of Veg-all
1   can whole kernel corn
2   cans of Campbell's Cream of Tomato Soup

Combine hamburger, onion, Veg-all, corn, and soup in a boiler and cook for at least 20 minutes. You can cook it longer, it will only get better.

Linda Pearce

Secret Soup

1   pound hamburger meat
3   medium potatoes, cubed
3   carrots, chopped
3   celery stalks, chopped
1   medium onion, chopped
1   26-ounce can stewed tomatoes
4   cups water
1   teaspoon salt
2   teaspoons sugar
1   can Campbell's Cream Soup (any flavor)

Brown hamburger and add remaining ingredients. Bring to a boil. Reduce heat and simmer for 3 to 4 hours. Optional: Add any leftovers or use mixed vegetables. Add water if needed. Try a little parsley and tarragon to perk it up even more.

Marjorie Mayfield Taylor

Years ago when long distance calls were rare, I phoned Aunt Mabel Van Landingham to find out how to make her wonderful soup. She assured me, "The secret is a can of Campbell's Cream of Any Flavor." Then she gave me this list of ingredients.

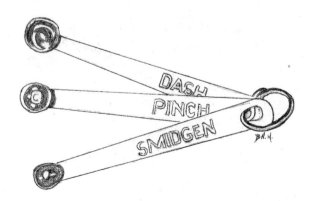

Spicy Eggplant Soup

2   slices bacon
1   small carrot, thinly sliced
¼   cup onion, chopped
1   small garlic clove, minced
4   cups cubed, peeled eggplant
2½   cups chicken broth
⅛   teaspoon ground red pepper
1   medium potato peeled and grated
½   cup light cream or milk
1   teaspoon curry powder added to bacon drippings
Salt and pepper to taste

Cook bacon, drain and save crumbled bacon. In drippings, cook the carrot, onion, and garlic until done but not brown. Add eggplant, broth, salt, and pepper. Simmer until vegetables are tender. Add potato and cook at least 20 minutes more. Mash vegetables slightly, stir in cream and heat through. Garnish with the bacon. I use white pepper, Swanson's broth, grate the potatoes and use half and half. It is absolutely outstanding and is every bit as good as the soup at Commander's Palace Restaurant in New Orleans.

Nancy Baker Beasley

I've been making this for over 30 years. I also add a dash or two of curry, thyme, and basil.

Tomato and Okra Gumbo

2   pounds fresh or frozen okra
1   #2 can of tomatoes or fresh tomatoes
½   teaspoon salt
1   tablespoon margarine
3   slices bacon (cooked and crumbled)

Cut okra in ½ inch pieces, pour tomatoes in deep sauce pan. Add okra along with seasonings. Cover and cook on medium heat for 20 minutes. Serves 8.

Alice McCorkle

My mother gave me this recipe. I remember eating it over rice.

Turnip Soup

3   large turnip roots, chopped
6   cups milk
Salt and pepper to taste
Butter to taste

Place turnips in large saucepan with 1 cup water; cook for about 10 minutes or until tender. Add milk, salt, pepper, and butter. Bring to a boil, stirring constantly. Serve hot with crackers. Similar in taste to oyster stew. Makes 4 to 5 servings.

Winnie Jean Hester

Recipe from Pilot International Fiftieth Anniversary Cookbook--1971. Macie M. Porter-Chester, South Carolina

Parmesan Potatoes

Wash potatoes and quarter, leaving peel on. Adjust amount according to crowd. Melt 1 stick of margarine in baking dish. In Ziploc bag, prepare a mixture of ½ Parmesan cheese and ½ flour. Coat potatoes and place in margarine. Bake 1 hour at 425 degrees. Turn ½ way through cooking.

Mary Thomas Ward

Potato Fritters

1½ cups left over mashed potatoes
1   egg
2   tablespoons flour
½   medium onion, finely chopped

In large bowl mix all ingredients. Drop 1 tablespoon at a time in hot cooking oil until all are golden brown. These go well with hamburgers or hotdogs. If you would like to reuse your cooking oil, cook French fries or a potato in it.

Katie F. Ansley

Mashed Sweet Potatoes in Orange Shells

3   oranges, halved crosswise
2   cups cooked, mashed sweet potatoes
¼   teaspoon salt
¹/₃   teaspoon pepper
2   tablespoons butter, softened
3   marshmallows, halved
¼   cup chopped pecans

Remove pulp from oranges, leaving rind intact. Press pulp through sieve or food mill to extract ¼ cup orange juice. Combine orange juice, sweet potatoes, salt, pepper, and butter. Fill orange shells with potato mixture. Top each with a marshmallow half and chopped nuts. Bake at 350 degrees for 20 minutes or until lightly brown. Serves 6.

Joyce M. Pickens

Roasted Sweet Potatoes with Garlic and Rosemary

1½   pounds sweet potatoes, peeled and cut into ½-inch thick slices
6   garlic cloves (or more if preferred)
3   tablespoons olive oil
2   teaspoons minced fresh rosemary (or 1 teaspoon dried)
Salt and fresh ground pepper

Place potatoes and garlic in sauce pan. Cover with water and bring to a boil. Simmer for about 5 minutes. Drain in a colander. Preheat oven to 425 degrees. Drizzle about half the olive oil in baking dish. Arrange potatoes and garlic in baking dish (with garlic on top of potatoes). Drizzle with remaining olive oil. Sprinkle with rosemary, salt, and black pepper. Bake 25 to 30 minutes or until golden brown.

Ruth Sims

Sweet Potato Pudding

2   cups grated raw sweet potatoes
1   cup sugar
1   cup milk
3   teaspoons margarine
1   teaspoon vanilla flavoring
1   egg

Mix all ingredients well. Bake at 350 degrees for 1 to 1½ hours. Bake in 5 x 9 x 2-inch casserole dish. Stir every 20 to 30 minutes to keep from burning.

Betty Hester

Sweet Potato Soufflé Crunch

3   cups cooked mashed sweet potatoes
1   cup sugar
2   eggs, slightly beaten
2½   tablespoons butter, melted
1   cup sweet milk
1   teaspoon vanilla

Topping
2½   tablespoons butter, melted
1   cup light brown sugar
¹/₃ cup all-purpose flour
1   cup chopped nuts

Mix all ingredients together. Pour into greased baking dish. Cover with topping. Bake at 350 degrees for 35 minutes. May add 1 cup coconut to topping.

Naomi Davis Scarbrough

Naomi Davis Scarbrough is the daughter of Confederate Veteran, Jonah Beal Davis.

Similar recipes submitted by Margaret Tyson and Sue C. Askew.

Homemade Baked Beans

2	cans pork and beans
½	teaspoon celery seed
1	small can chunk or crushed pineapple
1	large onion, chopped
1	bell pepper, chopped
⅓	cup dark brown sugar
¼	cup barbecue sauce

Mix all ingredients, place in casserole dish and top with bacon slices. Bake at 350 degrees for 1½ hours.

Betty Bannister

This recipe has been in my family many years.

Baked Beans

2	cups navy beans
4	inch square of fat back
1	large onion, chopped
1	teaspoon dry mustard
1	tablespoon salt
¼	cup sugar
½	cup molasses

Soak beans overnight. Drain and boil until skins curl. Drain. In a large baking dish put the fat back, onion, dry mustard, salt, sugar, and molasses. Pour beans in on top and just cover with hot water. Put lid on tight; bake at 250 degrees for 8 to 9 hours. Check every couple of hours; add just enough hot water to keep beans covered. Keep temperature as even as possible. Serve with hot cornbread, cole slaw, and pickles.

Helen Williams

Recipe of Mrs. A.H. Sprayberry, mother of a friend in Newnan, Georgia.

Tomatoes and Rice

Cook ham bone (or cut up pieces of ham) until tender. Add canned tomatoes that have been chopped and rice according to size of dish you need to make. Add salt and pepper. Small amounts of water may be added if needed. Some cooks do not use meat and add seasoning grease or butter instead.

Annette Harrell

Tomato Tart

1	15-ounce refrigerated piecrust
2	cups shredded Mozzarella cheese
3	tablespoons chopped, fresh basil
3	medium ripe tomatoes, peeled and cut into ½-inch slices
1½	tablespoons olive oil
¼	teaspoon salt
¼	teaspoon pepper

Fit pie crust into a 10-inch tart pan according to package directions, trim any excess pastry along edges. Generously prick bottom and sides of pastry with fork. Bake at 400 degrees for 5 minutes. Sprinkle cheese evenly into pastry shell, and top with 2 tablespoons basil. Arrange tomato slices on top. Brush with oil, and sprinkle with salt and pepper. Place on a baking sheet on lower rack of oven. Bake at 400 degrees for 35 to 40 minutes. Remove from oven, sprinkle with remaining 1 tablespoon basil. Let stand 5 minutes before serving. Yield 8 to10 servings.

Nancy Baker Beasley

Marinated Carrots

5   cups (1 pound bag frozen sliced) carrots, cooked, drained, and, cooled (Do not overcook.)
1   medium sweet onion, peeled and sliced
1   medium green pepper cut in ¼ slices
1   can tomato sauce (10¾-ounce)
½   cup oil (corn, vegetable, or canola)
1   cup sugar
¾   cup white vinegar
1   teaspoon prepared mustard
1   teaspoon Worcestershire sauce
1   teaspoon salt
1   teaspoon black pepper

Combine last eight ingredients. Mix well to dissolve sugar and mustard. Add carrots, onion, and pepper. Cover and refrigerate overnight. Lift carrots, onion, and pepper from liquid to serve. Store leftovers in liquid.

Thomas W. Brown

Recipe was used often by my mother, Aleyne W. Brown (1906-1991).

Fried Corn

Cut 2 cups corn from the cobs. Scrape cobs after removing kernels to get the juice that remained. Put about ⅓ to ½ stick margarine or butter into fry pan, pour in the corn. Add pinch of salt and sugar to taste and a little water. Cook about 20 minutes until done and thick as you like. You will need to stir frequently and may need to add additional water. The right maturity of corn could be tested by sticking a thumb nail in a kernel. If juice popped out, it was right! This stage of corn was referred to as "roast'n'ears" (roasting ears.) This is really stewed corn, but got its name because it was cooked in a fry pan.

Carolyn H. Chason

Ansley's Broiled Tomatoes

Tomatoes, slices of ¼ to ½-inch thickness
Butter or margarine
Parmesan cheese

Place tomatoes on foil-lined cookie sheet. Put a pat of butter on each slice. Sprinkle cheese on top of tomato and butter. Place in oven on broil until cheese slightly browns (about 3 to 5 minutes). Watch very carefully; can over brown easily.

Tad David

Fried Green Tomatoes

3   **slices bacon**
4   **green tomatoes, cut into ½-inch slices**
1   **cup fine ground cornmeal**
Salt and pepper to taste
½   **cup milk**

Fry bacon in heavy skillet. Remove to absorbent paper. Mix meal, salt, and pepper. Dip tomatoes into milk, remove and coat with cornmeal mixture. Fry tomatoes in bacon grease over medium heat until light brown, about 1½ minutes on each side.

Helen C. Bishop

Leather Britches

To preserve green beans through the winter, string on strong thread and hang to dry. To eat: unstring, break up, wash, and soak in water (overnight or several hours). Cook like fresh beans with fat back or streak o'lean for seasoning. Salt to taste.

Phillip Martin

My mother, the late Mildred Martin (Mrs. J.L.), grew up in Tennessee where these Leather Britches were a winter staple.

Mom's Potta Collards

2   bunches collards
Fatback or country cured ham bone
1   medium onion, cut in half
1   teaspoon pepper sauce
1   tablespoon finely chopped garlic
1   tablespoon cane syrup
¼   teaspoon black pepper
1   teaspoon sugar
Salt to taste

Pick out and strip the collard leaves from the tough stems. Wash well to get rid of the grit; takes about 3 to 4 washings. Put fatback or ham bone in plenty of cold water, bring to a good rolling boil. Drop in collards by handfuls and cover. If pot is too small, fill it then let them wilt, then there is plenty of room for the rest. When wilted, add enough water to cover. Add other seasonings. Turn down on low and cook for one and one half hours or until tender.

Polly A. Kincaid

My mother, while cooking for our family, used this recipe for years and I still use it.

Collards

Wash collard greens several times, removing all grit. Twist to break apart (do not cut). Put a dash of soda in last rinse water. Put in a large pot or skillet (use as little water as possible) and put in a few at a time and let wilt down, then add some more. Add a little hot water at the time while cooking. Add white salt meat, and smoked meat for seasoning and fried meat grease (a lot of fried meat grease-approximately ¼ cup). Add a touch of sugar and ¼ teaspoon soda. Let come to a boil; turn down to medium heat. It is better to cook on low heat for a very long time, at least two hours. After they are done, take up and chop greens (do this for a long period of time).

Esther H. Carter

This is one of the dishes I am asked to bring to all family gatherings and reunions.

Fried Okra

1 to 1¼ pounds okra
8   cups water
½   cup salt
Corn meal
Cooking oil

Wash okra well; drain. Cut pods into ½ inch slices. Combine water and salt. Pour over okra. Soak 30 minutes; drain; rinse well and drain again. Roll in cornmeal. Fry in hot oil until golden brown.

Carolyn H. Chason

New Year's Black-Eyed Peas

16   ounces dried black-eyed peas
½   pound salt pork
3   cups chopped onions
1   bunch chopped green onions
2   cloves garlic
1½   teaspoons salt
1   teaspoon pepper
1   teaspoon red pepper
3   dashes hot sauce
1   tablespoon Worcestershire sauce
1   8-ounce can tomato sauce
¼   teaspoon oregano
2   pounds smoked sausage cut into 1-inch pieces.

Sort and wash peas. Cover with water and soak overnight. Drain, add pork; cover with water and cook over low heat for 45 minutes. Add the remaining ingredients except sausage. Cover and cook over low heat for 1 hour. Stir occasionally. Add sausage and cook uncovered over low heat for 45 minutes. Serve over rice.

Dot Dalton

Hoppin' John

1	pound dried black-eyed peas
1	large onion, peeled and finely chopped
2	tablespoons vegetable oil
1	teaspoon garlic salt
1	teaspoon oregano
5	cups chicken stock
8	cups hot cooked rice

Soak peas overnight with water to cover by 2 inches. Drain peas; set aside. In large Dutch oven, sauté onion in oil until transparent; add peas, seasonings, and chicken stock. Cover and cook slowly until peas are tender, about 30 to 40 minutes. If made ahead, cover and reheat. For each serving, serve ½ cup of peas over ½ cup rice. Makes 16 servings.

La Vonne Childers

Greens and Pot Liquor Dodgers

1	quart greens, with pot liquor, cooked almost done
1	cup corn meal
½	teaspoon salt
½	teaspoon baking powder
1	cup pot liquor, drained from greens, hot
1	tablespoon fat, melted

Combine meal, salt, and baking powder. Stir in hot pot liquor and fat. Let mixture stand for 15 minutes. Shape mixture into cylinder biscuits, 2½ inches long and 1 inch wide. Arrange dodgers on top of greens from which almost all pot liquor has been drained. Cook, tightly covered for 20 minutes. Garnish tops of dodgers with a light sprinkling of paprika before cooking.

La Vonne Childers

Grits and Greens

4   cups half-and-half cream
1   cup quick cooking grits
1   pound package frozen collards, thawed
1½   cups Parmesan cheese
Butter, salt, pepper

Heat half and half on medium heat until warm; add grits and stir until thick. Sauté collards in butter. Add collards and cheese to grits. Add salt, pepper, and butter to taste. Mix well and serve hot.

Mary H. Chason

This is a strange sounding combination, but if you like greens, you'll love this dish! Perfect New Year's dish.

Stuffed Peppers

3   medium green peppers
1   beef bouillon cube
½   pound ground beef
1   clove garlic (minced) or garlic powder
1   cup shredded cheddar cheese
Salt
1   15-ounce can tomato sauce
½   cup chopped onion
1½   cups cooked rice
½   teaspoon Italian herb seasoning

Cut peppers in half length wise. Remove seeds and membrane. Sprinkle with salt. Place in 2-quart baking dish. Dissolve bouillon cube in half of tomato sauce in small bowl. In skillet cook beef, onions, and garlic until beef loses redness. Drain fat. Add rice, Italian herb seasoning, ½ teaspoon salt, 1 cup sauce mixture, and half of cheese. Fill peppers with equal amounts of beef mixture. Top with remaining sauce mixture and cheese. Cover and bake at 375 degrees for 45 minutes. Makes 6 servings.

Tommie Jean M. Cooper

Vegetable Casserole

1	can French style green beans
1	can white corn
1	can cream of celery soup
½	cup sour cream
1	cup cheddar cheese
1	2-ounce jar pimento
½	cup chopped onion

Season to taste

Drain corn and green beans and mix with remaining ingredients. Pour into lightly greased casserole dish. Top with onion rings. Bake at 300 degrees for 45 minutes.

Mary Allegood

Squash Casserole I

1½ to 2 pounds yellow squash

1	medium onion
1	green pepper, chopped
2	carrots, grated
1	stick butter
1	can of cream of chicken or cream of mushroom soup
½	pint sour cream
1	package herb dressing mix or croutons

Cook squash and onion; drain off liquid. Melt butter. Mix all ingredients together using only half of the dressing. Place in greased baking dish. Top with the rest of the herb dressing. Bake at 350 degrees for 35 minutes.

Mary Allegood

Similar recipe submitted by Thomas W. Brown.

Squash Casserole II

3   cups squash
3   tablespoons butter
1   beef bouillon cube
1   onion, grated or cut
2   eggs, well beaten
Salt and pepper to taste
1   cup sour cream

Topping
1   cup bread crumbs
½   cup shredded cheese
1   teaspoon paprika

Cook squash until tender. Drain, mash and add salt, pepper, butter, bouillon cube, and onions. Add eggs and sour cream. Put in casserole dish. Combine bread crumbs, cheese, and paprika. Sprinkle over top of squash. Bake at 325 degrees for 30 minutes.

Elizabeth Maxwell

Squash Casserole III

2   pounds yellow squash
1   can mushroom soup
¼   pound sharp cheddar cheese
Salt and pepper to taste

Slice squash; cook in salt water until tender. Drain. In a medium size casserole, layer squash, soup, cheese, salt, and pepper. Continue to top of dish. Bake at 450 degrees until cheese and soup are thoroughly heated. Serves 6 to 8.

Margaret Tyson

This was a recipe my grandmother, Margaret K. LeGette, used.

Stuffed Squash

6   medium sized yellow squash
¼   stick margarine or butter
Salt and pepper to taste
½   cup cracker or bread crumbs
1   egg, beaten

Cook squash in boiling salted water until tender, not soft. Remove from water and slice each squash lengthwise, making two halves. Scoop out inside pulp. Season pulp with butter, salt and pepper to taste. Add cracker crumbs to make a medium stiff stuffing. Season squash shells with salt, pepper, and dots of butter. Fill shells with stuffing. Sprinkle more cracker crumbs on top. Bake in 350 degrees oven until crumbs are brown. For added flavor, top with grated cheese.

Patsy C. Plant

During squash season, I grew tired of fried, stewed squash, and casseroles, so I experimented and came up with this in the seventies.

Mildred Allen Lennertz's Butternut Squash Casserole

2   cups cooked squash, drained and mashed
3   eggs
¾   stick margarine
1   cup milk
¾   cup sugar
½   teaspoon ginger
½   teaspoon coconut flavoring

Blend all. Cook in greased casserole in pan of water 45 minutes at 350 degrees. Cover with buttered Ritz cracker crumbs and brown. (Put crumbs on the last 15 minutes of cooking time.)

Helen Cooper Allen

Cheesy Broccoli Bake

1	package frozen chopped broccoli
½	cup mayonnaise
½	cup cream of mushroom soup
1	egg
1½	cups grated cheese
1	cup crushed crackers

Cook broccoli according to package directions; drain well and cool.
Combine mayonnaise, soup, egg, and grated cheese; stir in cooked broccoli.
Pour into a buttered casserole dish and sprinkle cracker crumbs on top.
Bake at 325 degrees for 30 minutes.

Laura M. Brinkley

When I went to college, I was given a book, "Where's Mom Now That I Need Her?"
Every roommate I had always loved the recipe, "Cheesy Broccoli Bake".

Broccoli-Egg Casserole

1	pound broccoli
2	tablespoons all-purpose flour
½	teaspoon baking powder
5	beaten eggs
1	cup cream style cottage cheese
4	slices bacon, cooked and crumbled
½	cup shredded Swiss cheese

Cut off flower buds and set aside. Chop remaining stalk. Cook stalks covered in small amount of boiling salted water for 5 minutes. Cook flower buds last 2 minutes. Stir flour, baking powder and add to beaten eggs. Stir in cottage cheese and bacon. Spread broccoli in a 10 x 6 x 2-inch baking dish. Pour egg mixture over broccoli. Bake 350 degrees for 20 minutes. Sprinkle with Swiss cheese and bake 3 minutes more. Let stand 5 minutes before serving. This recipe serves 6. It may be doubled or tripled. After cooking, cover with foil and wrap in thick beach towels. It will stay warm for 45 to 60 minutes. Great for large breakfast, brunch, or lunch gatherings with fruit, muffins and beverage.

Lequita LeGette

Broccoli Cheese Rice

1	package frozen chopped broccoli
1	8-ounce jar Cheez Whiz
1	can cream of chicken soup
1	can sliced water chestnuts

Rice for 6 to 8

Topping
1	stack Ritz crackers
½	stick butter

Mix first four ingredients and stir into cooked rice. Pour into a buttered or non stick cooking sprayed 9 x 13-inch dish. Crush crackers and top the casserole; use remaining butter sliced on top of crackers. Bake at 350 degrees for 30 minutes.

Lyn Robinson
174 Vegetables

Broccoli Casserole

2   packages frozen chopped broccoli
1   can cream of mushroom soup
¾   cup mayonnaise
1   small onion, diced
Shredded cheese

Cook broccoli according to package directions. Drain. Add other ingredients and mix well. Top with melted butter and bread crumbs. Bake at 350 degrees for 30 minutes.

Christine Cooper

Recipe was given to my daughter-in-law, Dianne, by a friend, Carolyn Hughes, of Camilla, over twenty years ago.

Asparagus Casserole I

1   can green asparagus spears, drained (handle gently)
2   hard-boiled eggs, chopped and divided into thirds
¼   cup milk
1   teaspoon prepared mustard
1   can cream of mushroom soup, mixed with milk and mustard
Cracker crumbs (approximately 6 saltine crackers per layer)

In loaf size baking dish place layer of asparagus, sprinkle ¹/₃ of eggs and ¹/₃ cracker crumbs. Spoon ¹/₃ soup, milk and mustard mixture over cracker crumbs. Repeat layers until all gone. Bake uncovered 30 minutes in 350 degrees oven.

Thomas W. Brown

My mother, Aleyne W. Brown (1906-1991), said this came from Aunt Mellie Brown, wife of Frances Thurston ("Uncle Buster") Brown, brother of William B. Brown (1863-1929) of Cairo, Georgia.

Asparagus Casserole II

2   cups Ritz cracker crumbs
½   pound grated cheddar cheese
1   can asparagus spears or tips
1   cup cream of asparagus soup
½   cup chopped pecans
½   cup butter

Mix cheese with cracker crumbs. Add liquid from asparagus to soup. Put a layer of crumbs and cheese in bottom of casserole dish. Add layer of asparagus and sprinkle with nuts. Cover with soup and repeat, ending with crackers and cheese on top. Garnish with nuts. Pour butter over casserole. Bake at 350 degrees for 20 to 30 minutes.

Sharon Whitfield

Accompaniments . . .

Kennemur
Mc Nair
House
Whigham,
Georgia

McNair-Kennemur House

This two story Victorian house was built circa 1870 for Samuel G. W. and Elizabeth Butler McNair of the North Carolina Settlement (now Calvary) on West Broad Street in Whigham. Later it became the Kennemurs' family home.

Fried Apples

Slice fresh (preferably green) apples with core and seeds removed. Place in cast iron skillet which has been greased with bacon drippings, sausage fat, or, for the healthy, vegetable oil. Add some sugar. Simmer apples in covered skillet till soft and beginning to candy. Serve with buttermilk biscuits.

Susan Y. Perkins

This came from my Grandmother Mitchell's farm in Virginia where fried apples were the daily breakfast fare along with country ham that came out of the smokehouse.

Hot Pepper Jelly

3	red bell peppers, seeded and finely chopped
2	green bell peppers, seeded and minced
10	jalapeno peppers, seeded and minced
1	cup cider vinegar
5	cups white sugar
1	package (1.75 ounces) powdered pectin

Sterilize canning jars. Measure 4 cups of prepared peppers and discard any extras. Put peppers into a 6 or 8-quart sauce pot. Stir in vinegar and fruit pectin. Bring mixture to a full rolling boil and boil exactly 1 minute, stirring constantly. Remove from heat. Skim off any foam with a metal spoon. Quickly ladle jelly into prepared jars, filling to within $1/8$ inch of the tops. Wipe jar rims and threads. Cover with flat lids and screw on bands tightly. Invert jars 5 minutes, then turn upright.

Andrea P. Webb

Strawberry Preserves ("Ma" Hunziker)

1   quart strawberries
3   cups sugar

Wash and cap strawberries. Put sugar over berries and let stand 20 minutes. Put on stove and boil hard for 5 minutes. Add 2 more cups sugar and boil 3 more minutes. Put in jars and seal while hot.

Cheryl Hunziker

Ma cooked up into her 90's, and died at 101.

Rozelle Jelly

8   cups Rozelle petals
6   cups water

Add Rozelle petals to water. Boil 5 minutes. Strain mixture through cheese cloth to get juice. Mix 4 cups juice, 1 package sure jell, and 5 cups sugar in large pot. Bring to rolling boil. Boil 1 minute and take off heat. Pour into sterilized jars and seal.

Mrs. Montine Miles

Each year my husband and I would grow Rozelle bushes in our yard. After the blooms fall off there is a seed pod left. Around each pod are the petals that you pick to make the jelly. You then have to pick the petals away from the seed pod. Wash thoroughly before using.

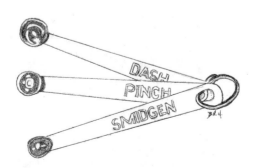

Strawberry Figs

3   cups peeled, chopped figs
3   cups sugar
1   small package strawbery gelatin

Boil for 10 minutes on medium high, stirring all the time. Remove from heat. Add 1 package strawberry gelatin, then bring to boil again. Skim off foam. Put in prepared jars and seal.

Danielle Lewis Jones

Pear/Peach Jelly

2   cups juice from pears or favorite fruit
1   cup sugar

Peel and cut fruit into small pieces. Cover with water and cook until tender. Drain juice. Measure juice and sugar in large boiler. Cook at low heat until it foams. The jelly is done when dropped by spoon onto plate and it does not run. Pour into sterilized jars and seal.

Rosaline Mills

As a child growing up on a farm with lots of brothers and sisters, we learned to cook at an early age. Everything was homemade. My mother taught us all how to cook and make things from scratch.

Mayhaw Jelly

4   cups prepared mayhaw juice (1 gallon of mayhaws covered with
         water in 6 or 8 quart sauce pan or Dutch oven)
5   cups sugar
1   box Sure-Jell fruit pectin

Prepare mayhaw berries by cooking over medium heat for 30 minutes, cool. Extract juice from berries, mash berries with potato masher and squeeze in cheesecloth, t-shirt, or pillowcase to strain the juice. Measure 4 cups of juice and pour into 6 or 8 quart saucepan or Dutch oven. Stir in Sure-Jell and bring to a full boil, stirring constantly. Stir in sugar and bring to full boil again. Boil for 1 minute, stirring constantly. Remove from heat, skim off foam. Pour hot jelly into hot, sterilized jars and seal with hot sterilized lids and rings. Yield 6 ½ pints.

Esther H. Carter

Similar recipe submitted by Donna C. Powell

Mayhaws are usually found in what is referred to as the 'sloughs' or on riverbanks. This area of the country (South Georgia) is the most prominent, if not the only, place this tree grows. You gather them usually in May and pick only the ripe ones. The easiest way to gather them is to place an old sheet on the ground beneath the tree and shake the tree so that the berries fall onto the sheet. Many of the berries fall into the river and you either wade into the river-if it is a shallow area- or get into a boat and use "dip nets" to gather them up. According to "Mr. Webster," the definition for mayhaw is "a small hawthorn common in the southern United States", (because the fruit ripens in May.) The best way to eat this jelly that "many would die for" is with good old homemade buttermilk biscuits hot from the oven.

Fried Syrup

Fry several slices of side pork meat in cast iron skillet. Pour off all grease except 3 tablespoons. Pour cane syrup into skillet with grease and cook until thick-not too thick or it will candy. Enjoy fried syrup with homemade buttermilk biscuits.

Esther H. Carter

Thanksgiving Dressing

½   teaspoon baking soda
2   tablespoons baking powder
2   cups self-rising corn meal
½   cup self-rising flour
1   teaspoon salt
1   teaspoon sugar
2   eggs
2   cups buttermilk
1   sleeve saltine crackers
6   slices white bread, crumbled
1   4-ounce package Pepperidge Farm seasoned bread crumbs
1   cup chopped onion
1   cup chopped celery
4 to 5 cups turkey or chicken stock (more if moister dressing desired)
¼   teaspoon celery salt
1   teaspoon poultry seasoning
½   teaspoon rubbed sage
¼   cup butter

Preheat oven to 425 degrees. Combine cornmeal, flour, baking soda, baking powder, salt, sugar, eggs, and buttermilk. Pour into greased 13 x 9-inch baking dish. Bake for 25 minutes for muffin bread. In large mixing bowl, combine crumbled muffin bread, crumbled saltine crackers, white bread crumbs and seasoned breadcrumbs. Steam onions and celery in broth and butter; add to bread mixture. Add broth and seasonings. Add additional broth to make moister dressing, if desired. Bake in two 13 x 9-inch baking dishes or larger baking pan for 45 minutes at 350 degrees. Serves 15. Serve with giblet gravy and cranberry sauce.

Donna C. Powell

My grandmother, Belle Banks McDaniel, gave me the basic muffin bread recipe to which I've added my measurements and additional ingredients.

Similar recipes submitted Cathy Walden Moore and Wynell Mitchell.

Dumplings

¹/₃   cup shortening
²/₃   cup milk
1½ to 2 cups all-purpose flour
Salt and pepper to taste

Place sifted flour in biscuit tray; add shortening and milk. Stir until moistened. Add more sifted flour, if needed, to make a soft dough. Pinch off small amount and roll out, then cut in strips and drop in broth. Salt and pepper while cooking.

Marilyn W. Joyner

My mother-in-law, Isabel Joyner, used this recipe and they were delicious. Mine don't taste like hers but, then she was a wonderful cook.

Corned Beef Gravy

½   can of corned beef
1   medium onion, chopped
4   tablespoons cooking oil
¹/₃   cup flour
2½   cups water
½   teaspoon salt
Pepper, if desired

Heat cooking oil until hot in a skillet. Mix in flour and stir. Mix in onions; stir until light brown. Add water, salt and stir. Break up the corned beef into the gravy and stir. Turn heat down and let the gravy simmer for 15 to 20 minutes. Serve over rice. Makes 6 to 8 servings.

Mabel Land

Hollandaise Sauce

3   egg yolks
$^1/_8$ teaspoon salt
$^1/_8$ teaspoon ground red pepper
2   tablespoons lemon juice
$^1/_2$ cup butter or margarine, cut into pieces

Whisk first 3 ingredients in top of a double boiler; gradually add lemon juice, stirring constantly. Cook until mixture thickens. Add about one third of the butter to egg mixture, cook over hot water, stirring constantly until butter melts. Add another third of butter, as butter melts, stir in remaining butter. Cook, whisking constantly until smooth and thickened.

Gloria R. Searcy

Tomato Gravy

Fry bacon. Add flour to 3 tablespoons grease and brown a little (not on high heat). Add salt and pepper. Add $^1/_2$ to 1 pint tomatoes (home canned tomatoes are best). Simmer ingredients. Add water as needed. Some cooks add milk. You can make as thick or as thin as you like. Delicious served on grits or homemade buttermilk biscuits or with both.

Nellie M. Harrell, Esther H. Carter

Lemon Gravy

Juice of 2 lemons (approximately $^1/_4$ cup)
$1^2/_3$ cups water
$1^1/_2$ cups flour

Blend all ingredients. Baste cooked turkey with gravy. Brown at 450 degrees, then turn and baste again. After turkey is browned, add water to gravy and let come to a boil. Serve gravy with turkey and dressing.

Nellie M. Harrell

I learned this from my mother, Mrs. Mary Ida Gray Murkerson.

Lemon Sauce

1   cup sugar
½   teaspoon salt
2   tablespoons flour
1   tablespoon butter
2   eggs
2   lemons (juice only)
1   lemon rind, grated
2   cups water

Mix dry ingredients, add remainder. Boil for about 10 minutes or until it thickens. Stir constantly while mixture boils. Good on gingerbread.

Gloria R. Searcy

My mother, Bessie L. Robinson, used this recipe for a variety of things. She would cook a layer cake and use this sauce for icing. Also, instead of using jelly for jelly roll, she would use this sauce. Mom loved lemon flavored recipes! She loved lemon pie.

Marinated Sweet Onion Rings

2   large sweet onions, peeled and thinly sliced
¼   cup water
½   cup sugar
²/₃   cup white wine vinegar
2   teaspoons salt
¹/₈   teaspoon crushed red chiles
1   tablespoon chopped cilantro

Break onions into rings and place in bowl. Combine water, sugar, vinegar, salt, and chiles; bring mixture to a boil. Add cilantro and cool. Pour over onion rings and refrigerate 6 hours or longer. Makes 1 to 1½ quarts. Variation: One teaspoon dill weed may be substituted for red chiles and cilantro.

La Vonne Childers

Pickled Beans

To pickle beans, wash, string, and break beans into pieces. Cook until done, then drain and wash in cold water. If you want corn with your beans, and they are good pickled together, cut as much fresh corn from the cob as you want. Boil until done, drain and rinse in cold water. Mix beans and corn together and pack into a clean crock. Make a salt water solution of ½ cup salt to 1 gallon water, and pour over beans to cover. Place a large plate over this and weight down with a heavy, clean crock rock. Tie a cloth over the top of the crock and allow to stand for about 2 weeks. As the beans pickle, a scum will form that has to be removed every day. The beans, when pickled, can be taken from the crock, heated and eaten; or they can be canned in a hot water bath like kraut. Notice that in this recipe the beans are pickled in a traditional salt brine solution and not canned with vinegar to make them taste pickled.

Hazel Logue

Sauerkraut

Chop cabbage finely and put in quart jars. Add 2 teaspoons table salt and pour boiling water over and seal. In two weeks, it will be made, or the cabbage can be put up in a large crock and left to stand with 2 teaspoons salt per quart for two weeks. Then it can be put in canning jars and sealed.

Hazel Logue

Never make kraut when astrological signs are in the bowels. My mother, who considered sauerkraut a necessary staple-- used this recipe as one of the ways she preserved food.

Sweet Pickles

7   pounds of cucumbers, sliced
6   gallons of water (2 gallons at a time)
2   cups pickling lime
2   tablespoons alum
1   small box ginger
2   quarts of vinegar
4½   pounds of sugar

Spice Recipe
1   tablespoon salt
1   tablespoon celery seeds
1   tablespoon whole cloves
1   tablespoon pickling spice

Soak cucumbers 24 hours in lime water, take out of water and rinse well in cold water. Put cucumbers in 2 gallons of water with alum and soak 24 hours; rinse well in cold water. Put cucumbers in 2 gallons of water with ginger and soak 24 hours; rinse well in cold water and drain. Take 2 quarts vinegar, sugar, and spice; let soak 24 hours. Boil 30 minutes from time of boil and put in jars and seal.

Linda Pearce

Mrs. Louise Voyles gave me this recipe, so it is special. I like to use this pickle (diced) in my potato salad.

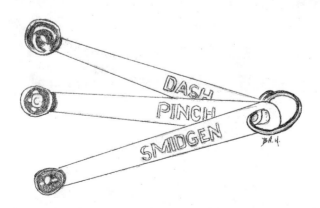

Nine-Day Cucumber Pickles

Wash and cut up cucumbers, about 5 to 7 pounds (after slicing). Make brine using 1 cup salt to 1 gallon water. Cover cucumbers with this brine and soak 3 days, making fresh brine each day. Make sure all cucumbers are covered with brine. Next three days soak cucumbers in alum water--2 scant tablespoons alum to 1 gallon water. Make fresh solution each day. Wash and let soak in clear water a short time. On seventh day make a vinegar solution, using 5 pounds sugar to ½ gallon vinegar and ½ cup mixed pickling spices. Place cucumbers in pot and pour vinegar solution over them. Heat to boiling point each day for two days. On ninth day, heat to boiling point; place in jars, and seal.

Helen C. Bishop

This was my mother's (Maggie H. Chason) favorite pickle recipe.

Corn Relish

12	ears of corn
2½	teaspoons celery seed or 1 stalk celery
4	large onions
2	green peppers
2	red peppers
1	large cabbage
4	cups sugar
1	tablespoon mustard
1½	quarts vinegar
2	tablespoons turmeric
1	tablespoon flour
1	teaspoon cayenne pepper

Salt to taste

Cut corn off cob. Grind cabbage, celery, onion and bell peppers. Cook until thick. Store in refrigerator, or store in jars until ready to eat.

Peggy A. Meyers

(Recipe was dated July 4, 1967 and in my mother's handwriting). I share this recipe because the art of making relish from scratch is about lost in my generation. My mother, Hortense Davis Johnson, owned and operated Davis and Wheeler Self Service Laundry during the early 1950s. When vegetables were in abundance, we took advantage of the season by canning almost all of them. Since my parents worked at full time jobs, I was given the opportunity to learn how to shell peas/beans, can and "put up" vegetables. My aunt, Lulu Mae Barrineau, and I would spend days at the canning plant by the old high school. At the end of the day, when the canning was done, we would divide the cans and go home...dog tired. I had a good teacher and excellent training.

Grandma Lewis' Pear Relish

1   gallon finely chopped pears
6   red bell peppers, finely chopped
6   green bell peppers, finely chopped
6   medium to large onions, finely chopped
3   cups sugar
Vinegar to cover well

Combine all ingredients in large non-reactive pot and bring to boil. Cook thirty minutes or until pears are tender. Put into sterilized jars and seal.

Shirley Maxwell Gale

Grandma Mary Virginia Kinsley Lewis (Mrs. Oscar Green Lewis) made this many times. I have the recipe in her handwriting where she put it for my mother, Edna Lewis Maxwell (Mrs. John Maxwell).

Donald McLean's Salsa

2   cups tomatoes, seeded and diced
1   cup cilantro
1   cup red onion, diced
Jalapeno peppers (to taste)
1   tablespoon garlic, minced
Juice of 1 lime

Combine all ingredients. Refrigerate before serving.

Kelly Scott

This is a Connecticut friend's recipe and is delicious!

Hot as Hell Pepper Sauce

½   cup chopped onion
½   cup chopped carrots
2   cloves garlic
12   whole habanero peppers
4   whole jalapeno peppers
2   ounces lime juice
1   tablespoon salt
1   tablespoon cumin
½   teaspoon oregano
1   teaspoon black pepper
½   cup distilled vinegar

Remove stems from the peppers and wash carefully. Place the peppers, onions, carrots, garlic, lime juice and heated vinegar in a blender. Blend until you have a well mixed, coarsely ground mixture. You may add more vinegar, if necessary. Then, add the remaining ingredients and blend slowly. This makes about 2 cups of hot sauce. This should keep for 4 months in the refrigerator. Be very careful handling the peppers. (I suggest you wear latex gloves while preparing this sauce!)

John L. Mason

Roasted Pepper Sauce

1   can roasted red pepper, diced
¼   cup fresh basil
¼   cup fresh oregano
2   teaspoons chopped garlic
3   cups tomato sauce
½   cup chopped onion (optional)
2   teaspoons sugar
Salt and pepper

Toss everything into saucepan and cook on low heat for 2 hours.

Donald McLean

Jim Van's Bar-B-Q Sauce

2   sticks oleo
1½   cups sugar (I use 1 cup)
1   pint apple cider vinegar
1   bottle cocktail sauce
2   large bottles catsup (36 ounces)
2   tablespoons prepared mustard
1   tablespoon red pepper-(add 1 teaspoon, taste, add as you like, 1
            tablespoon may be too hot)
1   tablespoon black pepper
Juice of 3 lemons

Mix together, cook on medium heat until all ingredients dissolve. This will
keep in refrigerator for a long time.

Carolyn J. Hopkins

Southwest Georgia Bar-B-Que Sauce

1   large onion, diced
1   tablespoon minced garlic
3   36-ounce bottles Hunts ketchup
1   16-ounce bottle Worcestershire sauce
½   cup brown sugar
½   cup cane syrup (I use Mr. Pye Harrison's)
1   stick butter
½   cup vinegar
Salt and pepper to taste

Melt butter. Sauté onion and garlic. Combine ketchup, Worcestershire sauce,
brown sugar, cane syrup and vinegar. Heat to simmer for 30 minutes. Makes
2 quarts.

Hubert de Sercey

Pickled Pears

1½   quarts pears
3   cups water
2   teaspoons whole allspice or 2 sticks cinnamon
1½   teaspoons whole cloves
¾   cup vinegar
2   cups sugar

Pare the fruit; remove core. Make a syrup of the vinegar, water, sugar and spice. Boil 15 to 20 minutes. Add pears and cook until clear, about 20 minutes. Seal in hot, sterilized jars.

Pearl Thomas

A recipe used by Aunt Virginia Thomas Rosser (Mrs. Adron V.) every year.

Spiced Grapes

5   pounds grapes
3   pounds sugar
1   tablespoon allspice
1½   cups apple cider vinegar
1   tablespoon cinnamon
1   teaspoon ground cloves

Separate hulls from pulp. Boil pulp in small amount of water until tender. Rub through colander to remove seeds. Boil hulls until tender in just enough water to cover them. Mix pulp and hulls; add sugar, vinegar, and spices. Cook until as thick as jam; seal in sterilized jars while hot.

Gloria R. Searcy

Recipe of mother-in-law, Anna Pidcock Searcy, from her mother, Willie Warren Ashburn Pidcock.

Pickled Peaches

8   pounds peaches (24 to 34 peaches), peeled
8½   cups sugar
2   cups water
4   cups apple cider vinegar
Couple of sticks of cinnamon
2   tablespoons pickling spice (wrap spices in cloth)

Boil sugar, vinegar, and water with spices (in cloth) five minutes. Add peaches. Boil 10 minutes, if ripe not as long. Place peaches in jars; pour syrup over peaches and seal.

Gloria R. Searcy

Mother (Bessie Lawrence Robinson) canned pickled peaches along with other pickles and vegetables every summer. Each year someone would come around selling peaches and other produce. Dad always bought several boxes. We would sit on the porch and peel peaches until finished. The soft peaches would be used for jams or either frozen. The peaches that were firm would be used to make the pickled peaches.

Green Tomato Pickles

7   pounds green tomatoes, sliced ¼-inch thick
3   cups pickling lime
2   gallons water
5   pounds sugar
3   pints vinegar
6   teaspoons pickling spice

Soak sliced tomatoes in lime water for 24 hours. Drain but DO NOT WASH! Soak 4 hours in clean fresh water. Make syrup of sugar, vinegar, and spices and bring to a boil. Pour over tomatoes and let stand overnight. Boil one hour. Pack in sterilized jars; seal while hot. Makes 10 to 11 pints.

Sheila Barnes Thornton

My grandmother, Louise Barnes, gave me this recipe since I helped her make these pickles when I was a teenager.

Cakes . . .

Powell-Mauldin-White House

In the late 1800s, this house was built for Mr. and Mrs. B.F. ("Doc") Powell. The Mauldins lived here for many years and now the White family owns it.

Chocolate Pound Cake

2	sticks butter or margarine
½	cup shortening
3	cups sugar
6	eggs
3	cups flour
½	teaspoon baking powder
½	cup cocoa
½	teaspoon salt
1¼	cups sweet milk
2	teaspoons vanilla extract

Cream butter and shortening with sugar. Add eggs one at a time and blend after each one. Sift all dry ingredients and add alternately with milk. Add vanilla. Bake in a greased and floured tube pan at 325 degrees for one hour and 25 minutes. Frost when cool.

Frosting

½	cup margarine
¼	cup cocoa
¼	teaspoon salt
2	cups sugar
²/₃	cup sweet milk
2	teaspoons vanilla extract

Cook all ingredients 2 minutes, stirring constantly. If too thick, add 1 tablespoon cream. Cool and frost cake.

Tommie Jean M. Cooper

Recipe from The Atlanta Constitution--1950s.

Old Fashioned Pound Cake

1	pound butter
3½	cups sugar
4	cups all-purpose flour
1	teaspoon baking powder
12	eggs
1	teaspoon vanilla extract
1	teaspoon almond flavoring

Cream butter thoroughly, gradually add sugar and cream until light and fluffy. Mix baking powder with flour. Add 3 tablespoons flour mixture and beat well, add 2 eggs and beat well. Add remaining flour and eggs alternately until all have been added. Add flavorings. Bake in two 10-inch tube pans at 325 degrees for 1 hour or one cake pan and bake 1½ hours. Serves 40.

Opal Lewis

Caramel Nut Pound Cake

1	cup butter
1	pound box light brown sugar
3	cups all-purpose flour
½	teaspoon baking powder
1	cup sweet milk
½	cup Crisco
1	cup white sugar
½	teaspoon salt
5	large eggs
1	tablespoon vanilla extract

Cream butter and Crisco, add sugars and beat until fluffy. Add eggs, one at a time and beat well. Add dry ingredients alternating with milk. Add vanilla. Bake in greased tube pan at 325 degrees for 1½ hours.

Frosting

1	cup chopped pecans, toasted
¼	cup margarine
1	teaspoon vanilla extract
2	cups confectioners sugar

Mix margarine and sugar, add vanilla and pecans. Enough milk to make spreading consistency may be added. Spread on warm cake.

Kathryn Miller Jones

Recipe from Helen Ponder.

Sour Cream Pound Cake

3	cups sugar
2	sticks butter
6	eggs
3	cups plain flour
¼	teaspoon baking soda
½	teaspoon salt
1	cup sour cream
1	teaspoon vanilla extract

Cream 2½ cups sugar and butter. Separate eggs, add yolks to sugar mixture. Mix flour with soda and salt, add to mixture. Alternate with sour cream. Beat until well blended. Beat egg whites until stiff, then add ½ cup sugar. Fold into mixture with vanilla. Bake at 300 degrees for 1½ hours.

Carolyn Trawick

Pound cake recipe is one which my Grandmother used and has always been a family favorite.

Peach Pound Cake

3	eggs
1½	cups Crisco oil
2	cups sugar
3	cups all-purpose flour
1	teaspoon salt
1	teaspoon baking soda
2	teaspoons vanilla extract
3	cups fresh peaches, peeled and chopped

Mix eggs, oil, and sugar; blend well. Sift flour, salt, and soda, and add to egg mixture. Add vanilla and peaches. Pour into greased tube pan. Bake at 350 degrees for 1 hour. While cake is hot, pour hot topping over it while still in the pan. Let cool before removing from pan.

Topping

1	cup brown sugar
¼	cup milk
1	stick butter or margarine

Cook for 2½ minutes in saucepan over medium heat. Pour over cake immediately.

Nancy C. Clark

Miss Myrt's Layer Cake

1   cup Crisco, plain or butter flavor
2   cups sugar
4   eggs
1   cup milk
1½   cups sifted all-purpose flour
1½   cups sifted self-rising flour
1   teaspoon vanilla extract

Cream shortening, add sugar. Add eggs one at a time. Beat together until fluffy and light yellow color. Alternately add milk and flours, beginning and ending with milk. Beat at medium speed until mixed well. Pour in greased layer cake pans. Bake at 350 degrees for 30 minutes.

Debbi Miller

Miss Myrt, my mother, worked with cake baking for many years. Her experience yielded us this recipe that we use for all birthday cakes and wedding cakes.

Crunchy Cake

2   cups sugar
2   cups flour
1   cup Crisco
6   eggs
1   teaspoon vanilla extract
1   teaspoon lemon flavoring

Mix sugar, flour, Crisco, and eggs until creamy and smooth. Add flavorings after mixing about halfway. With a mixer, beat about 8 to 11 minutes or by hand about 13 minutes. Pour into a lightly greased tube pan. Bake at 350 degrees for 1 hour until firm and brown.

Sharon Whitfield

Recipe submitted in memory of Rosa Lee Dyson, Home Economics Teacher, Cairo High School. A mimeographed sheet of paper was given to me while I was a student in Mrs. Dyson's class in 1971-1972 and has been used so often the paper is now very yellowed and fragile. Following her directions--it has never failed.

Similar recipe submitted by Carolyn Brown.

Jewish Apple Cake

4   large Granny Smith apples, cored, peeled, and sliced
3   cups flour
3   teaspoons baking powder
2   cups sugar, divided
4   eggs
1   cup Wesson oil
¼   cup orange juice
2½ teaspoons vanilla extract
Cinnamon

Place apple slices in bowl with cinnamon and ½ cup sugar until fully coated. (I use lots of cinnamon.) Beat all ingredients except apple mixture. Pour half of batter in a greased and floured tube or bundt pan. Add half the apple mixture; spread evenly. Add rest of batter and rest of apple mixture on top. Bake at 325 degrees for 1½ hours or until done.

Donna Wright

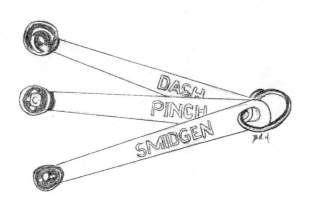

Applesauce Cake I

¼	cup butter
1	cup sugar
1	egg
1	cup nuts
1	cup figs or dates
1	cup raisins
2	cups plain flour
1	teaspoon ground cloves
1½	teaspoons cinnamon
1½	cups applesauce
2	teaspoons baking soda (dissolved in 2 tablespoons water)

Cream butter and sugar. Add egg and mix well. Add the nuts, figs, and raisins. Sift dry ingredients together and add alternately with applesauce to creamed mixture. Add soda mixture and mix thoroughly. Add vanilla. Pour into greased cake pan. Bake in 350 degrees oven for 1 hour.

Ruth Thomas Davis

This cake was a favorite of Janie Lou Doss Thomas (Mrs. George G., Sr.) handed down through her family.

Fresh Apple Cake

3	cups flour
1	teaspoon baking soda
1	teaspoon salt
1	teaspoon ground cinnamon
1	teaspoon ground nutmeg
2	large eggs
2	cups sugar
1	cup Wesson oil
3	cups tart apples, chopped
1	cup walnuts or pecans, chopped

Crisco, as needed

Mix flour, soda, salt, cinnamon, and nutmeg; sift 3 times and set aside. Beat eggs until creamy. Add sugar and cream well. Add oil. By hand, stir in flour and spices. Cake mixture will be difficult to mix. Add apples and nuts; mix well. Grease bundt pan with Crisco to prevent sticking. Bake at 300 degrees for 1½ hours. (Do not open oven.) Allow cake to cool before removing from pan.

Judy Treadaway Jordan

My mother and friends used wild, tart apples for this cake. It is an annual dessert for Christmas. Forty years after baking this cake for the first time at age 16, I still bake loaf cakes as Christmas gifts for my neighbors, family, and friends throughout the USA.

Sour Cream Nut Pound Cake

1	cup sweet whipped butter
3	cups sugar
5	eggs
3	cups plain flour
¼	teaspoon baking soda
½	teaspoon vanilla extract
½	teaspoon lemon flavoring
1	cup sour cream
1	quart pecans, chopped

Cream butter, add sugar gradually. Add eggs one at a time and beat well after each. Mix flour and soda and add alternately with sour cream to creamed mixture. Add flavorings and nuts. Bake at 325 degrees for 1½ hours.

Glaze

$^2/_3$	cup sugar
¼	cup melted butter
$^1/_3$	cup orange juice

Mix all ingredients to dissolve; pour over hot cake.

Fay Brannon

Pearl's Pound Cake

2   cups sugar
1   cup butter
6   eggs
3   cups flour
2   teaspoons baking powder
½   cup sweet milk
1   teaspoon vanilla extract

Cream sugar and butter. Add eggs one at a time. Sift flour and baking powder together. Add milk and flour alternately. Add vanilla. Bake in loaf pan at 350 degrees for 50 to 60 minutes. Can be used as layer cake.

Pearl Thomas

My mother, Pearl Maxwell Thomas, always made this cake for special occasions.

Better Than Sex Cake

1   box yellow cake mix
1   small box instant vanilla pudding
½   cup water
½   cup oil
4   eggs
1   8-ounce carton sour cream
1   6-ounce bag chocolate chips
1   cup chopped pecans
1   bar German chocolate, melted
1   cup coconut

Mix first 4 ingredients; add eggs and beat well after each addition. Add next 5 ingredients. Bake in well-greased tube pan at 350 degrees for 50 to 55 minutes.

Cheryl Hunziker

Rich and good, but only one person has ever said it was better than sex. She was 93 years old and somewhat "forgetful"!

Pound Cake

1   pound butter
1   pound sugar
1   pound flour
1   dozen eggs
1   teaspoon vanilla extract

Cream butter and sugar well. Add eggs one at a time, beat well after each egg. Sift flour 2 or 3 times. Add to creamed mixture gradually and beat thoroughly. Good beating is the secret. Bake in tube pan at 325 degrees for 90 minutes or until done. (Test by sticking a straw into it. If none sticks to straw, it is done.)

Alice A. Harrison

Our mother's recipe, it was probably handed down from her sister, Missouri Bryant Gainous, whom she lived with until she married in 1897.

Similar recipes submitted by Sue Askew, Linda Pyles Maxwell, and Elizabeth Maxwell.

Coconut Pound Cake

2½   cups sugar
½   cup Crisco
5   eggs
3   cups flour
1   teaspoon baking powder
¼   teaspoon salt
1   cup sweet milk
1   cup fine coconut
1   teaspoon coconut extract

Cream Crisco and sugar. Add eggs one at a time. Add dry ingredients alternately with milk gradually. Add coconut and flavoring. Bake in greased and floured tube pan for 1½ hours at 325 degrees. Let cool and remove from pan.

Tommie Jean M. Cooper

Sweet Cream Pound Cake

3   cups sugar
1   cup butter
6   eggs
3   cups all-purpose flour
1   carton whipping cream (do not whip cream)

Beat sugar and butter until smooth. Add eggs one at a time and beat on slow speed. Add flour alternately with whipping cream. Bake in 325 degrees oven an hour or until done.

Edith H. Sanders

Moonshine Cake

10   egg whites
$^7/_8$ teaspoon cream of tartar
1½   cups sugar, sifted 5 times
1   cup pastry flour, sifted 5 times
¼   teaspoon salt
7   egg yolks
1   teaspoon almond extract

Beat whites until light (add salt). Sift in cream of tartar, beat until stiff. Beat yolks in separate bowl; add 2 teaspoons whites. To whites, add sugar, almond extract. Combine mixtures, fold in flour. Bake one hour in tube pan, place in a pan of hot water.

Nancy Nichols

Recipe from "The Chastain Family Cookbook-A Collection of Favorite recipes from the A.Y. and Lela Chastain Family and Friends Kitchen" of 2001 Family Reunion.

Brown Sugar Pound Cake

1	cup shortening
1	stick margarine
1	box light brown sugar
5	eggs
3	cups plain flour
½	teaspoon baking powder
1	cup milk
1	teaspoon vanilla extract
1	cup nuts, cut fine

Cream shortening, margarine, and sugar. Add eggs and beat well. Mix flour and baking powder; add alternately with milk. Stir in vanilla and nuts. Bake in tube pan at 325 degrees for 1½ hours or until done.

Alice Shores Dodson

A delicious cake recipe that has been handed down through my family for years.

Rum Cake

1	cup chopped pecans
1	18½-ounce box yellow cake mix
1	small package instant vanilla pudding
4	eggs
½	cup cold water
½	cup oil
½	cup dark rum

Preheat oven to 325 degrees. Grease and flour a 10-inch tube pan. Sprinkle nuts on bottom. Mix all other ingredients together. Pour over nuts. Bake one hour. Cool and invert on plate. Prick top and sides, drizzle glaze over cake.

Glaze

½	cup butter
¼	cup water
1	cup sugar
½	cup dark rum

Combine ingredients; boil 3 minutes. Pour slowly over cake until all liquid is absorbed.

Pam Mason

Cream Cheese Pound Cake

3	sticks butter, softened
3	cups sugar
1	8-ounce package cream cheese, softened
6	eggs, at room temperature
3	cups cake flour
1	tablespoon vanilla or almond flavoring

Cream butter and sugar, add cream cheese. Add eggs alternately with flour. Add flavoring. Bake 1½ hours at 325 degrees.

Pam Mason

Applesauce Cake II

3½   cups plain flour, sifted
1   teaspoon baking soda
½   teaspoon salt
2   teaspoons ground cinnamon
1   teaspoon ground cloves
1   cup butter
2   cups sugar
3   eggs, well beaten
2   cups raisins, cut and floured
2   cups chopped nuts, floured
2   cups applesauce, strained, hot, and thick

Sift flour; measure. Add soda, salt, cinnamon, and cloves; sift together 3 times. Cream butter , add sugar until light and fluffy. Add eggs, raisins, and nuts; beat until smooth. Add flour alternately with applesauce, a small amount at the time, beating until smooth after each addition. Pour in greased tube or bundt pan. Bake at 350 degrees for 1 hour or until done (when clean straw comes out clean).

Gloria R. Searcy

Recipe of Willie Warren Ashburn Pidcock given to daughter, Anna Pidcock Searcy, who gave it to, Floyd H. and Gloria R. Searcy. Miss Anna always cooked Floyd's favorite cake for his birthday each year.

Apple Upside Down Cake

3   large Rome Beauty Apples, peeled, cored, and cut into wedges
½   cup brown sugar
4 . tablespoons butter
2   cups sifted flour
1½   teaspoons baking soda
½   teaspoon salt
2   teaspoons ginger
1   teaspoon cinnamon
½   teaspoon cloves
½   cup butter
½   cup firmly packed brown sugar
2   eggs, beaten well
¾   cup molasses
1   cup boiling water

Preheat oven to 325 degrees. In 12-inch skillet, heat apples, sugar, and butter over medium heat 7 to 8 minutes or until fork tender, golden and mixture begins to bubble; gently stirring. In medium bowl, sift flour once and measure. Add baking soda, salt, and spices; sift together 3 times. In mixing bowl, work butter with spoon until creamy. Add sugar gradually, beating after each addition until light and fluffy. Add eggs. Add ½ cup of flour and blend. Add molasses and beat until smooth. Add remaining flour and beat well. Add boiling water and stir until blended. In greased 9-inch square baking dish, pour apple mixture, arranging apple wedges cut side down. Pour gingerbread batter over apple mixture. Bake for 45 minutes. Immediately invert cake onto wire rack to cool. (May use 14½-ounce box gingerbread mix per box directions.)

Andrea P. Webb

Syrup Cakes

Just a little meal, A lot of flour, Syrup, Any spice you had

Mix all together and bake in iron spider.

Margaret Courtney (1912-2003)

My mother, Alice Johnson Prince, would make these in her wood burning stove.

Mississippi Mud Cake

2   sticks margarine, melted
½   cup cocoa
4   eggs, beaten
1½   cups self-rising flour
½   cup milk
2   cups sugar
Dash of salt
1½   cups pecans, chopped
1   teaspoon vanilla extract
1   small package miniature marshmallows

Combine margarine and cocoa with eggs, flour, and milk. Add sugar and salt; beat well. Stir in nuts and vanilla. Pour into greased 9 x 13-inch pan. Bake for 35 minutes at 350 degrees. Pour marshmallows over cake while still hot. Put cake in warm oven until marshmallows melt.

Icing
1   box confectioners sugar, sifted
½   stick margarine
⅓   cup cocoa
1   teaspoon vanilla extract
½   cup milk

Mix ingredients and beat well. Pour over cake and marshmallows.

Celeste C. Tyler

Agnes' Sheet Cake

2½   cups self-rising flour
2½   cups sugar
2   sticks oleo, softened
4   tablespoons cocoa
1⅓   cups water
¾   cup buttermilk
1   teaspoon baking soda
1   teaspoon vanilla extract
2   eggs, slightly beaten

Preheat oven to 400 degrees. Grease 11 x 17 x 1-inch sheet cake pan, line with waxed paper, spray with baking spray and sprinkle with flour. Mix flour and sugar in bowl. Heat oleo, cocoa, and water in heavy saucepan and bring to boil; pour over flour and sugar. Mix well. Combine buttermilk, soda, vanilla, and eggs and add to cake mixture; mix well. Pour into prepared pan and bake about 20 minutes.

Topping
1½   sticks oleo
4   tablespoons cocoa
6   tablespoons canned milk
1   box confectioners sugar
1   teaspoon vanilla extract
1   cup chopped nuts

Bring oleo, cocoa, and milk to a boil. Add sugar, vanilla, and nuts. Spread over hot cake as soon as it comes out of the oven. Yield 40 squares.

Shirley C. Womble

Recipe of my mother, Lavelle Cox

Bernice Porter's Apple Cake

2   eggs
2   cups sugar
1   cup cooking oil
2½   cups plain flour
1   teaspoon baking soda
1   teaspoon baking powder
1   teaspoon salt
1   teaspoon cinnamon
4   cups raw apples, peeled and diced
1   cup chopped pecans
1   6-ounce package butterscotch morsels

Combine eggs, sugar, and oil. Add dry ingredients, then apples, then nuts.
Pour into greased and floured 9 x 13-inch pan. Sprinkle with butterscotch
morsels. Bake at 350 degrees for 55 to 60 minutes.

Sonya Porter

Similar recipe submitted by Dot Dalton

Carrot and Pineapple Cake

1½   cups all-purpose flour
1   cup sugar
1   teaspoon baking soda
1   teaspoon baking powder
½   teaspoon salt
²/₃   cup salad oil
2   eggs
1   cup finely shredded carrots
½   cup crushed pineapple with syrup
1   teaspoon vanilla extract

In large mixing bowl, sift together dry ingredients. Add oil, eggs, carrots, pineapple, and vanilla. Mix until moistened. Beat 2 minutes at medium speed of electric mixer. Bake in grease and lightly floured 9 x 9 x 2-inch pan in 350 degrees oven about 30 minutes or until done. Cool 10 minutes, remove from pan. Cool and frost with Cream Cheese Frosting.

Cream Cheese Frosting

1   3-ounce package cream cheese, softened
1   tablespoon butter, softened
1   teaspoon vanilla extract
2   cups sifted confectioners sugar
½   cup chopped pecans (optional)

In small mixing bowl, combine cream cheese, butter, and vanilla. Beat at low speed of electric mixer until light. Gradually add sugar, beating until fluffy.

Curtis Darus

Mayonnaise Cake

1½	cups mayonnaise
1½	cups sugar
1½	cups warm water
6	drops red food coloring
3	cups flour
3	teaspoons baking soda
5	heaping tablespoons cocoa

Cream mayonnaise and sugar. Mix in water, vanilla, and coloring. Sift in flour, baking soda, and cocoa. Blend until smooth. Bake in 13 x 9-inch cake pan at 375 degrees for about 30 minutes. Cool and ice with cream cheese icing.

Shirley Kaye

This cake is a family favorite passed down from my grandmother, to my mother, to me. It originated in Ohio and was served by my mother many times at family gatherings and church potlucks. It is a surprisingly moist, rich chocolate cake that is easy to make.

Date Nut Cake I

1	cup flour
1	cup sugar
2	teaspoons baking powder
1½	cups chopped dates
2½	cups assorted nuts
1	cup shredded coconut
4	eggs, separated and beaten
1	teaspoon vanilla extract
1	teaspoon almond flavoring
½	cup bourbon or wine

Sift flour, sugar, and baking powder over dates, nuts, and coconut. Fold in egg yolks, then whites. Pour into lightly greased and floured pan. Bake at 350 degrees for one hour. Invert and sprinkle with bourbon or wine. Let age, tightly covered, for at least a week.

Marjorie Mayfield Taylor

Growing up, this was our favorite Thanksgiving and Christmas cake. It was greatly preferred over traditional fruitcakes. The first one was made in early November, then another after Thanksgiving. I still make this cake for the holidays.

Date Nut Cake II

½   cup butter or margarine
1   cup sugar
2   eggs
1   package chopped dates
1   cup boiling water
2   cups plain flour
1   teaspoon baking soda
Pinch of salt
1   cup chopped nuts

Cream butter and sugar. Add eggs. In separate bowl, pour boiling water over the dates and let cool. Stir dates into above mixture, add flour, soda, salt, and nuts. Pour into a 9 x 13-inch baking dish. Bake at 350 degrees for 45 minutes. Cut into squares. Serve with Cool Whip.

Laurie Carlisle Conradi

This is a recipe from my grandmother, Mrs. Ira Carlisle.

Pineapple Upside Down Cake

½   cup shortening
1   cup sugar
2   eggs
2   cups flour
2   teaspoons baking powder
¼   teaspoon salt
¾   cup syrup drained from pineapple
4   tablespoons butter
1   cup brown sugar
1   No. 2 can sliced pineapple, drained (save syrup)
Cherries

Cream shortening, sugar, and eggs. Sift together flour, baking powder, and salt. Add to creamed mixture alternately with pineapple syrup. Mix well. Put butter and brown sugar in 9-inch skillet. Heat until dissolved. Place pineapple on top of this mixture; put cherries in centers of pineapple. Pour batter over all. Bake at 350 degrees about 50 minutes. Turn out at once.

Evelyn Hester

Wash Day Cake

1   cup cane syrup
2 or 3 eggs (fresh from hen house)
2   cups flour
½   cup milk
1   cup lard or butter
Vanilla and/or lemon flavoring

Mix well and bake in skillet in wood stove.

Annette Harrell

This recipe originated with Pashie P. Davis Oliver, wife of Confederate Veteran Jonah Beal Davis, Company B, 8th Florida Infantry CSA and daughter of Confederate Veteran, William G. Palmer, Company A, 29th GA Battalion CSA Cavalry. It was given to me by Fannie Davis Tinsley and Naomi Davis Scarbrough, daughters of Pashie and Jonah Beal Davis.

Eggless Nut Cake

1½	cups water
1½	cups sugar
½	cup oil
1	teaspoon cinnamon
½	teaspoon cloves
1	cup raisins
1	cup chopped pecans
3	cups flour

Combine ingredients, except pecans and flour, and boil for 5 minutes. Add pecans and flour and mix well. Pour into baking pan. (I use an iron skillet). Cook for about 45 minutes at 375 degrees.

Betty W. Harrison

Chocolate Sheet Cake

2   cups sugar
2   cups all-purpose flour
1   teaspoon baking soda
1   teaspoon ground cinnamon
1   cup water
1   stick margarine
½   cup vegetable oil
4   tablespoons cocoa
½   cup buttermilk
2   eggs, slightly beaten
1   teaspoon vanilla extract

Sift together sugar, soda, and cinnamon; set aside. In a saucepan, mix water, margarine, oil, and cocoa; bring to a boil. Pour dry ingredients, mixing well. Set aside. Mix together buttermilk, eggs, and vanilla; add to chocolate batter. Pour into greased and floured 13 x 9 x 2-inch pan. Bake at 400 degrees for 20 minutes. Start icing about 5 minutes before cake is done. Frost cake in pan.

Icing

1   stick margarine
4   tablespoons cocoa
1   pound box powdered sugar
6   tablespoons milk
1   teaspoon vanilla extract
1   cup chopped pecans

Mix margarine, cocoa, and milk into saucepan and bring to a boil. DO NOT SCORCH! Add powdered sugar, vanilla, and pecans. Spread on HOT cake.

Carolyn Brown

My mother, Helen Coats, made this often and it is the best dessert ever!

Earthquake Cake

1½   cups coconut
1½   cups pecans
1   box Betty Crocker German Chocolate cake mix
1   stick butter
1   8-ounce package cream cheese
1   box confectioners 4X sugar

Grease a 9 x 13-inch pan. (I use Baker's Joy.) Mix coconut and pecans; spread over bottom of pan. Mix cake mix as directed; spread over nuts and coconut. Melt butter and cream cheese; pour over sugar and mix together. Pour this over uncooked cake mix. Bake at 350 degrees for 45 to 50 minutes.

Marilyn W. Joiner

Given to me by a friend.

Nine Layer Cake

1   cup Crisco
2   cups sugar
5   eggs
1   cup sweet milk
3   cups flour (2½ cups cake flour
      and ½ cup self-rising flour sifted together)
1   tablespoon vanilla extract

Cream Crisco; add sugar. Add eggs all at once. Beat on high speed 5 minutes; reduce speed to low and add flour and milk alternately. Add vanilla. Cut wax paper circles and place in lightly greased 9-inch pans; grease paper also. Put 5 heaping tablespoons of batter in each of 9 pans. Bake at 325 degrees for 20 minutes or until done. Cool layers completely before frosting.

Cooked Chocolate Icing

1   pound margarine
4   cups sugar
1   cup evaporated milk
¾   cup cocoa
2   teaspoons corn syrup
1   teaspoon vanilla extract

In a large bowl, combine sugar, cocoa, milk, and syrup; mix well. In a heavy boiler, melt margarine (watch carefully, do not brown). Add wet sugar mixture to margarine and mix well; bring to boil. Let boil for 4 to 5 minutes, stir as needed. Remove from heat. Add vanilla. Beat over cold water until thick and cool. Spread between 9 cake layers; ice top and sides.

Shirley C. Womble

Lavelle Cox (my mother) makes the family favorite, a 9 layer chocolate cake. She developed the recipe over 20 years by using the best parts of recipes that she found in cookbooks or that she received from friends. Myrtle Hollingsworth gave her the original icing recipe and Eilene Murphy suggested the mixing instructions. Mother tried to keep at least one or two cakes in the freezer for those requests that came from her family or her church. She did sell to a few outsiders but really considered this cake her mission. To receive this cake was indeed an honor.

Grandma Kate's Lane Cake

3	cups cake flour
2	teaspoons baking powder
1	cup butter
2	cups sugar
1	cup milk
8	egg whites
1	teaspoon cream of tartar

Pinch of salt

1	teaspoon vanilla extract

Sift flour and baking powder together 2 times; set aside. Cream butter and sugar. Add milk and flour alternately to creamed mixture. Beat egg whites until foamy, add cream of tartar and salt. Beat until stiff. Add egg whites. Add vanilla. Bake in 7 layers in greased and floured cake pans at 350 degrees. Just keep checking to see when it is done.

Filling

8	egg yolks
1	cup milk
½	cup butter
2	cups sugar
1	cup raisins
1	cup chopped pecans
1	cup coconut
1	teaspoon vanilla extract
3	tablespoons of cake batter

Beat yolks, add butter, sugar, milk, and batter. (¾ cup of wine and ¼ cup sweet milk could be substituted for the cup of milk. Winifred Maxwell says, "This is what Mama did.") Cook in double boiler until thick. Add other ingredients. Put between layers and on top of cake; or put between layers and ice with 7 minute icing topped with nuts. (Mama never had time to make the icing, she just used the filling.)

Susan Y. Perkins

This was always a holiday favorite at the home of Sheriff and Mrs. Perkins and their family of 5 boys and 5 girls (3 additional children died as infants). David Daniel Perkins served as Sheriff of Grady County for 16 years. At that time, the sheriff was the embodiment of law and order and Sheriff Perkins took his position quite seriously. He loved his family very much and was known as a "people person." There was a time when the family all lived in the "new jail house." The youngest daughter, Winifred Perkins Maxwell, was born there. The jail housing was not adequate so 2 of the sons, Roy and Jack, had to sleep on a porch. Later the family moved to the Providence Community. There was little money but always plenty of good food and lots of company! It has been said, "I'd rather go to the Perkins' than a 3 ring circus."

Grady County Jail

In 1908, the jail and courthouse were completed for the new county. The jail was located on 2nd Avenue, west of Broad Street. Many of the sheriffs lived in the jail with their wives being responsible for the inmates' food.

Lane Cake

½   **pound butter**
2   **cups sugar**
6   **egg whites**
2   **cups cake flour**
½   **teaspoon baking soda**
1   **cup buttermilk**
1   **teaspoon vanilla extract**

Cream butter and sugar until creamy. Add egg whites, beat well. Add flour, soda, milk, and vanilla. Bake in layers at 350 degrees until done.

Filling
8   **egg yolks**
2   **cups sugar**
1   **lemon, juice and rind**
1   **cup nuts, chopped**
1   **cup raisins**
4   **ounces Wild Turkey whiskey**
Butter the size of large egg

Cook eggs, sugar, and lemon in a double boiler until thick; add butter, nuts, and raisins. Add whiskey; cook until thick enough to spread on cake. Put cake in cold, dark room for the filling to soak into the layers.

Sheila Barnes Thornton

This cake has been a holiday favorite for many, many years. A four generation cake recipe, it was given to me as a teenager when I helped Granny (Louise Barnes) make this cake every Thanksgiving and Christmas. I have passed it down to my daughter, Jamie Thornton Faircloth.

Foundation Layer Cake

1   cup sugar
½   cup butter
2   eggs, well beaten
2   cups flour, sifted
2   teaspoons baking powder
²/₃   cup milk
1   teaspoon vanilla extract

Cream butter and sugar until very light. Add eggs and add flour with baking powder and milk alternately. Bake in 3 or 4 greased pans for thin layers at 350 degrees for 25 minutes.

Chocolate Filling

3   cups sugar
1   cup milk
½   cup butter
2   squares unsweetened chocolate
⅛   teaspoon baking soda
1   teaspoon vanilla extract

Put all ingredients except vanilla in large saucepan, allowing plenty room for rapid boiling. Cook, boiling rapidly, stirring constantly until a heavy trace of spoon shows and mixture is quite thick (about 8 minutes). Place in cold water, stir and beat constantly until thick and creamy. Add vanilla and spread between layers and on top.

Winnie Jean Hester

My mother (Mrs. Guss M. Maxwell) always used this recipe.

Aunt "John's" Fresh Coconut Cake

¼   cup fresh grated coconut
¾   cup coconut milk
¾   cup shortening
1   cup sugar
4   eggs, separated
½   teaspoon almond extract
2¼   cup sifted cake flour
½   teaspoon baking powder
½   teaspoon salt
½   cup sugar

Preparation of coconut: Pierce 3 holes in coconut; drain out milk and save. Heat coconut in 350 degrees oven for 20 minutes; cool. Break shell and chisel out meat. Peel off brown skin. Cut white meat into pieces and grate.

Cream shortening and sugar. Add egg yolks and almond extract; beat well. Mix in ¼ cup grated coconut. Sift together flour, baking powder, and salt. Add coconut milk (if necessary, add milk to make up amount ¾ cup) alternately with dry ingredients. Beat egg whites until peaks are formed; gradually beat in ½ cup sugar until whites are stiff. Fold into batter. Bake in 3 greased and floured 9-inch pans at 350 degrees for 25 to 30 minutes. Cool.

Icing
1   cup sugar
⅓   cup water
⅓   teaspoon cream of tartar
2   egg whites
1½   teaspoons vanilla extract
Fresh grated coconut

Boil first 3 ingredients in saucepan until 242 degrees is reached on candy thermometer. Keep pan covered for the first 3 minutes. Beat egg whites until very stiff. Pour hot syrup very slowly into egg whites, beating constantly. Add vanilla. Frost between layers, top, and sides of cooled cakes, sprinkling as much coconut as desired.

Claire Chason Willett

Japanese Fruitcake

1	cup margarine
2	cups sugar
4	eggs
1	cup milk
3	cups self-rising flour
1	tablespoon allspice
1	cups nuts, chopped
1	cup raisins, chopped

Grease and flour 3 or 4 cake pans. Cream margarine and sugar. Beat in eggs. Add milk , flour, and allspice. (May divide mixture and put allspice in half.) Stir in nuts and raisins. Bake at 350 degrees until brown.

Filling

1	can coconut
2½	cups sugar
2	tablespoons flour
2	lemons, grated rind and 1 juice
½	cup hot water

Mix all ingredients except coconut together and cook until thick. Add coconut. Cool slightly and put on cake layers.

Hilda McKinney

Mother always cooked this cake for Christmas when we were growing up. It was the best!

Red Devil's Food Cake

1½	cups plus 2 tablespoons all-purpose flour
1½	cups sugar
1¼	teaspoons baking soda
1	teaspoon salt
½	cup cocoa
½	cup shortening
1	cup milk
1	teaspoon vanilla extract
2	medium eggs

Preheat oven to 350 degrees. Grease and flour 2 8-inch round pans. Sift dry ingredients into bowl; add shortening, milk, and vanilla. Beat 2 minutes on medium speed mixer or 30 vigorous strokes by hand. Scrape sides and bottom of bowl constantly. Add eggs, beat 2 more minutes, scrapping bowl constantly. Pour into prepared pans. Bake 30 to 35 minutes. Cool in pans on rack about 10 minutes. (I use 7 minute frosting and top with coconut--really good.)

Doris Harrison

Recipe given to me in the 60s by a friend.

Red Velvet Cake

1½	cups sugar
1½	cups Crisco oil
2	eggs
1	$1^5/_8$-ounce bottle red food coloring
1	teaspoon vanilla extract
2½	cups cake flour, sifted
2	tablespoons cocoa
1	cup buttermilk
1	teaspoon vinegar
1	teaspoon baking soda

Combine sugar and oil; beat slightly. Add eggs, coloring, and vanilla. Add flour and cocoa alternately with buttermilk. Beat until smooth. Mix vinegar and soda, fold into mixture. Pour into 3 greased and floured cake pans. Bake at 350 degrees oven for 25 minutes.

Filling

1	8-ounce package cream cheese, softened
1	stick butter
1	box 4X confectioners sugar, sifted
1	teaspoon vanilla extract
1	cup chopped nuts

Combine cream cheese and butter. Add sugar; mix well. Add vanilla and nuts. Spread on cake.

Wynell Mitchell

Strawberry Cake

1   package Duncan Hines white cake mix
4   eggs
1   small package strawberry Jell-O
½   cup cooking oil
½   cup water
4   tablespoons plain flour
½   cup strawberries, cut in small pieces

Mix all ingredients together in order as listed. Pour batter in 4 greased and floured cake pans. Bake at 350 degrees for 20 to 25 minutes.

Filling
½   stick margarine
½   cup strawberries, cut in small pieces, drained well
1   box confectioners sugar

Mix all ingredients for filling and spread between layers and on sides and top.

Carolyn Trawick

This is an old family recipe from my grandmother and has been used for many birthday cakes for my children and grandchildren. It was a favorite for people at my office.

Butternut Cake

2¼   cups sifted cake flour
1½   cups sugar
2½   teaspoons baking powder
1   teaspoon salt
¾   cup shortening
¾   cup milk
1   teaspoon butternut flavoring
3   eggs

Sift together flour, sugar, baking powder, and salt. Add shortening, ½ cup milk, flavoring, and 1 egg. Mix on low to medium speed for 2 minutes and add remaining milk and eggs. Beat 2 minutes longer. Bake in 3 greased and floured 9-inch pans at 375 degrees for 20 to 25 minutes.

Filling
1   box 4X confectioners sugar
1   stick butter, melted
1   8-ounce cream cheese, softened
1   teaspoon butternut flavoring
1   cup nuts, chopped

Mix all ingredients except nuts with mixer. Stir in nuts.

Mary Allegood

This recipe was one of Ruby Cooper's (mother of Mary Allegood and Joy Reed) and is very good.

Blueberry Cake

1	Duncan Hines Butter Cake mix
1	8-ounce sour cream
½	cup canola oil
¼	cup sugar
¼	cup water
4	eggs

Mix all ingredients in a large bowl and beat for 3 minutes. Bake in 3 layers for 20 minutes at 350 degrees. Cool.

Frosting
1	8-ounce package cream cheese
1	large Cool Whip
1	cup 4 X confectioners sugar
1	can blueberry pie filling

Mix cream cheese and sugar. Fold in Cool Whip. Assemble layers spreading with frosting, leaving a slight ridge around the edge. Use about 1/3 of pie filling on each layer.

Ruth Sims

Jelly Cake

We would make our basic cake layers cooked in wood stove. Whatever jelly we had made would be the icing.

Margaret P. Courtney (1912-2003)

At Christmastime, we would buy a coconut and break it open with a hammer, cut brown edges off and peel out coconut. We would grate the coconut by hand and sprinkle over the jelly. This was our Christmas cake. This recipe was passed down from my mother, Alice Johnson Prince, who died in 1936.

Similar recipe submitted by Donna C. Powell using Blackberry or Mayhaw Jelly.

Buttermilk Chocolate Cake with White Chocolate Frosting

2   cups cake flour
½   teaspoon salt
1½   teaspoons baking soda
¾   cup unsalted butter, softened
1½   cups sugar
2   teaspoons vanilla extract
4   ounces unsweetened chocolate melted with 2 teaspoons
           vegetable oil
4   eggs
1½   cups buttermilk

Preheat oven to 325 degrees. In medium bowl, mix flour, soda, and salt. In large bowl, beat butter, sugar, and vanilla until fluffy, 3 minutes. Add eggs, one at a time, beating after each. Beat in chocolate. On low speed, beat flour mixture into butter mixture in 3 additions, alternating with buttermilk. Beat 1 minute. Divide batter between 4 greased and floured 9-inch pans. Bake for 35 minutes. Cool cakes in pans on wire racks for 15 minutes. Turn out onto rack; cool.

White Chocolate Frosting
1   12-ounce package white chocolate chips
1   8-ounce container sour cream
3   cups confectioners sugar
½   cup unsalted butter, softened

In large glass bowl, microwave white chocolate on medium power for 30 seconds; stir. Microwave another 30 seconds until completely melted and smooth. Let cool slightly. With mixer, beat in sour cream and butter until smooth. Refrigerate 10 minutes. On low speed, beat in sugar until blended; continue to beat until fluffy and good spreading consistency. Spread frosting between layers and on top of cake. Refrigerate until set, about 20 minutes.

Donna C. Powell

Best Cake Layers You'll Ever Eat

1   cup butter flavor Crisco
2   cups sugar
5   eggs
1   cup milk
1   cup all-purpose flour
1   cup self-rising flour
1½   teaspoons vanilla flavoring

Cream Crisco and sugar; add eggs one at a time and beat well after each addition. Sift together flours and add to creamed mixture alternately with milk mixed with vanilla. Bake in 4 or 5 pans prepared with cooking spray at 350 degrees for 10 minutes. Delicious with any type filling--great for jelly cake. Freezes well.

Cathy Walden Moore

This recipe is from Mrs. Virginia (Henry) Webb, mother of Twila Bearden. It is great for thin layer cakes. She made cakes for many people.

Ten Layer Chocolate Cake

Mix 2 boxes yellow cake mix as directed on box, except add ¹/₃ cup more water than directions calls for. Prepare pans with baking spray. Put ½ cup of batter in each pan and spread evenly. Bake in preheated 350 degrees oven until very lightly browned. Cool just long enough to turn out on plate. Icing can begin right away. (I prepare my icing after first four pans.)

Icing
1   pound butter
3   cups sugar
1   cup evaporated milk
1   cup cocoa

Mix ingredients in heavy saucepan and bring to a boil; stir briskly while boiling for two minutes. Icing is now ready to use when needed. (Cake and icing recipes can be doubled.)

Jamie C. Lewis

Hummingbird Cake

3   cups all-purpose flour
2   cups sugar
1   teaspoon baking soda
1   teaspoon salt
1   teaspoon cinnamon
3   eggs, beaten
1   cup canola oil
1   cup chopped bananas
1½ teaspoons vanilla
1   8-ounce can crushed pineapple
1   cup chopped pecans
1   cup shredded coconut (optional)

Combine flour, sugar, soda, salt, and cinnamon. Add eggs and oil, stirring until flour mixture is moistened. Do not beat. Stir in vanilla, pineapple, pecans, and bananas. Bake in 3 greased and floured 9-inch cake pans at 350 degrees for 25 to 30 minutes or until a wooden toothpick inserted in the center comes out clean. Cool completely in pans.

Frosting
1   8-ounce package cream cheese, softened
1   stick butter, softened
1   box powdered sugar
1   teaspoon vanilla extract
Chopped pecans (optional)

Combine cream cheese and butter, beating until smooth. Add powdered sugar and vanilla. Beat until light and fluffy. Spread between layers, top, and sides of cake. Sprinkle nuts on top, if desired.

Pam Mason

Ten to Fifteen-Layer Chocolate Cake

2   boxes Duncan Hines yellow cake mix
3   cups water
6   eggs

Mix ingredients together. Bake in layers in iron skillet 10 to 15 minutes at 375 degrees.

Cooked Icing
1   pound margarine
4   cups sugar
1   cup evaporated milk
1   cup cocoa

Put all ingredients in a heavy boiler and bring to a boil; stir briskly and let boil 2 minutes. Remove from heat; cool. Frost the cake layers.

Mary Gainous

Similar recipe submitted by Kathryn Miller Jones.

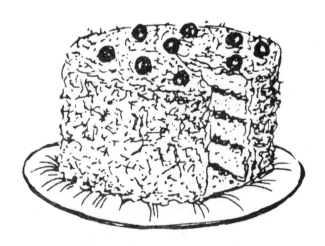

Lemon Cheese Cake

1   cup butter
2   cups sugar
3   eggs
3   cups cake flour
½   teaspoon baking soda
1   cup buttermilk
1   teaspoon vanilla extract
1   teaspoon lemon flavoring

Preheat oven to 350 degrees. Cream butter and sugar. Add eggs one at a time, beating after each addition. Alternately add sifted flour and soda with buttermilk. Add flavorings. Pour batter into 4 well greased and floured 9-inch pans. Bake about 20 minutes or until lightly browned. While warm, frost with Lemon Cheese Frosting.

Lemon Cheese Frosting
4   eggs, slightly beaten
1½   cups sugar
2   tablespoons butter, melted
3   lemons, juice and grated rind

Place all ingredients in top of double boiler over boiling water until thick, stirring constantly. (Can be microwaved--cook all ingredients on High for 2 to 3 minutes; stir, cook another 2 to 3 minutes; repeat until thick and bright yellow.)

Donna C. Powell

Similar recipe submitted by Linda Pyles Maxwell.

Apple Stack Cake

2	cups sugar
1	cup shortening
2	eggs
6	cups plain flour
3	teaspoons baking soda
1	teaspoon salt
½	cup molasses
½	cup buttermilk
2	teaspoons vanilla extract
2	teaspoons cake spices

Mix all ingredients as you would biscuit dough. Divide into six equal parts and press into six 9-inch cake pans that have been greased and floured. Pat out with floured hands. Bake at 450 degrees for 10 minutes.

Apple Filling

2	pounds dried apples
1¾	cups brown sugar
1	cup white sugar
2	teaspoons cinnamon
1	teaspoon cloves
1	teaspoon allspice

Cook and mash the dried fruit. Add brown sugar. Mix all ingredients together and spread between layers and on sides. Do not put fruit on top layer. Leave overnight for fruit to soak into layers. Place in a plastic cake box and refrigerate until serving time.

Hazel Logue

We were a very large family and our mom had to do everything on a large scale. We had many apples and she always dried lots of them, as well as peaches.

Cake with Caramel Filling

5   eggs, stir good
1½   cups of sugar
½   cup of sweet milk
½   cup of butter, melted
1   teaspooonful of baking powder
1   teaspoonful of vanilla
2¹/₃ cups of flour

(No directions given for mixing cake in Grandma Holt's cookbook selections.)

Caramel Filling
2   cups of sugar
1   cup of milk
Butter the size of egg
Pinch of soda

Cook in double boiler until thick. Stir into the whites of two eggs lightly beaten. Can add 1 teaspoonful vanilla.

Linda Pyles Maxwell

Birthday Cake Icing

1   cup Crisco shortening
½   cup water
2   pounds 10X or 4X confectioners sugar
1   teaspoon vanilla extract

Cream Crisco. On low speed, add powdered sugar and water. Add vanilla. Beat at high speed until light and fluffy. Will cover 3 layer cake or a 9 x 13-inch sheet cake. Make extra recipe for decorating. Colors well.

Debbi Miller

Recipe has been used for many years in our area because Miss Myrt requires it to be used in her cake decorating classes. She says always use Crisco shortening.

Marshmallow Frosting

1   cup sugar
¹/₃   cup water
¹/₃   teaspoon cream of tartar
2   egg whites
8   large marshmallows, chopped or 80 miniature
1½   teaspoons vanilla extract

Mix sugar, water, and cream of tartar in saucepan. Boil rapidly, stirring until it spins a thread when spoon is lifted above pan. Remove from heat. While syrup is cooking, beat egg whites stiff. Add marshmallows to syrup to melt, stirring until dissolved. Pour mixture into egg whites, beating until mixture forms peaks and is glossy. Add vanilla and coloring as desired. Frost cooled cake.

Donna C. Powell

My mother made a Crunchy Pound Cake for my sisters and me on each birthday and we could choose the color for the frosting. I continued this tradition with my daughter and son on their birthdays.

Sarah Courtney's Chocolate Icing

2 ½   cups sugar
½   cup cocoa
1   stick margarine
1   cup evaporated milk
1   tablespoon vanilla extract

Mix all ingredients except vanilla. Bring to a boil; cook 4 minutes. Do not stir. Add vanilla. Cool. Ice cake.

Catherine Lacy

Handed down from family.

Caramel Icing

¾ cup sugar
¼ cup water
4 cups sugar
1 cup evaporated milk
½ pound butter
Pinch of soda
1 teaspoon vanilla extract

Cook ¾ cup sugar in heavy boiler until browned, add water and stir until it dissolves. Add remaining sugar, milk, and butter; cook approximately 4 minutes. Take off heat; add soda and vanilla and beat. Spread on cake. If it is not stiff enough, re-heat. If too stiff, add a little milk.

Catherine Lacy

Handed down from family, one of Hazel Prince's recipes.

Seven Minute Frosting

2 egg whites
1½ cups sugar
Dash of salt
5 tablespoons water
2 teaspoons white corn syrup
½ teaspoon vanilla extract

Beat all ingredients except vanilla in top of double boiler until mixed well. Place over boiling water and continue beating about 7 minutes or until frosting thickens and stands in peaks. Remove from boiling water, add vanilla and beat until stiff enough to spread. A few drops of red food color will make pink frosting. Good topped with coconut.

Doris Harrison

Boiled Frosting

2   cups sugar
1   cup water
Pinch of salt
1   teaspoon vinegar
2   egg whites, beaten
¾   teaspoon vanilla

Stir sugar, water, salt, and vinegar over medium heat until clear. Don't be tempted to stir anymore. Cook syrup until you can see a long thin thread when syrup is dropped from tip of spoon. Add syrup in thin stream over beaten egg whites. Continue beating until frosting keeps its shape. Add vanilla.

Linda Pyles Maxwell

Pineapple Cake Icing

2½   cups sugar
6 to 9 tablespoons flour
1½   cans crushed pineapple (or 1 large and 1 small can), drained
¾   cup orange juice
3   tablespoons butter

Mix flour and sugar together. Add orange juice and pineapple; bring to a boil.
Add butter and cook a little longer until thick.

Shirley C. Womble

A pineapple cake from Kathryn Davis in 1981 was the inspiration for this recipe and was a favorite of Ellen Cox and Mary Anne Willis. Mother (Lavelle Cox) adjusted the amounts to her liking and made 1½ "makings" for her thin 9 layers.

Orange Sauce for Angel Food Cake

2   egg yolks
2   oranges, juice and grated rind
½   cup sugar

Cook ingredients until thickened. Let cool. Fold into ½ pint whipping cream (whipped) and serve over slices of cake.

Lucy Singleton

Icebox Fruitcake I

1   pound Vanilla Wafers, crushed
1   pound Angel Flake coconut
½   box raisins, seedless
2   cups pecans, chopped
1   can condensed milk

Mix all ingredients well. Press into pan or casserole dish. Refrigerate for at least 24 hours before cutting. Will keep for a long time in refrigerator.

Geraldine Gleaton

My mother had this recipe for a long time. Our family enjoyed it, especially at Christmas.

Variation using graham crackers submitted by Esther Carter.

Icebox Fruitcake II

2   boxes Vanilla Wafers, crushed fine
½   cup raisins
1½   cups pecans, diced
1   can condensed milk
Candied fruit (optional)

Mix ingredients thoroughly be hand. Pour onto waxed paper covered cookie sheet; spread as thinly as you wish or desired shape. Cut small squares if desired.

Anita Singletary

Moma's Christmas and Thanksgiving dessert every year for Hopkins family gatherings. I have taken on her tradition for my family.

Similar recipe submitted by Sue Askew.

Nut Cake

2   cups sugar
½   pound butter
6   eggs, separated
4   cups flour
2   teaspoons baking powder
1   nutmeg, grated
1   glass grape juice
1½   boxes raisins
1   quart pecans

Cream butter and sugar. Add egg yolks. Add flour, baking powder, and nutmeg with grape juice. Add beaten egg whites. Dredge raisins and pecans with flour; add to mixture. Bake at 250 degrees approximately 3 hours or until done.

Katherine S. Cook

Recipe from my great grandmother, Mary Morrison McDaniel.

Fruitcake-Ettes

1 package spice cake mix
¼ cup shortening
½ cup boiling water
2 eggs
¼ cup cooking sherry
3½ cups mixed candied fruit
1 cup raisins
2 cups chopped nuts

Mix cake mix, shortening, and water until moistened. Let stand 30 minutes. Add remaining ingredients. Fill paper cups or greased and floured muffin pan ¾ full. Bake at 300 degrees for 45 minutes. Yield 7 dozen.

Carole Booth

Recipe has been in my family and was always made at Christmas. Aunt Katie put them in red and green papers and we always looked forward to our Fruitcake-Ettes.

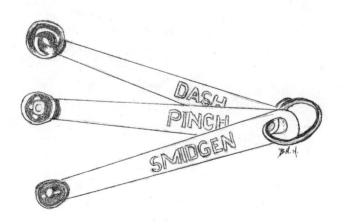

White Fruitcake (Fruitcake Cookies)

1	pound butter
1	pound sugar
1	pound plain flour plus 1 cup for dredging fruit
1	dozen large eggs
1	cup apricot brandy
1	teaspoon nutmeg
1	teaspoon cinnamon
1	pound candied cherries, red and green
1	pound candied pineapple, red, white and green
1½	pound nuts, chopped
3	pounds white raisins

Cream butter and sugar. Add flour alternately with eggs; beat well. Add brandy, nutmeg, and cinnamon. Mix extra cup of flour with fruit, nuts, and raisins. Add to batter. (I do this with my hands.) Pack tightly into 3 loaf pans lined with greased brown paper extending slightly above top of pan. Bake at 275 degrees for 2 hours. Place a baking pan of water on rack below rack holding loaf pans. Recipe makes 11 pounds of batter. It will make 15 to 18 dozen cookies.

Frances Mitchell

My mother (we called her "Mutha", others called her Mrs. Nora), Nora Dalton Mitchell, got this recipe from Mrs. Joe Higdon of Calvary. Mutha took care of her during her last days.

Large Size Dark Fruitcake

13   eggs
1   pound of butter
1   cup of sugar
1   cup of syrup

Add enough flour to make thick. Add nutmeg and cinnamon.

1   pound cherries
5   pounds raisins
2   pounds dates
1   pound almonds
1¼   pounds citron
1   pound currants
1   cup of coffee

Mix all together and bake in slow oven until done.

Linda Pyles Maxwell

Recipe from Grandmother Holt's cookbook selections.

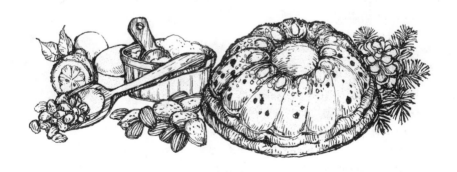

Fruitcake I

8   eggs
3   cups of sugar
1½   cups of butter
²/₃   cup of sweet cream
Flour (enough to thicken)
2   pounds of white raisins
1   teaspoon each, lemon and vanilla flavoring
8   ounces orange juice
3   ounces citron
3   ounces pineapple
6   ounces cherries
3   ounces dates
½   pound almonds, shelled
1   pound pecan kernels, chopped
1   pound Brazil nuts, shelled

Beat eggs. Add sugar, butter, and cream. Add flour to thicken. Add flavorings, nuts, and fruits. Bake until cooked enough.

Linda Pyles Maxwell

Fruitcake II

½   pound butter
1   cup sugar
5   eggs
2   cups plain flour, sifted 3 times
1   tablespoon lemon flavoring
1   tablespoon vanilla extract
1   8-ounce jar pineapple or fig preserves
1   pound red cherries
1   pound green or white pineapple
4   cups chopped pecans

Cream butter and sugar; add eggs one at a time. Cream well. Add flour, flavorings, and preserves; add well floured fruit and nuts to batter. Bake at 275 degrees for 2 hours or until done.

Gladys Ponder

252 Cakes

Grandma's Fruitcake

1	cup butter
1	cup sugar
1	cup blackberry jelly (homemade)
7	eggs
1	quart flour
1	teaspoon baking soda
1	teaspoon cinnamon
1	teaspoon nutmeg
1	teaspoon mace
½	pound orange peel
½	pound citron
2	pounds raisins
1	pound candied cherries
1	pound candied pineapple
1	pound dried figs
1	pound dates
1	pound hulled nuts

Cream butter and sugar, stir in jelly. Beat in one egg at a time. After each egg, stir in some flour and baking soda. (Save out one cup of flour to roll the fruit and nuts in.) Stir in spices. Fold in floured fruits and nuts. Put paper in the bottom of a tube pan and pack the batter firmly in the pan. Bake 4 hours in a slow oven. (Grandma baked the cake early and each day would pour a little homemade blackberry shrub on the cake to keep it moist.)

Mabel V. Kral

My mother got this recipe from her mother-in-law. Grandma was Eliza (Mrs. W. R.) Van Landingham, grandmother of R.R. Van Landingham. She ran a boarding house called Drummer's Retreat, located across the street from the courthouse where the school board is now.

Annie Lee's Fruitcake

6	eggs
¾	pound butter
1	16-ounce box powdered sugar
1	16-ounce sugar box full of plain flour
4	cups pecans
1½	pounds candied pineapple, red, green, and natural
1	pound candied cherries, red and green
½	pound citron
1	whole fresh coconut, reserve milk

Mix eggs, butter, sugar, and flour as any pound cake. Add nuts and fruit. Grate coconut; add meat and the milk. Mix with hands. Grease tube pan with Crisco; line pan with wax paper and coat with Crisco. Bake in preheated oven at 275 degrees for 3 hours.

Nancy Herring Stingley

This cake is worth the time and trouble!

Dried Fruit Fruitcake

4½   cups all-purpose flour
1½   teaspoons baking soda
½   teaspoon salt
1½   teaspoons ground cloves
1½   teaspoons ground cinnamon
1½   teaspoons ground allspice
1½   teaspoons ground ginger
1½   teaspoons ground nutmeg
2   cups butter flavor Crisco
3   cups dark brown sugar
5   eggs
3   cups or 2 packages dried fruit, reconstituted (we like apple and
     peach)
1   pound golden raisins
1   cup candied cherries, chopped
1   cup candied pineapple, chopped
2 to 3 cups pecan pieces

Sift all dry ingredients together. Cream Crisco, sugar, eggs, and reconstituted
fruit. In a large dish pan, mix 1 cup of flour with fruits and nuts; coat well.
Add 3½ cups of flour to the creamed mixture. (You will probably have to
mix by hand as mixture gets thick.) Add fruit and nuts; mix well. Pour into 1
tube pan and 1 loaf pan. Bake at 250 degrees for 3 hours or until knife blade
inserted comes out clean.

Cathy Walden Moore

*My own recipe after experimenting with different fruitcake recipes; I have been making
this for about 15 years. Moist! Moist!*

Whigham Street Scene
Broad Avenue

Whigham is home of the Rattlesnake Roundup. The Roundup, which is sponsored by the Whigham Community Club, began in 1960 and is held the last Saturday of January each year. Hunting and exhibiting snakes are featured as well as snake handling and milking demonstrations, arts and crafts, and continuous entertainment around the grounds on the day of the Roundup.

Candy . . .

Prince Home

Relocating from Alabama to the Spence community, the J.L. Prince family occupied this home, built around 1904, when W.L. "Ellie" Prince was about 6 months old. Mrs. W.L. (Donie Wilder) Prince still owns this home and the barns and other farm buildings associated with the turpentine business of years ago that still stand on the property. An upstairs and terrace were added to the original home. Today, many in the Spence community refer to Mrs. Prince as the "flag lady". She has several different flags waving from the terrace of the home, even though she now resides in the Camilla Retirement home. She will celebrate her 100th birthday in January of 2004.

Caramel Candy (Frosting)

4   cups sugar
2   cups milk
½   pint cream
¼   teaspoon soda
4   tablespoons butter
2   cups nuts

Melt ½ cup sugar, remove from fire. Add other sugar, milk, cream, and butter. Mix well. Add soda when mixture boils. Cook until soft ball has formed. Beat until light in color. Add nuts, spread on cake immediately, as it hardens quickly after it begins to harden. Cook additional time (to firm ball stage) for candy. Spread onto flat buttered pan to cool, cut into pieces.

Betty Hester

Mrs. Lucille Sholar Nowell's recipe.

Pecan Candy

3   cups pecans
3   cups sugar
½   cup corn syrup
1   cup water
1   teaspoon salt
1   tablespoon butter
1   teaspoon baking soda

Cook sugar, corn syrup, and water until it reaches 260 degrees, then add pecans and cook to 290 degrees. Add salt, butter, baking soda. Stir together and pour on marble or greased surface. Spread with knife to have thin candy. Break in pieces when cool enough to handle.

Maggie Roddenbery

Recipe of Mrs. Walter C. Jones, Sr., wife of a beloved Methodist minister in Cairo.

Easy Pralines

1	small package pudding mix (Chocolate, Vanilla, or Butterscotch)
½	cup brown sugar
1	cup granulated sugar
1	tablespoon butter
1	teaspoon vanilla extract
½	cup milk

Nuts, chopped

Mix all ingredients except vanilla and nuts. Cook to soft ball stage. Add vanilla and whip until cool. Add nuts and drop on wax paper.

Carolyn Brown

This recipe has been used in our family for many years. Taste is very much like New Orleans Pralines.

Syrup Candy

Cane Syrup
Pinch of baking soda

Cook syrup until it strings when spooned up from pan; let cool. Add a pinch of baking soda. Pull candy from one hand to the other until very cool. Twist or flip over to make long rope. Lay out on dish curled in circles. When dried, cut in small stick pieces.

Margaret Courtney (1912-2003)

I would help my mother, Alice Johnson, make this candy which would last a long while.

Variation submitted by Hannah Rogers: Add 1 cup nuts and 1 teaspoon vanilla extract.

Brown Sugar Candy

2   cups white sugar
1   cup evaporated milk
1   cup brown sugar (the darker the better)
2   tablespoons butter
Nuts or fruit
1   teaspoon vanilla

I use an iron frying pan. Melt one cup of granulated sugar (slowly to keep from scorching it). Add one cup evaporated milk (undiluted), slowly, it will get gummy, but cook until it is free of lumps again. Add brown sugar, cook until completely melted. Add another cup of white sugar (cook until the mixture will form a soft ball in cool water). Add butter and vanilla, remove from fire and add nuts and/or fruit and beat as you would fudge, pour on greased platter and cut before it gets too set.

Kathryn Miller Jones

This is my grandmother's recipe.

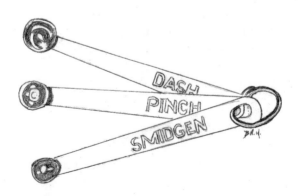

Divinity

3   cups sugar
$^2/_3$ cup cold water
Dash of salt
½   cup white corn syrup
2   egg whites
Dash of sugar
1   teaspoon vanilla
1   cup coarsely broken pecans

Bring sugar, water, salt, and syrup to boil. Boil until syrup threads to "hair" thread from spoon. Meanwhile, beat egg whites adding the dash of sugar (about 1 tablespoon) until they hold a stiff peak. Slowly pour syrup, beating at high speed in mixer. Add vanilla and when mixture is cool enough and just beginning to lose glossiness, stop beating. Add nuts and stir with spatula and drop with spoon and knife onto waxed paper.

Rusty Moye

Fun times were had by all the kids in the 50s when my Mom, Norma Claire, would cook up some divinity and "us kids" would stand around her dress tails and help spoon the candy out on wax paper. It was so rich you could only eat one piece per day.

Potato Fondant

1   Irish Potato (size of egg)
1   pound box confectioner's sugar
Crunchy peanut butter

Boil potato covered in water until well done (approximately 30 minutes). Remove peeling and mash. Place in bowl and add sugar. Mix well. Roll out mixture on wax paper coated with confectioner's sugar to ⅛ inch thickness. Spread with peanut butter. Roll up beginning on longer edge until a long roll is formed. Place in refrigerator and chill for 1 hour or longer. Slice in thin slices. May also wrap well and freeze. Keep refrigerated.

Hilda McKinney

Recipe was made in a Home Economics class in Cairo High School, 1952-53.

Peanut Brittle

1½   cups sugar
½   cup white corn syrup
½   cup water
1½   cups raw peanuts
1½   teaspoons butter
1   teaspoon baking soda

Boil sugar, syrup, water until when spoon is lifted from pot a thin thread forms. Add peanuts. Cook until caramel color. Remove from heat. Add butter and soda. Mix well. Pour into buttered pan. Let cool.

Ann Bracewell

Recipe handed down from mother, Bessie Robinson. We made it quite a lot through the holidays.

Edwin's Coconut Curls

Punch out eyes of a fresh coconut with ice pick and pour "milk"(juice) in a cup. Place coconut on a rack in oven at 250 degrees for 45 to 60 minutes, or until shell breaks. Remove from oven (be careful about steam). Complete breaking of shell. Sometimes the coconut will come out whole. Break into pieces and use potato peeler to sliver all the coconut into a heavy baking pan with sides. Sprinkle about 1½ cups of sugar over the coconut curls. Pour coconut "milk" over these. If no "milk", add a cup of water and stir. Bake at 250 degrees, stirring all along until all of the curls are caramelized. Be sure you leave the brown edge on the white coconut.

Laurie Carlisle Conradi

Daddy, Edwin Carlisle, made these every Christmas. We all, including grandchildren, didn't think we had had Christmas without these.

Old Fashioned Molasses Taffy

1¼   cups sorghum or dark molasses
¾   cup sugar
1   tablespoon vinegar
1   tablespoon butter
⅛   teaspoon soda
⅛   teaspoon salt

Combine sorghum, sugar, and vinegar and cook to 270 degrees or to the soft crack stage; stir occasionally to prevent burning. Remove from heat, add butter, soda, and salt, and stir just enough to blend. Pour into buttered pans. When cool enough to handle, gather into a ball and pull between ungreased fingertips until firm and light in color. Cut into pieces and wrap in waxed paper. Add a few drops of oil of peppermint.

Hazel Logue

We used to make this candy on rainy, snowy days when we had to stay inside. We also popped corn and mixed it with this candy for popcorn balls.

Millionaire Fudge

2   6-ounce packages milk chocolate chips
1   pint marshmallow cream
1   teaspoon vanilla
4½   cups sugar
1   large can evaporated milk
¼   pound margarine
1   cup chopped pecans

Place chips, marshmallow cream, and vanilla in large mixing bowl and slightly mix. In heavy saucepan put sugar, milk, and margarine. Bring to a boil and let boil 7 minutes, stirring constantly. (Best to use a timer.) Add this mixture along with nuts to first part. Mix until all chocolate is melted. Pour into 14 x 8 x 2-inch greased pan. Let cool. May substitute semi-sweet chocolate chips or omit nuts, if desired. May be placed in refrigerator to set and speed cooling. Cut into pieces.

Sharon Whitfield

Prince Turpentine Commissary

Items for purchase at the commissary included sugar and rice. Twenty-five hogs were butchered at a time and sold as well as the lard. Mrs. Prince also had cloth for purchase as well as dress forms to custom-make clothes for the customers.

Cookies . . .

Shoemaker- Harrison House

Mrs. Gusie Cobb built the Jimmy T. Harrison house. She was a sister of Judge Tom Mills. Mrs. Cobb sold to Mr. J. S. Shoemaker, who had a lumber company in Whigham. Mr. Shoemaker sold to Jim T. Harrison in October 1940. Now the house belongs to Mrs. Frank Johnson.

Tea Cakes I

1   cup butter Crisco
2   cups sugar
3   eggs
3   cups self-rising flour
1   teaspoon vanilla extract

Mix Crisco and sugar together with a spoon. Add eggs and vanilla, then mix in flour. Dough will be stiff. Drop by teaspoonful about 2 inches apart on cookie sheet. Bake at 325 degrees for 8 to 10 minutes. Do not overcook.

Betty Hester

Tea Cakes II

4   eggs
1½   cups sugar
¼   cup Crisco
¾   cup butter
4   cups sifted flour
2   teaspoons baking powder
1   teaspoon vanilla extract

Cream butter, shortening, and sugar. Add eggs and vanilla. Sift dry ingredients together; add small amount at the time and mix well. Chill dough, roll out on floured surface and cut in rounds or other shapes. Bake at 400 degrees on greased baking sheet.

Edith M. Prevatte

Tea Cakes III

5 to 6 cups self-rising flour
2   eggs
2   cups sugar
3   teaspoons vanilla extract
1   cup butter or solid vegetable shortening
3   tablespoons buttermilk

Cream sugar and butter. Add balance of ingredients. Mix well. Flour
fingertips and roll dough into small balls. Place on greased cookie sheet and
press with fork or fingertips. Bake at 350 degrees for 8 to10 minutes.

Fannie Davis Tinsley

Fannie Davis Tinsley is the daughter of Confederate Veteran Jonah Beal Davis.

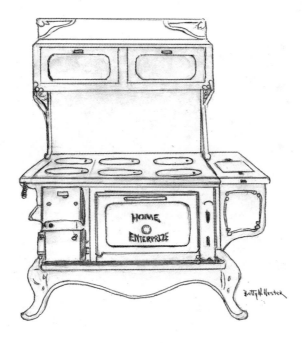

Old Fashioned Tea Cakes I

4   cups self-rising flour, sift, measure, and set aside
2   cups sugar
2   sticks oleo or 1 cup Crisco
3   eggs
2   teaspoons vanilla
2   teaspoons lemon extract

Mix sugar and shortening until creamy. Beat in eggs; mix well. Begin adding flour gradually until all is added. Add flavorings and mix well. An additional 4 to 6 cups of flour is necessary to add gradually to small portions of the batter until desired consistency to roll out on a floured pastry sheet. Cut cookies with desired designs. In other words, pinch off a handful of the batter, flour the pasty sheet, add flour gradually, kneading until can be rolled and cut with cookie cutters. Continue this process until all batter is used. Bake at 325 degrees on ungreased cookie sheets until done (light golden in color). This recipe yields well over 200 cookies.

Yvonne Childs

Recipe was given to me by Mrs. Emmye Maxwell. It was passed from her great grandmother, Charlotte Pilcher Davaney (1823-1901). Charlotte produced 15 children, so we can only imagine how many teacakes she made through the years. Mrs. Emmye told me it was passed on to her grandmother, then her mother, and now to her. She estimates this recipe to have been in use for over 161 years.

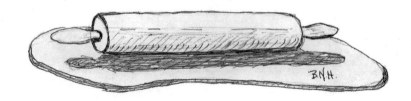

Old Fashioned Tea Cakes II

2	sticks butter, melted
2	cups sugar
2	teaspoons vanilla flavoring
3	eggs
¼	cup sweet milk
3	cups all-purpose flour and enough flour to roll out cookies

Beat eggs slightly. Add sugar, vanilla, butter, and milk, mix well. Stir in flour and cream well. This will be stiff enough to roll out on floured board. Do not mix too much flour while rolling out into ¼-inch thickness. Cut with cookie cutter the size you would like to have. Bake in 375 degrees oven until golden brown.

Pamela C. Forrester

Recipe was handed down from my Great Grandmother (Emma Simpson Edmondson). My mother (Lena Faye Winters Carter) taught me how to make these delicious Tea Cakes when I was small. Mother was one of five girls who grew up on a farm in Morven, Georgia where good cooking was a way of life.

Old Fashioned Tea Cakes III

2	sticks real butter
2	cups sugar
5½	cups plain flour
1	teaspoon vanilla
1	teaspoon soda
2	tablespoons buttermilk
3	eggs

Beat butter and sugar together. Add vanilla. Sift flour and soda together twice. Add buttermilk and one egg at a time to flour and soda with your mixer on low speed. Refrigerate dough overnight. The next day roll out and bake in 400 degrees oven for 5 minutes.

Mary B. Gainous

Recipe from Mrs. Mildred Jones from Climax, Georgia.

Ginger Tea Cakes

1   cup sugar
1   cup syrup
1   cup shortening
1   cup buttermilk
1   egg
1   tablespoon baking soda
2   teaspoons ginger
Pinch of salt
Plain flour (enough for firm dough)

Mix ingredients except flour and shortening and beat well. Add shortening and flour. Knead until dough becomes firm. Roll out and cut. Bake at 350 degrees until lightly browned.

Annie Mae Perkins

My mother, Mamie Ulmer Jones (1900-1995), made these for us to take to school in our lunches.

Syrup Tea Cakes

1   cup lard
1   cup sugar
1   cup cane syrup
1   egg
¾   cup buttermilk
1   tablespoon soda
¼   teaspoon ginger
Plain flour, sifted
Pinch of salt

Mix all ingredients, adding flour to make a stiff "biscuit-type" dough. Turn out onto a floured surface and knead as you would for biscuits. Roll thin and cut with biscuit cutter. Bake at 350 degrees for 10 minutes.

Kay Johnson Harder

My grandmother, Idella Johnson, always had these in her kitchen. They were stored in a large Dutch Oven with a glass lid. Before baking she pressed the dough, so her fingerprints were on the cookies! Lots of people have used the recipe to make the cookies for me and my 82 year old dad, but none have tasted just like Grandma's.

Old Fashioned Syrup Tea Cakes

1   egg
1   cup margarine
1   cup sugar
1   cup cane syrup
1   teaspoon vanilla extract
Flour (self-rising) as needed

Mix all ingredients well, then mix in flour until stiff enough to pat out on floured surface. Cut into squares. Bake at 325 degrees for 10 to 12 minutes.

Eleanor Lee

My mother's recipe, a favorite of the family.

Soft Tea Cakes

1¾   cups self-rising flour
1   cup sugar
½   cup butter
1   teaspoon vanilla
2   tablespoons milk
1   egg

Mix flour and sugar. Add melted butter, vanilla, milk, and egg. Drop on greased or sprayed cookie sheet and bake 8 minutes at 375 degrees. May add M&M's, chocolate kisses, or any colored candies that would melt after removing cookies from oven.

Alice McCorkle

Given to me by my late sister-in-law, Sarah S. Courtney.

Molasses Ginger Cookies

¾   cup shortening
¾   cup sugar
1   egg
¼   cup molasses
2   cups flour
1½   teaspoons baking soda
1   teaspoon cloves
1   teaspoon cinnamon
1   teaspoon ginger
½   teaspoon salt

Mix all ingredients together. Roll dough into balls. Roll balls in sugar. Place on greased cookie sheet. Bake 10 minutes at 350 degrees. For crisp cookies, bake longer.

Keith and Andrea Powell Webb

We shared this recipe with Andrea's family after we were married. It is a Webb family Christmas tradition and has become a favorite of the Powell family as well.

One Pot Brownies

1 stick margarine
2 blocks unsweetened chocolate
1 cup sugar
¼ teaspoon salt
¾ cup flour
2 eggs
1 teaspoon baking soda
1 cup chopped nuts

Melt margarine in a 3 quart pot. Add blocks of chocolate and melt. Add sugar, stir; add baking soda, salt, and flour, stir. Add eggs, stir. Add nuts. Pour in 10 x 10-inch vegetable spray coated pan. Bake at 350 degrees for 25 to 30 minutes.

Laurie Carlisle Conradi

Crispy Cookies

1 cup margarine
1 cup white sugar
1 cup brown sugar
2 eggs
1 teaspoon vanilla
1 teaspoon baking soda
½ teaspoon salt
2 cups uncooked oatmeal
2 cups flour
1 cup Wheaties or 40% bran flakes

Cream margarine and sugars together. Add eggs and vanilla, beat well. Add soda, salt , and oatmeal, beat again. Add flour and cereal together and stir into batter with spoon or spatula until well mixed. Form into balls and press down some to flatten out. Bake at 350 degrees about 10 minutes.

Carolyn Fulton

Ma-Maw's Sugar Cookies

1	cup shortening
2	cups sugar
2	eggs
6	tablespoons sweet milk
3	teaspoons vanilla
½	teaspoon soda
3½ to 4	cups plain flour

Cream sugar and shortening, add well beaten eggs, milk, flavoring, and soda. Add enough flour to make stiff dough. Knead well. Roll out and cut with cookie cutter or jar lid. Use plenty of flour to keep from sticking to counter or wax paper. Bake at 350 degrees for 10 to 15 minutes. If stored in airtight container, teacakes will keep for months (if they last!)

Annette Prince Blackmon

A favorite for the grand kids—quick, easy and good!

Similar recipes submitted by Julie Stewart and Annette Lodge.

Hermits

2	cups brown sugar
1	cup shortening
1	teaspoon soda in a little hot water
2	eggs
4	teaspoons sour milk

Combine above ingredients. Mix well. Add citron, cinnamon, cloves, nuts, and raisins, as desired. Mix well. Drop by teaspoons on greased baking sheet. Bake at 350 to 375 degrees until browned.

Nancy Nichols

The old way was a pinch or palm full and you just knew what temperature and how long to bake. Grandma always had a 5-pound tin of lard she used for baking on the wood stove.

White Sugar Crunchies

½   cup shortening
²/₃   cup sugar
1   egg
½   teaspoon vanilla
1½   cups sifted flour
½   teaspoon soda
½   teaspoon baking powder
½   teaspoon salt
Dash of grated nutmeg

Cream shortening, add sugar gradually, and beat until light and fluffy. Add egg and vanilla, and continue beating until blended. Add sifted dry ingredients, mixing well. The dough should be stiff enough to handle. Roll into ½ or 1-inch balls, then roll in granulated sugar. Place on greased cookie sheet and flatten each ball with a fork. Bake about 10 minutes in a 400 degrees oven. Yield 25 large or 50 small cookies.

La Vonne Childers

Brilliant Candy Slices

Cream 1 cup butter. Add 1 cup sifted powdered sugar, creaming well. Blend in 1 unbeaten egg and 1 teaspoon vanilla. Add 2¼ cups sifted Pillsbury's Best all-purpose flour; mix well. Stir in 1 cup pecan halves and 2 cups soft candied cherries, cut in halves. Chill 1 hour. Divide in thirds. Shape into rolls 10 inches long. Wrap in wax paper; chill at least 3 hours. Cut into ⅛-inch slices; place on ungreased cookie sheets. Bake at 325 degrees for 12 to 15 minutes until delicately browned on the edges. Makes 7 dozen cookies.

Sue Askew

Recipe from Shirley Skeen---our favorite Christmas cookie for many years.

Monster Cookies

6   eggs
1   pound brown sugar
½   teaspoon vanilla
2   teaspoons light corn syrup
4   teaspoons baking powder
½   pound butter
1½   pounds peanut butter
9   cups oatmeal
½   pound chocolate chips
½   pound M & M's
2   cups sugar

Preheat oven to 350 degrees. Mix ingredients in very large bowl in given order. Drop from tablespoon (make them big) onto cookie sheet and flatten slightly. Eight cookies to sheet. Bake 12 minutes. Makes 8½ dozen.

Betty W. Harrison

Mud Hens

1   cup sugar
½   cup Crisco
2   eggs, 1 white saved
1½   cups self-rising flour
1   teaspoon vanilla
1   cup chopped pecans
1   cup brown sugar

Cream sugar and Crisco. Add eggs and beat well. Add flour and vanilla. Spread on pan ½-inch thick. Sprinkle 1 cup chopped pecans on top and press in mixture. Mix 1 cup brown sugar and 1 beaten egg white. Spread on top of mixture and bake 25 to 30 minutes at 325 degrees.

Gladys Ponder

Perfect Drop Raisin Cookies

2	cups raisins
1	cup water
1	teaspoon soda
2	cups sugar
1	cup shortening
3	eggs
1	teaspoon vanilla
4	cups plain flour
1	teaspoon baking powder
½	teaspoon salt
1	teaspoon cinnamon
¼	teaspoon nutmeg

Cook raisins and water for 5 minutes; cool and add soda. Cream together shortening and sugar. Add vanilla and eggs; mix well. Add cooled raisins and liquid. Sift together flour, salt, baking powder, cinnamon, nutmeg; add chopped nuts, if desired. Mix well and drop on greased cookie sheet. Bake in a 350 degrees oven for 10 to 12 minutes.

JoAnn Humphries

Recipe was a family hit. My mother gave it to me about 40 years ago. She made it when I was a child.

Crisp Sugarless Gingersnaps

2   cups medium heavy cane syrup
Pinch of salt
2   teaspoons soda
1   cup lard (or butter)
1   tablespoon ground ginger
5½   cups flour (or enough to make a soft dough)

Boil together syrup, shortening, salt, and ginger. Let boil 2 minutes or longer if syrup is thin. Set aside to cool. Add soda and beat thoroughly. Add flour to make dough as soft as can be handled. Roll out to $^1/_8$-inch thickness. Cut and bake on greased cookie sheet at 300 degrees (these cookies will burn easily, so watch them closely.) Yield 6 to 7 dozen.

Kathryn Miller Jones

Mrs. Jesse Miller gave me this recipe, which she said is 240 years old.

Chewy Cookies

2   cups brown sugar
3   eggs
1   cup chopped nuts
½   cup melted butter
1   rounded cup flour
1   teaspoon baking powder
1   teaspoon vanilla

Mix all ingredients together. Bake in a buttered pan at 350 degrees for about 15 minutes.

Mabel Van Landingham Kral

Armetta Hines, "Metta", came to work for "Miss Mabel" in 1932 and was a loved member of the family for many years. These cookies had no recipe, but Metta finally, at our insistence, wrote this one.

Similar recipes submitted by Carolyn Brown and Cheryl Hunziker.

Easy Cookies

1   box yellow cake mix
2   eggs
½   cup oil

Mix by hand and spoon onto cookie sheet which has been sprayed with cooking spray. Bake at 350 degrees for 8 minutes.

Alice McCorkle

Recipe given to my daughter, Laura, by Geneva Owens. The youth group made Valentine cookies for the entire church.

Granny's Coconut Cookies

½   cup margarine
1   cup sugar
1   teaspoon coconut flavoring
1   egg
1   package biscuit baking mix
1   package spud flakes

Mix all ingredients; mixture will be thick. Chill. Roll dough in hand--size of small ball. Bake at 375 degrees for 12 to 15 minutes. Dough will keep in refrigerator up to 1 week.

Cheryl Hunziker

Cinnamon Toasties

2   cups flour
¾   cup sugar
2   teaspoons baking powder
1   teaspoon salt
1   cup raisins
1   cup milk
2   tablespoons melted butter or margarine
1   teaspoon vanilla

Topping
2   tablespoons melted butter or margarine
2½   tablespoons sugar
1   teaspoon cinnamon

Prepare dough: sift flour, sugar, baking powder, and salt into mixing bowl. Add raisins. Combine milk, butter and vanilla; add dry ingredients, stirring just until moistened. Spread in greased 10 x 15-inch jelly roll pan. Bake in 350 degrees oven 15 minutes. Remove from oven. Brush 2 tablespoons butter over cake. Sprinkle with mixture of cinnamon and sugar. Bake 10 to 15 minutes more, or until golden brown. Cut into 3-inch squares. Cool 5 minutes on rack. Serve warm or cool.

Betty W. Harrison

Ice Box Cookies

1   cup butter
2   cups brown sugar
1   cup chopped nuts
3½   cups all-purpose flour
½   teaspoon salt
1   teaspoon soda
2   eggs

Combine all ingredients and roll into logs. Wrap in wax paper. Refrigerate overnight. Slice and bake at 375 degrees for 12 to 15 minutes or until desired brownness. The logs keep in the refrigerator for several weeks.

Annette M. Lodge
280 Cookies

Peach Refrigerator Cookies

¾   cup butter
1½   cups dark brown sugar
1   egg
¼   cup milk
1   cup chopped dried peaches
2½   cups flour
3   teaspoons baking powder
1   teaspoon salt
1   cup chopped nuts

Cream butter, sugar, and egg. Sift dry ingredients, add to first mixture alternating with milk. Add nuts and peaches and mix well. Shape into rolls, wrap in waxed paper and place in freezer until ready to cook. Slice thin and bake in 400 degrees oven for 12 to 15 minutes. Makes 5 dozen cookies.

Carolyn H. Chason

Betty Foy Sanders "invented" these peachy goodies to accompany her famed Peach Punch when her husband, Carl Sanders, was Governor of Georgia. She gave me this recipe in 1965.

Pecan Sandies

1   cup buttermilk baking mix
¼   cup butter
1   tablespoon sugar
1   tablespoon boiling water
½   teaspoon vanilla
½ to 1 cup pecans, chopped
¼   cup confectioners sugar

Put first 5 ingredients into mixing bowl. Stir until well mixed. Add nuts; stir to blend into dough. Stir until dough forms a ball and cleans the sides of the bowl. Shape dough into finger like shapes. Place on ungreased cookie sheet 1 inch apart. Bake at 350 degrees for 12 to 15 minutes until lightly browned. Cool on wire rack. Roll in confectioners sugar while warm.

Martha Ruth Elkins

Fruit Bars

2	cups finely chopped pecans
1½	cups light brown sugar
1	stick butter
1	cup unsifted plain flour
2	eggs
1	tablespoon vanilla
½	pound candied cherries
½	pound candied pineapple

Grease and flour 7 x 11-inch pan. Sprinkle pan with chopped nuts. Cream butter and sugar; add eggs and vanilla. Fold in flour and chopped fruit. Bake an hour at 300 to 325 degrees, depending on your oven.

Lucy Singleton

A neighbor in Elberton, Georgia, where we lived for a year, shared this recipe with me. After coming to Cairo in 1954, I shared it many times.

Toffee Fingers

1	cup chopped pecans
1	cup real butter, melted and hot
1	cup sugar

Graham crackers to cover bottom of 11 x 13-inch pan

Mix together pecans, butter, and sugar; pour over graham crackers. Bake for 10 minutes at 350 degrees.

Tommie Jean Cooper

Coconut Bars

4   eggs
1½   cups sugar
½   stick oleo
2   cups self-rising flour
1   teaspoon vanilla
2   cups milk
1   cup coconut

Beat eggs and add sugar, oleo, and flour. Mix well, add vanilla, milk, and coconut. Pour in greased pan and bake 1 hour at 300 degrees. When cool, cut into bars.

Elizabeth Maxwell

Lemon Bars

1   box Pillsbury lemon cake mix
1   egg
1   cup chopped nuts
1   stick margarine
1   8-ounce cream cheese
1   box powdered sugar
2   eggs

Mix cake mix, egg, nuts, and margarine, press in 9 x 13-inch baking dish. Mix cream cheese, powdered sugar, and eggs. Pour on top. Bake at 325 degrees for 35 to 45 minutes.

Deborah Phillips

Barn on Wendell Gainey Farm

'The Storm' of 1929 or 1930 blew down the barn, killed a mule, and damaged the family home on the Robert Gainey farm. Wendell's grandfather, Robert, and father, Cullen, rebuilt the barn. After Wendell's retirement, he and his wife returned to the family land. The Gaineys were early settlers of what is now Grady County.

Desserts...

Betty N Hester

Singletary House

Now owned by Emogene Strickland Miller, this typical early Grady County house was well suited to the needs of settlers and their families. Some have referred to it as "Aunt Dink's house" because Claudia Singletary Dinkins (born 1875) lived there many years ago.

Bishop Whipple

$^2/_3$ **cup flour**
½ **cup sugar**
2 **eggs**
1 **tablespoon baking powder**
1 **cup pecans**
1 **cup dates**

Beat eggs, add sugar, flour and baking powder. After beating, add nuts and dates. Bake for 1 hour at 300 degrees or until done in lightly greased 8 x 8-inch square pan.

Tommie Jean M. Cooper

Given by Mrs. Gladys Clark in 1958.

Chocolate Chip Goodie

2 **20-ounce chocolate chip cookie rolls**
2 **8-ounce packages cream cheese**
2 **cups sugar**
2 **eggs**

Slice 1 cookie roll in ⅛-inch slices. Put cookie slices in bottom of pan. Press to make crust. Mix other ingredients and put on top of crust. Slice other cookie roll and put on top of mixture. Bake at 325 degrees for 45 minutes.

Opal Lewis

Shortnin' Bread (Similar to Gingerbread)

2   cups all-purpose flour
½   teaspoon ground cinnamon
¼   teaspoon ground nutmeg
1½   teaspoons baking soda
½   cup buttermilk
¼   cup plus 2 tablespoons butter or margarine
1   cup molasses
1   egg, slightly beaten

Combine flour, cinnamon, nutmeg in large bowl; mix well and set aside. Dissolve soda in buttermilk, stir well and set aside. Combine buttermilk and molasses in a heavy sauce pan; bring to boil, stirring constantly. Add to flour mixture. Stir in buttermilk mixture and egg. Pour batter into greased and floured 10-inch cast iron skillet. Bake 350 degrees for 25 to 30 minutes or until toothpick comes out clean. Cool 10 minutes in pan.

Cheryl Hunziker

Ginger Bread

1   cup sugar
1   cup cane syrup
1   egg
1   teaspoon soda
¼   teaspoon ginger
¼   teaspoon allspice
¼   teaspoon cinnamon
¼   teaspoon ground cloves
¾   cup buttermilk
2   cups all-purpose flour
8   tablespoons butter, melted

Put all in bowl and mix well. Pour into a large 11 x 17-inch pan. Bake at 350 degrees for about 20 to 30 minutes.

Annette M. Lodge

This recipe is over 100 years old.

White Chocolate Cheesecake

1   8-ounce package cream cheese, softened
2   cups cold milk divided
2   packages (4 serving size each), white chocolate flavor instant
     pudding and pie filling, sugar free
1   8-ounce tub cool whip
1   prepared graham crackers crumb crust (6 ounces)

Beat cream cheese and ½ cup of the milk in large bowl with wire whisk
until smooth. Add remaining 1½ cups milk and pudding mix. Beat with wire
whisk 1 minute. Stir in whipped topping until smooth and well blended.
Spoon into crust. Refrigerate 4 hours or until set. Garnish with white
chocolate curls made with Baker's Chocolate.

Carolyn Fulton

Oreo Cheesecake

3   8-ounce packages cream cheese, softened
3   eggs
¾   cup sugar
12   Oreo cookies
6   squares Baker's chocolate, melted
1   8-ounce Cool Whip, thawed

Place 12 cupcake liners in muffin pan. Place an Oreo in each liner. Mix
cream cheese and sugar; add eggs one at a time until blended. Pour creamed
mixture on each Oreo. Bake at 350 degrees for 15 to 20 minutes until center
is almost set. Cool. Drizzle melted chocolate on each. Top with Cool Whip.

Kelly Scott

Recipe of my mom, Donna Wright

Candied Rose Petals

18   small rose petals
1   cup sifted powdered sugar
1½   teaspoons meringue powder
3   tablespoons water
½   cup superfine sugar

Rinse rose petals, let dry on paper towel. Beat powdered sugar, meringue powder, and water at low speed until blended. Beat at high speed 4 to 5 minutes until fluffy. Brush mixture on all sides of petals. Sprinkle with superfine sugar. Let stand on wire rack 24 hours.

Gloria R. Searcy

Delicious Centerpiece

1   stick butter or margarine
30   large marshmallows
1 to 2 teaspoons green food color
½   teaspoon vanilla flavoring
4   cups corn flakes
Cinnamon red hots

Melt margarine in large pot. Add marshmallows, stirring constantly, until melted (low heat). Add food coloring and flavoring. Mix well. Add corn flakes and mix gently until corn flakes are covered. Remove from stove. Dip mixture and place in a curve on a round plate or tray. Leave a round place in the center for a candle. Use a case knife and arrange the mixture in the shape of a wreath. Arrange cinnamon red hots to resemble holly berries. Place 2 or 3 inch candle in center. Delicious to eat, if eaten soon after making.

Martha Ruth Elkins

My students in Grady County Schools' cooking classes enjoyed making these centerpieces for the holiday season.

Ambrosia

1   large ruby red grapefruit (sweet)
5   medium sweet juicy oranges
1   8-ounce can crushed pineapple
¾   cup sweetened flaked coconut
¹/₃   cup liquid from maraschino cherry jar
2   tablespoons of sugar (sweeten to taste)
Maraschino cherries with stems
Mint leaves

Scoop fruit and liquid from grapefruit and oranges into a medium to large sized bowl (2 quart). Cut wedges of fruit in half. Add the crushed pineapple along with its liquid. (Note: I use the pineapple canned in its own juices. If pineapple canned in a heavy syrup is used, taste the Ambrosia for sweetness before adding sugar.) Add the flaked coconut, maraschino cherry liquid, and sugar. Mix well. Chill in refrigerator. Serve in crystal compote stemware and top each serving with one stemmed maraschino cherry and mint leaf. Serves 6 to 8. Note: Can be frozen in freezer. Best served with almond pound cake.

Lunelle Mizell Siegel

Recipe of Nellie Butler Mizell by her granddaughter.

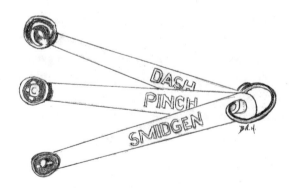

Old Fashioned Ambrosia

6   navel oranges
Sugar (to taste)
¾   cup coconut
½   cup chopped pecans
2   sliced bananas

Peel oranges, removing all membranes and cut in small pieces. Add sugar to taste. Add coconut and pecans; combine and stir. Add bananas when ready to serve.

Myrt McCorkle

Recipe of my mother, Ma Betty Knowles. It was simple because this was what we had at this time of year.

Variation submitted by Gloria Searcy: May add grapefruit, raisins, strawberries, and apples.

Heavenly Hash

1   pint whipping cream
25   marshmallows, chopped or 250 small marshmallows
25   maraschino cherries, chopped
1   small can crushed pineapple
1   cup chopped pecans

Whip cream. Add other ingredients. Mix and chill several hours.

Tommie Jean Cooper

Lemon Fluff

1   small package lemon gelatin
1½   cups hot water
1   large can evaporated milk
1   cup sugar
Graham cracker crust

Mix gelatin and water; chill until thick. Beat evaporated milk that has been partially frozen; until it is thick. Beat sugar and milk, fold in gelatin that has been whipped. Pour into cracker crust and chill well.

Carolyn Brown

Peggy Clark Williams and I grew up making this dessert. You may use any flavor gelatin.

Blue Willow Squares

1   18-ounce package yellow cake mix
½   cup (1 stick) butter or margarine, softened
1   cup chopped pecans
4   eggs, divided use
1   8-ounce package cream cheese, softened
1   16-ounce package confectioners sugar

Preheat oven to 350 degrees. Lightly grease an 8 x 11-inch baking pan and set aside. In a bowl, mix cake mix, butter, pecans, and 2 eggs with a large spoon; transfer dough to baking pan. Use plastic wrap or chill your hand with ice water to press mixture into pan making it even; will be very sticky. In a separate bowl, lightly beat remaining 2 eggs. Add cream cheese, gradually add sugar and lightly mix. It should be slightly lumpy. Spoon cream cheese mixture over cake mixture and use spatula to spread it evenly. Bake 45 to 50 minutes or until golden brown. Cool for 1 hour. Run knife around sides of pan and cut into squares.

Orine C. Bulloch

Strawberry Surprise

1   angel food cake cut up in chunks
1   can condensed Eagle Brand milk
1   8-ounce cream cheese (room temperature)
1   large cool whip
2   cartons of strawberries
Trifle bowl

Mix milk, cream cheese, and cool whip together. Set aside. Cut up strawberries. Set aside. 1st layer: Cream cheese mixture, spread in the bottom of bowl, $^1/_3$ of mixture. 2nd layer: Half of angel food chunks. 3rd layer: Half of strawberries with the exception of a few for decoration on top. Continue layering in order listed. Top with strawberries. Preparation time--30 minutes. Serves 16 to 24.

Danielle Lewis Jones

Tortoni

$1^2/_3$ cups (1 tall can) evaporated milk
1   13½-ounce can pineapple tidbits, well drained
1   cup maraschino cherries, well drained
1   cup roasted pecans or almonds (cut up)
1   cup broken vanilla wafers (about 12)
1   cup sugar
1   envelope lemon instant Kool-aid drink mix

Chill milk in flat pan until almost frozen around edges. Have pineapple, cherries, nuts, and wafers prepared in large bowl. Put ice-cold milk into cold small bowl of electric mixer whipping at high speed until fluffy. Gradually beat in sugar and Kool-aid until stiff. Fold whipped mixture into fruit mixture. Spoon into foil lined muffin cups. Freeze until firm, about 3 to 4 hours. This dessert may be made in advance; put the frozen individual servings in a freezer bag until needed.

Carolyn H. Chason

This is a simplified version of a very old recipe used by an Italian cook at a Jacksonville boarding house in the 1950s. It was always served when spaghetti or other Italian dishes were on the menu.

Vanilla Pudding

1/3   cup sugar
1/4   cup cornstarch
1/8   teaspoon salt
2¾   cups milk
2   tablespoons butter or margarine
1   teaspoon vanilla

Mix dry ingredients. Add milk. Cook until it begins to thicken, stirring frequently. Add butter and vanilla. Enjoy! (For chocolate pudding, add ²/₃ cups sugar and 3 tablespoons cocoa.)

Buddy West

Recipe of Marguerite Stagner (Mrs. Harrell B.) West

Egg Custard

3   slightly beaten eggs
1/4   cup sugar
1/4   teaspoon salt
2   cups milk, scalded
½ to 1 teaspoon vanilla extract

Combine eggs, sugar, and salt. Slowly stir in slightly cooled milk and vanilla. Put in quart baking dish. Place in shallow pan on oven rack. Pour hot water in pan to about an inch deep. Bake in slow oven, 350 degrees about 60 minutes, or until knife inserted off-center comes out clean.

Susan Y. Perkins

This is one of Pat Perkins' favorite dishes of his mother. She was not known for following directions and therefore did not use many recipes.

Similar recipe submitted by Ann Robertson.

Chocolate Pudding

2   cups sugar
½   cup self-rising flour
Dash of salt
4   eggs, separated
²/₃   cup powdered cocoa (can be omitted for vanilla pudding or base
         for banana pudding.)
4   cups milk
1   teaspoon vanilla

Cook in double boiler. Mix dry ingredients, slowly add milk. Cook over
boiling water until smooth and slightly thickened. Mix small amount of hot
pudding and beaten egg yolks; slowly add to pudding. Cook until thickened:
add vanilla flavoring. Pour into 1 or 2 cooked pie crusts.

Meringue

Beat egg whites and ¼ teaspoon cream of tartar; add 4 tablespoons sugar.
Beat until stiff. Put on pies and bake 350 degrees until light brown. Cool.
Can be put in casserole and served without crust.

Hedy B. Donaldson

*This was always served as a Sunday lunch dessert, cooked by my brother or me on
Sunday morning. A favorite of children, grandchildren, and cousins who happened to
show up for lunch.*

Rice Pudding

²/₃   cup uncooked regular rice
1¹/₃ cups water
2   eggs or 4 egg yolks
½   cup sugar
½   cup raisins
2   cups milk
½   teaspoon vanilla or 1 tablespoon grated orange peel
¼   teaspoon salt
Ground nutmeg

Heat rice and water to boiling, stirring once or twice; reduce heat. Cover and simmer for 14 minutes. (Do not lift cover or stir). All water should be absorbed. Heat oven to 325 degrees. Beat eggs in ungreased 1½ quart casserole. Stir in sugar, raisins, milk, vanilla, salt, and hot rice. Sprinkle with nutmeg. Bake uncovered, stirring occasionally, until knife inserted halfway between center and edge comes out clean, 50 to 60 minutes. Serve warm or cold. 6 to 8 servings.

Gwen Maloy

Banana Pudding

2   small packages or 1 large package vanilla cook and serve
            pudding mix
2   large bananas
Vanilla wafers

Cook pudding mix according to package directions. Line serving dish with vanilla wafers. Cover vanilla wafers with banana slices. Pour pudding over bananas and wafers. Let cool.

Paulette Robinson Daughtry

Quick and easy, this recipe was prepared for our Sunday dessert.

Boots Hunziker's Jelly Roll

3   eggs
1   cup sugar
1   cup plain flour
½   teaspoon salt
1   teaspoon vanilla
2   teaspoons baking powder
Jelly of choice

Mix all ingredients well. Line jelly roll pan with waxed paper. Pour in batter. Bake at 400 degrees for about 12 minutes. Turn out on cloth and cool about 5 minutes. Roll up, then unroll and let cool a few minutes. Spread on jelly and roll up again. Can sprinkle with powdered sugar.

Cheryl Hunziker

My mother-in-law won first prize at the county fair with this recipe.

Apple Dumplings

1   cup water
1   cup sugar
¼   cup margarine
2   apples
Salt
2   cans crescent rolls
Cinnamon (pinches)

Boil water, sugar, margarine, and salt for 4 minutes. Peel and cut 2 apples (16 pieces). Take 2 cans crescent rolls and wrap 1 piece of apple in 1 roll. Place wrapped apples in vegetable spray coated pan. Pour sauce over all pieces. Sprinkle cinnamon on each wrap (just a pinch). Bake at 375 degrees for 35 minutes.

Alice McCorkle

My daughter's (Allison) mother-in-law, Celia Bass, made this dessert for a family get together. We added ice cream on top.

Chocolate Torte

1 cup plain flour
1 stick margarine
¾ cup pecans, finely chopped

Mix and pat into casserole dish and bake 15 minutes at 350 degrees. Set aside and completely cool.

1 8-ounce package cream cheese, room temperature
1 cup powdered sugar
1 9-ounce carton Cool Whip, divided
1 large package instant chocolate pudding mix

Mix cream cheese, sugar, and 1 cup Cool Whip and spread on crust evenly. Prepare pudding mix according to directions on package and spread over cream cheese mixture. Add rest of cool whip on top of pudding. Garnish with finely chopped nuts or shavings of chocolate. When mixing pudding with milk as directed, use less milk to be thicker. When the torte is cooled, cut with knife in squares and serve.

Julie W. Stewart

This recipe will keep my family coming for refills until it's all gone. This is a great dessert for Sunday dinners and for family gatherings.

Peach Delight

First layer

1	cup flour
1	tablespoon sugar
1	stick margarine, softened
½	cup pecans finely chopped

Mix flour, sugar, margarine, and nuts. Press in the bottom of an ungreased 9 x 13-inch baking pan. Bake at 350 degrees for 15 minutes. Cool.

Second layer

1	8-ounce package cream cheese, softened
1	cup confectioners sugar
1	cup Cool Whip

Blend cheese and sugar. Fold in Cool Whip. Spread over crust.

Third Layer

1	cup sugar
3	tablespoons peach gelatin
4	tablespoons cornstarch
1	cup water
8 to 10 fresh peaches	

Mix sugar, gelatin, cornstarch, and water. Cook over medium heat stirring constantly until thick. Cool. While mix is cooling, peel and slice peaches. Combine cooled filling with peaches. Spread over the second layer in dish. Cover with Cool Whip. Store in refrigerator until serving time. Serves 10 to 12.

Celeste C. Tyler

Chocolate Dessert

1	package German chocolate cake mix
1	cups nuts, chopped
$^1/_3$	cup evaporated milk
$^3/_4$	cup butter, melted
60	pieces caramel candy
$^1/_2$	cup evaporated milk
1	cup chocolate chips

Combine, and mix well, cake mix, nuts, $^1/_3$ cup milk, and butter. Press half of the mixture into the bottom of a greased 9 x 13-inch baking dish; bake at 350 degrees for 8 minutes. Melt caramel candy in top of double boiler with half cup of milk. When caramel mixture is well mixed pour over baked mixture. Cover with chocolate chips, and pour rest of dough on top of chips. Bake for 18 minutes at 350 degrees. Cool before slicing. Quite Simply Divine. Yield 18 to 20 squares.

Agnes Williams

Fruit Pizza

Crust

Slice refrigerated sugar cookie dough very thin. Lay pieces of cookie dough in and around sides of pan. Flatten dough with your fingers. Bake 10 to 12 minutes at 350 degrees or until brown.

Cream Cheese Filling

1	8-ounce package cream cheese
2	tablespoons sugar
$^1/_4$	teaspoon vanilla

Mix cheese, sugar, and vanilla well. Spread on baked crust. Use any assortment of fruit washed, dried, and sliced thinly: bananas, strawberries, cantaloupe, kiwi, grapes, apples, and blueberries (whole). Place attractively on cream cheese filling. Top with glaze of 2 to 3 tablespoons preserves (orange is good) and 1 tablespoon water, mixed well.

Martha Ruth Elkins

Cherries in the Snow

1 8-ounce package cream cheese
2 cups thawed Cool Whip
1 20-ounce can cherry pie filling
½ cup powdered sugar

Mix cream cheese and sugar until smooth. Gently stir in Cool Whip. Layer ¼ cup cream cheese mixture and 2 tablespoons pie filling in each of 4 stemmed glasses or dessert dishes. Repeat layers.

Donna C. Powell

Blackberry Crisp

4 cups blackberries
1¼ cups sugar, divided
½ cup water
1 teaspoon vanilla
1 cup flour
1 teaspoon baking powder
½ teaspoon salt
1 egg lightly beaten
⅓ cup butter, melted and cooled

Combine blackberries, ½ cup sugar, water, and vanilla; place in 8 x 8 x 2-inch baking dish. Combine flour, baking powder, salt, and ¾ cup sugar; add egg and mix until crumbly. Sprinkle on berry mixture and drizzle with butter. Bake at 350 degrees for 35 minutes. Serve warm or cold. Yield 6 to 8 servings.

Patsy Childs Moye

It was a hallmark of summer: hands and mouth stained purple from smacking on blackberries!!! Picking the brambles, up one side and down the other, along fence rows on our granddaddy's farm. I would wear my Auntie Estella Sasser's apron with deep pockets and carry a basket as well.

Biscuit Pudding I

4   cold biscuits
$^2/_3$ cup sugar
1   tablespoon cocoa
1   egg
¾   cup whole milk

Crumble biscuits; pour enough hot water over this to moisten crumbs well and mix. Add sugar and cocoa, then add beaten egg and milk. Pour in greased baking dish and bake on 350 degrees for 45 minutes. Variations to above: add chopped pecans, raisins, or pineapple. Vanilla flavoring can be substituted for cocoa. Also, you can make an icing from one egg white and add some coloring for a quick surprise for a loved one.

Esther H. Carter

This special recipe was made by Sarah Palmer Harrison Phelps for her 7 children.

Biscuit Pudding with Fruit

3   cups biscuit crumbs, cold
2   eggs
2   cups milk
1½   cups sugar
½   stick butter
1   can fruit, drained

Mix well. Pour in greased casserole dish and bake at 350 degrees until brown. Cut into squares when cool.

Eunice Robinson Griner

Our mother, Bessie Laurence Robinson, made this recipe from leftover biscuits.

Biscuit Pudding II

10	left over biscuits
1½	cups sugar
²/₃	cup cream
½	cup raisins
1	teaspoon lemon extract
4	eggs
1	cup milk

Crumble biscuits in pan; pour sugar over crumbs. Pour enough warm water over this to moisten crumbs well. Add eggs, cream, raisins, milk, and extract; stir until well mixed, adding a little more milk if needed. Pour into well-greased pan and bake in 300 degrees oven until done.

Peggy A. Meyers

This recipe was copied from the Spring Hill's Kitchen Secrets published in 1951 and compiled by the W.S.C.S. of the Spring Hill Methodist Church. This recipe was prepared long before the early 50s. My Aunt Laura would rise early in the morning and prepare her dough for biscuits long before the family got ready for school and working the field. She was known in the Spring Hill Community of Grady County for her biscuit pudding. No matter when you visited her home day or night she would have her safe full of goodies. After you greeted, you could head to the safe and find biscuit pudding. It would be freshly made. Even when my husband, Frank Meyers, went hunting with her son, J.B. Martin, Frank would look forward to going in the house for some hot coffee and biscuit pudding.

Ansley's Bananas Foster

¾ to 1 whole banana for each person (quartered long ways)
1   stick butter or margarine
1   cup brown sugar
½   cup banana liqueur
½   cup rum (not over 100 proof)
½   cup brandy

Put bananas and brown sugar in pan with melted butter. Reduce or caramelize; pour banana liqueur and rum over bananas. Let simmer about 2 minutes. Pour brandy, stir, then light it (flambé), shaking during flaming to insure all alcohol is burned off. Tip: Flambé with low or no light to be able to see alcohol flames, these are hard to see in light. Serves 4.

Tad David

Ansley fixed this dessert when my friends and I would eat with him. I was glad I watched him make this so many times.

Yummy Cheese Bars

1   box Betty Crocker butter recipe yellow cake mix
½   cup margarine, melted
1   box powdered sugar
3   eggs
1   cup chopped pecans
1   8-ounce package cream cheese

Mix cake mix, 1 egg, melted margarine, and nuts. Spread mixture into greased 9 x 13-inch pan. Dough will be stiff. Mix together cream cheese, sugar, and 2 eggs. Spread over dough mixture. Bake in preheated 325 degrees oven for 45 minutes. Let cool at least 2 hours in pan. Cut into small bars.

Mary H. Chason

Served at Grady County Historical Society's 2003 Big Picnic at Susina.

Pumpkin Soufflé

2 cups cooked pumpkin
$^2/_3$ cup sugar
2 eggs
½ cup yellow cake mix
1 teaspoon lemon flavoring (see history below)

Combine these ingredients into bowl and beat together. Pour in baking dish. Sprinkle 1 cup cake mix on top of mixture. Melt 1 stick margarine and pour over top. Bake at 350 degrees for 30 to 45 minutes or until brown.

Peggy A. Meyers

Recipe was given to my mother, Hortense, in the early 70s by our friend and relative, Vera Hunter. Mother was active in her church and would often invite members of her circle for lunch. One day when mother was preparing this dish for her church friend, she did not have any flavoring so she used a great amount of liquor in place of the flavoring. Needless to say, she received favorable comments on her pumpkin soufflé and after that luncheon, the church ladies always wanted mother to bring the "Special Soufflé". They never knew that Miss Hortense had enhanced the flavor with alcohol.

My Bread (Tennis Shoe) Pudding

8   slices round top bread
1   stick margarine
8   eggs
1   cup sugar
Nutmeg
2   teaspoons vanilla
4   cups milk

Place bread slices on cookie sheet and put margarine in chunks on the slices. Place bread in oven on broil until margarine is melted and bread is slightly brown. Place bread in 3 quart casserole (oblong) dish. Beat eggs with whisk slightly. Add sugar, mix well. Pour milk and vanilla in egg mixture. Pour over bread and mash until completely mixed. Sprinkle nutmeg over casserole. Bake at 350 degrees until puffy and knife will come out clean. Pudding will be pretty brown.(45 minutes to1 hour.) Serves 10 to12.

Laura Carlisle Conradi

Once when making pudding, grandson had lost his tennis shoe. Pop Pop said "Granny put it in that pudding." It was called Tennis Shoe Pudding from then on. This was Annie Laura Carlisle's recipe.

Ambrosia Cakes

There is nothing "ticky tacky" about ambrosia cakes, a "food for the gods" creation when guests number 10. Prepare a package of lemon pudding mix according to directions. Center sponge cake shells on individual dessert plates. Generously fill each shell with 3 tablespoons pudding, letting it overflow onto plate. Sprinkle with toasted coconut, using ½ cupful in all. Garnish with slices of banana and strawberries. Decoration with sprig of mint.

La Vonne Childers

Bread Pudding with Vanilla Sauce

3	cups stale bread crumbs
3	cups scalded milk
½	cup sugar
¼	cup melted butter
2	eggs, slightly beaten
½	teaspoon salt
1	teaspoon vanilla or rum flavoring
½	teaspoon nutmeg

Soak bread crumbs in milk. Set aside until cool. Add other ingredients. Bake 1 hour in buttered dish in 325 degrees oven. Serve with your favorite sauce while still warm.

Vanilla Sauce for bread pudding

1	tablespoon cornstarch
½	cup sugar
$^1/_8$	teaspoon salt
1	cup boiling water
1	tablespoon butter
½	teaspoon vanilla or lemon flavoring

Mix dry ingredients and add boiling water slowly, stirring constantly. Cook several minutes until corn starch loses raw taste. Add butter and flavoring.

Gwen Maloy

Peach Ice Cream

4½   cups mashed fresh ripe peaches
2¼   cups sugar
3   eggs
¼   cup all-purpose flour
¼   teaspoon salt
3½   cups milk
2   cups half and half
1   cup heavy cream
1   tablespoon vanilla extract

Combine peaches and ¾ cup of sugar; stir well and set aside. Beat eggs with an electric mixer on medium speed until frothy. Combine remaining sugar, flour, and salt; stir well. Gradually add sugar mixture to eggs; beat until slightly thickened. Add milk; mix well. Pour egg mixture into a large saucepan. Cook over low heat, stirring constantly, until mixture thickens enough to coat a metal spoon (about 15 minutes). Cover and refrigerate mixture until thoroughly chilled (about 2 hours). Stir in half and half, cream, vanilla, and reserved peaches. Pour mixture into freezer container of a 1 gallon hand turned or electric freezer. Freeze according to manufacturer's instructions. Let ripen 1 or 2 hours before serving.

Nancy Herring Stingley

My version of my mother's ice cream.

Frosty Ice Cream

½   gallon chocolate milk
1   12-ounce cool whip
1   can condensed milk

Mix together and put in churn. Do not add anything else. Very, very, good!

Betty W. Harrison

Cherry Pineapple Ice Cream

2   cans condensed milk
1   small jar cherries
1   8½-ounce can crushed pineapple
½   gallon milk

Mix the condensed milk and fruit in blender and put in freezer 'can'. Finish filling this container with milk to the fill line. Follow manufacturer directions for freezing.

Carolyn C. Brown

Recipe came from the Bethesda Church in North Carolina where my ancestors worshipped.

Hester's Frozen Dessert

1   bag Famous Amos Cookies
½   cup sweet milk
Cool Whip

Dip cookies in milk and place one layer of cookies in bowl which can be frozen. Cover with Cool Whip. Repeat layers until bowl is full. Freeze until ready to serve.

Evelyn G. Hester

Broome's Hay Mower

Two mules pulled this hay mower on the farm from 1930 until after World War II.

Pies...

Susina

This colonial home designed by the noted architect, John Wind, was built circa 1840 for the James Blackshear family. A. H. Mason put together a larger plantation in the 1890s and moved his family from Pennsylvania to the Duncanville area. The home is now owned by Mr. and Mrs. Randall Rhea.

Old Fashioned Egg Custard Pie I

1½   cups sugar
3   tablespoons flour
3   eggs
2   cups evaporated milk
A little butter
Vanilla flavoring to taste
1   unbaked 9-inch pie shell

Mix ingredients well and pour into pie shell. Bake at 350 degrees for 30 to 35 minutes or until set.

Christine Cooper

Old Fashioned Egg Custard Pie II

3   eggs, beaten
¾   cup sugar
¼   teaspoon salt
1   teaspoon vanilla extract
½   teaspoon ground nutmeg
2   cups milk, scalded
1   unbaked 9 inch pie shell
Ground nutmeg

Combine eggs and sugar, beating well; add salt, vanilla, and ½ teaspoon nutmeg. Gradually add scalded milk, stirring constantly. Pour mixture into pie shell; sprinkle with additional nutmeg. Bake at 400 degrees for 10 minutes. Reduce oven temperature to 325 degrees and bake additional 25 minutes or until a knife inserted halfway between center and edge comes out clean. Cool thoroughly before serving. Yield one 9-inch pie.

Frederick Perkins

This is an old, good recipe used by my mother.

Similar recipe submitted by Dot Dalton.

Aunt Clyde's Buttermilk Pie

1½   cups sugar
3   tablespoons flour
2   eggs
½   cup butter (or oleo)
1   cup buttermilk
2   teaspoons vanilla flavoring
1   lemon, juice and pulp (optional)
1   unbaked 9 inch pie shell

Combine sugar and flour; beat eggs and add to mixture. Add melted butter and buttermilk; mix well. Fold in vanilla, lemon pulp, and juice. Pour into chilled pastry shell and bake at 425 degrees for 10 minutes. Reduce heat to 350 degrees and bake for 35 minutes longer, without opening door. Meringue can be added if desired or whipped topping is very good.

Winifred Maxwell

My father-in-law often talked of how delicious his mother's Buttermilk Pie was. I looked until I found this recipe in Bay Leaves cookbook and tried it...it is delicious.

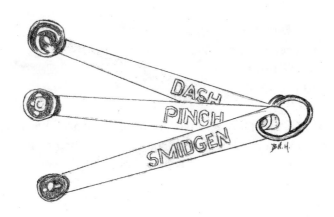

Two Small Egg Custard Pies

4 Eggs, 2 whole and 2 yolks, stir good and add flour until kindly thick and add 1½ cups of sugar. Add 3½ cups of sweet milk and 1 teaspoonful of lemon extract. For crust, fix a paste like you make biscuits and roll out and put in pan. Add mixture above and cook slowly. Then beat the whites of 2 eggs good and stiff; add a little lemon extract and sugar over pies and bake just a little. Chocolate pie: Same as above only add cocoa after eggs.

Linda Pyles Maxwell and Patsy Childs Moye

Today's women add to their income by joining investment clubs. During The Great Depression, the women of Grady and Decatur Counties took economic measures of their own for earning money. A farming woman earned income by raising chickens and selling eggs; hence the phrase "egg money" and "nest egg". The Old Egg Road in Grady County got its name from such activity. Linda Pyles Maxwell's grandmother, Viola Jones Holt of Climax, Georgia, and Patsy Childs Moye's grandmother, Jessie Sasser Childs, of Cairo, Georgia, were both such women. We offer this simple but delectable recipe as a tribute and testimony to the efforts by those pioneer women and in thanksgiving for the many pies that were baked, thanks to the Egg!

Syrup Custard Pie

1	cup syrup
2	eggs
½	stick butter, melted
½	cup sour cream
1½	tablespoons flour
1	unbaked pie shell

With a whisk, beat all ingredients well; pour into unbaked pie shell and bake at 350 degrees until set. Check for doneness by inserting a knife with a thin blade. When it comes out clean, it is done.

Yvonne H. Childs

Old Fashioned Vinegar Pie

½   cup butter
1½   cups sugar
3   eggs, beaten well
Pinch of salt
½   teaspoon vanilla extract
1   tablespoon vinegar
1   unbaked pie shell

Cream butter and sugar. Add beaten eggs. Add vanilla, vinegar, and salt. Pour into unbaked pie shell. Start cooking at 300 degrees. Raise heat after 10 minutes to 350 degrees. It takes about 45 minutes in all to cook.

Hazel Logue

Mrs. John Emory Trawick gave me this recipe 40 years ago.

Chess Pie

Combine 1 stick of margarine and 1¼ cup of sugar in a saucepan and bring to a boil. Stir in 1 tablespoon of vinegar. Put 3 eggs in electric mixer bowl and while they are beating pour in the margarine mixture slowly. Sprinkle in 2 tablespoons of cornmeal. Add 1 teaspoon of lemon extract (or vanilla). Stir. Pour into an unbaked pie crust. Bake at 325 degrees for approximately 45 minutes.

Julia Lewis Gainey

This pie was a favorite when my sister, Sarah Lewis, served it at her coffee shop in Perry, GA.

Coconut Pie

4	eggs, beaten
1½	cups sugar
½	cup buttermilk
¾	stick butter or oleo, melted
1	teaspoon vanilla flavoring
1	cup coconut, shredded or flaked

Dash of salt

1	unbaked pie shell

Stir together everything but coconut. Mix well. Add coconut. Pour into unbaked pie crust. Bake at 300 degrees for 1 hour.

Faye S. Miller

My mother, Louise Kelly Stephens, was often asked to cook and bring Coconut Pies to gatherings. She was using this recipe in the early 1950s.

Similar recipe submitted by Kathryn Miller Jones.

Jamie's Chocolate Pie

1½	cups sugar
6	tablespoons flour, heaping
6	tablespoons cocoa, heaping
6	egg yolks
1	tall can evaporated milk
1	can of water
1	stick of butter
2	pie shells, baked and cooled

Stir sugar, flour, and cocoa together. Stir yolks, milk, and water together. Combine the two mixtures in a double boiler; cook on medium heat. Stir until it starts to thicken. Remove from heat and add butter. Spoon into pie shells. Makes enough for 2 regular pie shells or one deep dish pie shell and several pudding glasses. Meringue can be made with egg whites; browned in oven.

Jamie C. Lewis

Fudge Pie

½   cup melted butter
1   cup sugar
2   eggs
½   cup flour, sifted
1   teaspoon vanilla flavoring
1   square bitter chocolate, melted

Beat sugar and butter together, add eggs and flour, mix thoroughly. Add chocolate and vanilla. Pour into greased pie plate and bake in preheated 325 degrees oven for 25 minutes. Serve with vanilla ice cream.

Lola L. Tyson

Hoover Pie

1½   cups sugar
6   tablespoons self-rising flour
3   cups milk
5   tablespoons cocoa
5   egg yolks, (reserve whites)
1   stick oleo
1   teaspoon vanilla flavoring

In boiler over medium heat, combine the first 5 ingredients. Cook until thick, stirring constantly. When thickened, add oleo and vanilla. Meringue: Beat 5 egg whites until stiff and slowly add 8 to 10 tablespoons sugar and ½ teaspoon vanilla.

Sadie W. Voyles

From the depression era, this pie has no crust. Passed down from her grandmother, it was one of Ina G. Wilson's favorite chocolate recipes.

Lemon Pie

2   cups sugar
4   eggs
2   tablespoons flour, heaping
2   cups water, boiling
1   teaspoon grated lemon peel
Juice of 2 lemons
1   pie shell, baked

Beat sugar and eggs; add flour. Stir into boiling water. Add lemon juice and peel. Cook on low heat, stirring often until thick. Pour into pie shell, top with meringue. Bake at 400 degrees for 6 to 10 minutes, until light brown.

Meringue
3   egg whites
6   tablespoons sugar
$^1/_8$ teaspoon cream of tartar

Beat egg whites until frothy; add cream of tartar and beat to soft peaks, gradually adding sugar. Beat until meringue holds a peak.

Helen C. Bishop

Elmera Jane Maxwell (Mrs. Ellis), who had gotten it many years ago from her sister-in-law, Vera W. Maxwell (Mrs. Howard) gave this recipe to me.

Strawberry Icebox Pie

1   pint strawberries
¼   cup sugar
1   can condensed milk
½   cup lemon juice
Vanilla wafers

Mash strawberries and add sugar. Mix together milk and lemon juice. Layer vanilla wafers, strawberries, and milk mixture; ending with milk mixture. Save a few whole berries to garnish. Best when made a day ahead.

Connie Butler

My mother got this recipe at a cooking school during the 1940s. Every strawberry season, my mother would make several pies.

Strawberry Pie

1½   pints fresh strawberries
½   small box strawberry gelatin
¾   cup sugar
3   tablespoons cornstarch
¾   cup cold water
1   deep dish pie shell, baked and cooled
Whipped topping

Wash and slice strawberries and place in pie shell. Bring gelatin, sugar, cornstarch, and cold water to a boil, stirring constantly. Boil for 5 minutes on medium heat, stirring constantly. Pour mixture over strawberries and place in refrigerator to set. Cover with whipped topping.

Christine Cooper

Lazy Day Cobbler

2   20-ounce frozen peach pies
$^2/_3$ cup sugar
4   cups water
1   stick margarine
Nutmeg (optional)

Thaw pies enough to cut into large pieces and arrange in a 13 x 9-inch pan. Sprinkle with sugar. Add water and dot with margarine. Sprinkle with nutmeg. Bake in a 400 degrees oven for 1 hour until top is lightly brown. Yield 12 servings. Apple pies with cinnamon can be substituted.

Mary Robertson

Apple Pie with Cheese Topper

½   cup light raisins
8   tart apples, peeled, sliced, cored
½   teaspoon grated lemon peel
1   teaspoon lemon juice
¾   cup sugar
2   tablespoons flour
½   teaspoon ground nutmeg
Dash of salt
Cheese topper

Preheat oven to 400 degrees. Make a pastry for double crust 9-inch pie shell. Pour boiling water over raisins and let stand for 5 minutes; drain. Toss apples with lemon peel, juice, and drained raisins. Combine sugar, flour, nutmeg, and salt. Mix with apples. Pour in the pastry lined pie plate. Place top crust over apples; seal and flute edges. Cut slits for escape of steam. Bake for 50 to 60 minutes or until done. Cover edges with foil after 15 minutes to prevent over browning. Serve warm pie with Cheese topper—Combine ½ cup shredded cheese and 3-ounce package of cream cheese (both at room temperature) and 2 tablespoons milk; beat until fluffy and nearly smooth.

Nancy C. Clark

Dixie's Raisin Pie

1½ cups raisins, dark or golden
2 sticks butter, softened
1 cup sugar
1 cup brown sugar, light or dark
6 large eggs
2 teaspoons vanilla extract
2 teaspoons ground cinnamon
1 cup chopped nuts
1 cup flaked coconut
2 unbaked pie crusts
Whipped topping

Line pie crusts with double thickness of heavy-duty foil. Bake at 450 degrees for 10 minutes; discard foil and cool. Place raisins in saucepan and cover with water. Bring to boil, remove from heat and set aside. In mixing bowl, cream butter and sugars; add eggs, vanilla, and cinnamon. Beat until smooth. Drain raisins. Stir raisins, nuts, and coconut into creamed mixture. Mixture will appear curdled. Pour into pie crusts. Bake at 350 degrees for 30 to 35 minutes. Cool. Garnish with whipped topping.

Sheila Barnes Thornton

This recipe, from his daughter, Thelma Chastain Crew, was a favorite of my great grandfather, A. Y. (Dixie) Chastain. This pie has always been a favorite of the Chastain and Dock Crew families.

Edith Stanfill's Prize Winning Cherry Pie Recipe

3	cups unsweetened red cherries (2 #2 cans)
$^2/_3$	cup of cherry juice
4	tablespoons cornstarch or 8 tablespoons flour
1	heaping cup sugar
¼	teaspoon salt
1	teaspoon almond flavoring
1½	tablespoons butter

Several drops red food coloring

1	unbaked pie crust

Drain cherries; cook cornstarch and juice until clear and thick. Remove from heat and add everything but cherries. Then add cherries very gently. Pour into a pie crust that has been baked for 5 minutes (to prevent it from getting soggy). Put lattice strips on top and bake in moderate oven for 30 to 40 minutes or until done.

Mrs. J. B. Roddenbery, Jr.

In February 1952, Edith represented the state of Georgia in a Cherry Pie Baking Contest (sponsored by the National Cherry Association) in Chicago.

Rancher's Pie

1	8-ounce can crushed pineapple, do not drain
1	cup flaked coconut
1½	cups sugar
3	tablespoons flour
3	eggs, slightly beaten
¾	stick butter, melted
1	unbaked 9-inch deep dish pie shell

Mix all ingredients together, adding melted butter last. Pour into unbaked pie shell and bake in 350 degrees oven until lightly brown and set, approximately 1 hour.

Julie W. Stewart

Peach and Blueberry Cobbler

2   cups peaches, fresh or frozen
1   cup blueberries, fresh or frozen
1   cup self-rising flour
2   cups sugar
¾   cup milk
1   stick butter or margarine

Melt butter or margarine in a 13 x 9-inch baking pan. Mix 1 cup sugar, flour, and milk together; pour mixture into baking pan. Mix 1 cup sugar with fruits; pour over mixture in baking pan. Bake at 350 degrees for 45 minutes or until golden brown. Good served with whipped cream or ice cream.

Katie F. Ansley

Variation submitted by Agnes Williams: May substitute cherries for peaches and blueberries

Aunt Ruth's Pecan Pie

1   cup dark Karo syrup
½   cup sugar
3   eggs
1   cup pecans, broken
¼   cup butter
1   pinch salt
1   teaspoon vanilla flavoring
1   unbaked pie shell

Bring sugar and syrup to boil. Remove from heat and add butter. Let cool. Break eggs into bowl and beat; slowly add syrup mixture. Add nut meats, vanilla, and salt. Pour into pie shell. Bake at 400 degrees for 15 minutes. Reduce to 350 degrees and bake 30 to 35 minutes longer or until knife blade comes our clean.

Frederick Perkins

Similar recipes submitted by Gladys Ponder, Mrs. J. B. Roddenbery, Jr., and Evelyn Hester

Fried Apple Pies

Apples, (pears, peaches, or berries)
Cornstarch
Self-rising flour
Sugar
Cinnamon (optional)
¼ **cup Crisco**
1 **cup sweet milk**
Oil

Peel fruit; sweeten to taste. Cook slowly in juice until tender. Do not add water. Use cornstarch dissolved in water to thicken. Make a nest in self-rising flour in a biscuit bowl. Mix in Crisco and milk. Mix in enough flour to make stiff dough. Pinch off in small pieces; roll out in thin circle. Fill with small spoonful of fruit. Fold over, mash together with fingers and seal edges with fork. Fry in deep fat until lightly brown. (Fruit filling can be made a day ahead and refrigerated.)

Mamie Taylor Crapps

This recipe came from my Grandma Mamie Jones and was always a hit, especially with the grandchildren. If you wanted fried apple pie at a reunion, you got it first or it would be gone by the time you made your way down the food line.

Cushaw or Pumpkin Pie

3   cups cushaw or pumpkin, cooked and mashed
4   tablespoons flour
1½   cups sugar
1½   sticks butter or oleo
3   eggs, beaten
1   cup milk
½   teaspoon salt
2   teaspoons lemon extract
½   teaspoon cinnamon, ground
½   teaspoon nutmeg, ground
½   teaspoon ginger, ground
2   unbaked pie crusts

Mix butter and hot cushaw; add sugar and flour. Add remaining ingredients; beat. Pour into pie crusts. Bake at 325 degrees for approximately 1 hour.

Carolyn H. Chason

My mother got this recipe from Cousin Lil Higdon's (Mrs. Joe) cook, Rosa Maynor, in 1952.

Pumpkin Pie

1   15-ounce can pumpkin
1   can sweetened condensed milk
½   cup sugar
3   eggs, beaten
¾   teaspoon cinnamon
¾   teaspoon nutmeg
2   teaspoons lemon flavoring
2   unbaked pie crusts

Combine all ingredients. Pour into pie crusts. Bake at 350 degrees for 30 to 40 minutes.

Mary Robertson

Peanut Butter Pie

Crust

2	cups flour
½	teaspoon salt
¾	cup Crisco
¼	cup ice water (may take little more)

Mix flour, salt, and Crisco together with fingers until it forms little clumps. Add water and mix with fingers until it sticks together, not too long. Be tender with it; the more you work with dough, the tougher it becomes. Roll out about ¼-inch thick, place in pie plate. Take a fork and lightly make holes all around crust to prevent bubbles when baked. Bake at 400 degrees for 12 to 14 minutes, until brown.

Peanut Butter Layer

¾	cup crunchy peanut butter
¾	cup powdered sugar

Mix peanut butter and sugar together with fingers until it forms little clumps. Pour this mixture into the hot crust.

Pudding

1	cup granulated sugar
3	eggs
1	teaspoon vanilla flavoring
1½	cups milk
3	tablespoons plain flour

Separate eggs. Beat egg yolks and put into heavy pan. Add milk; heat. Mix flour in sugar; slowly add to the milk and eggs. Cook slowly until thick. Add vanilla. Pour into pie shell on top of peanut butter layer. Beat egg whites until stiff, adding 1 tablespoon of sugar while beating. Place on top of pudding and bake in 350 degrees oven about 10 minutes until brown.

Louise Anderson

Oil Pastry Pie Shell

1   cup all-purpose flour
¼   cup vegetable oil
½   teaspoon salt
2½   tablespoons cold water

Sift together flour and salt; add oil and water. Stir lightly with fork. Form a ball and roll between waxed paper to make a 9 to 10-inch circle. Place in pie plate and prick with fork to prevent shell from bubbling while baking. Bake at 425 degrees for 10 to 12 minutes.

Donna C. Powell

Aunt Ida Hunziker's Pie Crust

¹/₃   rounded cup of refrigerated Crisco
1   cup plain flour
½   teaspoon salt

Mix together all ingredients until it resembles cornmeal. Add 2 tablespoons cold water until firm dough forms. Pour out on floured surface and knead with hands until mixed thoroughly. (Use as little flour as possible.) Round out and put in the pie plate, trim or flute edges. Place another pie plate over crust and bake at 400 degrees for 5 minutes; remove empty plate from top of crust and bake 5 minutes more.

Cheryl Hunizker

Aunt Ida, of Deland, Florida, catered numerous parties and weddings for state dignitaries.

Pie Crust

1   cup plus 1 tablespoon plain flour
$^1/_3$ cup Wesson oil
3   tablespoons cold milk
Dash of salt

Mix all with fork. Dough will be soft. Roll between sheets of waxed paper. Remove top paper and place crust in pan. Should a tear appear as you remove bottom wax paper, repair with your fingers.

Emogene Miller

Recipe from a 1949 Wesson oil cookbook.

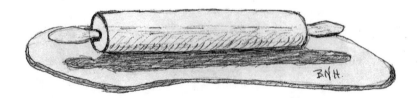

This 'n That...

Trulock House

The construction of the G.B. Trulock, Sr. house in Whigham, Georgia, began in 1876 was completed in 1877. The builder, Mr. Sanders, was paid $200. The heart of pine lumber used was the size of each room, 17 x 17 with ceilings 14 feet tall. Handmade bricks, prepared in a pit near the Baptist church, were used in the foundation and chimneys. G.B., Jr. and his wife, Jenny, lived in the house until their deaths. They added in-door bathrooms, one being the former pantry. They changed the location of the kitchen and renovated the area into a bedroom. The house was purchased by Embree and Karen Robinson in 1984 and sold back to the Trulock family in 2001. During the time the Robinsons owned the house, it was painted inside and out and the shutters were replaced.

Soap by the Moon

Mother always made soap before the New Moon on a cool or cold day. She used a clean wooden paddle or stick and the big iron wash pot. To one can of potash lye, she added about four pounds of pure fat meat scraps, or grease in the pot over the fire. Ingredients began cooking slowly. She added one quart of water at a time until ten quarts were used, stirring often to keep from scorching. She cooked it slowly until soap threads from the paddle thickened. She added some borax to have thicker suds. She said making soap just before the moon news dries and hardens quicker, and by adding a cup of fresh turpentine would keep the worms out of the soap. It took lots of soap for washing, bathing, and moping during the raising of her family.

Alice A. Harrison

Similar recipe submitted by Lyn Robinson.

Cold-Water Soap

2½   pints cold water
2½   quarts used grease
1   can lye
2   tablespoons Borax (optional)

Pour cold water into small glass or stone bowl. Carefully empty can of lye into the 2½ pints of cold water. Stir slowly until lye is dissolved. Allow to stand until just barely lukewarm. Pour used grease into a large stone bowl or enamel (unbroken) container. Using a wooden spoon, slowly stir, while pouring dissolved lye mixture into grease. Continue stirring for about 15 minutes or until mixture begins to harden (very thick). If soap mixture appears to harden before 15 minutes is up, immediately pour up soap into a wooden or packing box that has been lined with waxed paper. Should soap or mixture tend to separate while stirring, then beat harder--otherwise just a continual moderate stirring should be sufficient. If color is desired, add 1 ounce food coloring just before pouring mixture into box.

Lyn Robinson

I found this clipped in an old recipe book that belonged to my mother-in-law, Martha Vaughn Robinson of Whigham, Georgia. She lived in Whigham from 1930 to 1977. She was married to Rufus Hill Robinson and they raised six boys.

Bratty Diet

For an upset stomach, get on the BRATTY diet:

Bananas   Rice   Applesauce   Tea   Toast   Yogurt

Celeste C. Tyler

Homemade Liniment

Beat 1 egg very well to a very foamy state. In a quart container, pour the egg, 1 cup of turpentine (pure gum spirits), and 1 cup apple cider vinegar. Shake well until mixture is white. Works better than what you can buy.

Beulah G. Cox

From Medical Notes of Cal Thomas (A 9-Dime Doctor from Whigham area in early 1900s). All his medicine was made from roots and herbs.

Burn Salve

2   **cups strong fireweed tea**
        (Fireweed is a wild plant, St. John's Wort. The tea would be made by boiling the leaves in water.)
½   **cup tallow**
½   **cup lard**

Combine above ingredients and simmer until all water has boiled out. When cool, place in a jar or tin with a cover. Spread salve on soft cloth and place on burned area.

Jean Miller Merritt

Recipe came from my grandmother, Mary Kinsley Lewis' old doctor book.

Cough Remedy

½   cup whiskey
½   cup honey
½   cup lemon juice

Blend all ingredients. Store in refrigerator. Use about 1 to 2 tablespoons for cough as needed.

Peggy A. Meyers

This cough formula has been in my family for two generations. My mother, Hortense R. Johnson, and my grandmother, Dora Martin, used this medicine to treat chronic coughs.

Roach Poison

1   pound boric acid
1   cup plain flour
¼   cup sugar
1   onion, grated or chopped fine
½   cup lard or shortening
Small amount of water

Mix and roll into small balls. Put on waxed paper to dry. Place in area where roaches or water bugs are a problem–away from children and pets. Store excess in airtight containers till needed.

Annette Prince Blackmon

Recipe of Gladys G. Prince passed down from her mother, Mittie "Mitt" Bradley Gainous (born 1896).

Gruntin' for Worms

Pound a 2 x 2 board that is about 3 feet long, into the ground approximately a foot deep. You will find that a board that is pointed or slanted will be easier to drive into the ground. Take another board or ax handle and rub back and forth on the top of the post. This vibrates the ground causing the earthworms to come to the surface. Do this near flowerbeds or where you notice very small holes in the yard where worms have dug down.

This is an easy way to get fish bait!

Alice Courtney McCorkle

Home Remedies

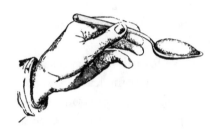

Sardine oil rubbed on neck will help cure mumps.

Janice Tillis

My grandmother, Ruth Dollar, recently told me that when she was young and had mumps, her daddy bought a tin of sardines and they rubbed her jaws and neck with the oil. The rest of the family ate the sardines . She said in those days, her family never bought sardines unless someone had mumps.

Gloria Dollar

To cure a headache, put a few drops of fresh lemon juice into a cup of black coffee and drink it in small sips. (This is not for people with sensitive stomachs.)

To relieve a headache, cut two large unpeeled potatoes into quarters and boil until tender. Mash and press out the excess moisture. Wrap the warm mixture in a cloth; place this on the back of neck for about 15 minutes.

With help from acupressure, use your thumb and index finger to press against bridge of your nose at the corners of your eyes or, rub the center of the fleshy webbing between your index and thumb to relieve a headache.

A soothing footbath diverts the blood supply from your head to your feet. For relief of headache, bathe feet in a basin of warm water (95 degrees). Add hot water at 5-minute intervals until 115 degrees is reached. After soaking feet for 5 minutes, pour in cold water until temperature is lukewarm. Put on wool socks and lie down for about 20 minutes.

Take one tablespoon of juice made from sea-buckthorn berries daily for the extra vitamin C that smokers need.

Help for hay fever can be found in honey. Honey contains grains of pollen that, over time, may have a desensitizing effect, making it useful for relief of allergies. You should eat honey that has been harvested locally.

Drink catnip tea as a sedative for calming nerves and inducing sleep. Gather catnip when it is flowering. Take some leaves and stems; wash. Pour boiling water over stems and leaves in this proportion: 1-cup water over ¼-cup leaves and stems. Let steep for about 4 minutes. Strain. Now it's ready to drink. Catnip is also known as rabbit tobacco.

To relieve tension headaches and relax blood vessels, run a tub of warm water. Combine the following essential oils with an emulsifier (cream or honey): 3 drops of chamomile, 3 drops of lavender, and 3 drops of rosemary. Add this mixture to bathwater and soak.

To stop bleeding, find spider webs and pat on bleeding spot.

Mix equal parts of vinegar and honey; sip for relief of coughing.

For a bad chest cold, mix together 1 tablespoon turpentine, 1 tablespoon kerosene, 1 teaspoon salve, tallow (beef fat). Rub on chest. Wrap with flannel; keep on overnight.

For measles or any breaking out, tie a string with asafetida on it around the neck.

To ease the pain of the earache, a smoker should blow smoke in hurting ear, then cover.

To ease the pain of the earache: Warm syrup in a spoon, and then pour in ear, place cotton in ear.

Put chewed tobacco on bee sting, or place snuff on bite, or put turpentine on bite.

To make an iron smooth, rub the bottom over beef tallow.

For dry skin, apply melted beef tallow.

For cough or sore throat, mix a teaspoon of sugar with a few drops of turpentine. Gradually sip.

Contributed by Margaret P. Courtney

For cough medicine, mix together 4 tablespoons honey and 1 tablespoon vinegar; stir real well. Take a teaspoon as needed for coughing.

If you have arthritis, make a tea using leaves of alfalfa and add whiskey. Drink.

To calm an irritable child, boil catnip leaves to make a tea. Have him drink ¼ cup.

To treat ringworm, apply juice of green walnut hull.

Pour ½ cup of syrup over a hot boiled turnip root and let it stand for 15 minutes. Squeeze turnip and pour off liquid. Take this liquid warm on going to bed for a cough and cold.

To regulate blood pressure, dig and wash several briar roots. Boil in 1-quart water. Drink ¼ cup daily for a few days.

For a congested chest, warm Vicks Salve and pour on a flannel cloth. Place on patient's chest and leave until cool. Reheat cloth and keep replacing on chest to break up the congestion.

To heal ground itch, take a large collard leaf and hold it over a fire until it becomes wet and juicy. Then apply to infected feet.

For relief of a bad fever, get weed from woods (has a pink bloom) and boil and make a tea to drink.

Go to woods and get chips of bark from Red Oak tree and boil down low to make a tea. Good for curing cancer. Can be taken orally or as a douche. This was actually done in the early 1900s by Sarah Harrison Phelps and cured the cancer in Pashie Palmer Davis Oliver.

Contributed by Esther H. Carter

To relieve ground itch, take a mullen leaf and heat in oven until wilted. Wrap it around foot while hot. Wrap a cloth around it to hold in the heat.

To heal Seven Year Itch, rub the body with light coat of yellow axle grease. Repeat as necessary.

To ward off diseases, take a piece of asafetida and make it into a small ball. Put it in a cloth, and tie a string to the ball, and wear around the neck.

Contributed by Carolyn Chason

Mix some kerosene, Vicks salve, Vaseline, pine tar from fat wood, and beef tallow. Spread on soft cloth; apply to chest to cure bronchitis and pneumonia.

To stop coughing, melt peppermint candy and add some whiskey. Sip as needed.

To cure chickenpox, get under the chickens roosting; flush them out and let them fly over you.

To cure shingles, catch a black chicken, cut off the head, and drain the blood over the shingles.

Contributed by Yvonne Childs

Remedies were told to me by my mother, Zelda Sanders Hiers (age 92) and my aunt, Lillian Sanders Durham, (age 90).

Whiskey in baby bottle for colic.

Sip hot tea, lemon, and honey for a cold.

Gargle with salt water for a sore throat.

Blow pipe smoke in ear for earache.

Eat oatmeal for heart problems.

Put baby on bare chest to lower fever.

Use baking soda to brush teeth.

Use cornstarch for deodorant.

Lemon juice for pain from hot peppers.

Use baking grease for suntan oil.

South window is best for houseplants.

Wear damp jeans to bed to stretch, but place pants under mattress to press.

Put heated brick or hot potato under blanket to keep feet warm.

Contributed by Nancy Nichols

To clean toilet of water stains, add 1 cup of vinegar in bowl. Leave overnight.

Add 1 cup vinegar in dishwasher monthly to remove residue from glasses..

Remove sticky stickers and decals with warm vinegar. Saturate cloth with vinegar and place on stickers.

Permanent marker on carpet? Clean area with cloth dipped in alcohol.

To remove greasy stains, apply cola to clothes and let set. Apply more and wash.

To determine if eggs are good, put them in water deep enough to cover; the good eggs will lie flat at the bottom while the bad ones will stand upright.

Contributed by Carolyn H. Chason

Home Comfort Cookbook, 1928-1931

Keep a powder puff in a flour canister for dusting greased cake pans. There are many ways to say "I Love You". Cooking is a wonderful way.

Contributed by Allison M. Bass

To help rid the house of the odor of cooking vegetables, put a little vinegar in an open saucepan on the stove.

A piece of charcoal in the refrigerator will absorb odors and keep the refrigerator smelling sweet.

A little finely grated cheese added to thin soup improves the taste immensely.

When silver becomes dull, rub it with a piece of lemon; wash and dry well. It acquires extra brilliancy and it will keep clean longer than with ordinary cleansing.

Aluminum ware may be cleaned with a cloth dipped in lemon juice.

When the glue thickens in the bottle, moisten it with vinegar instead of water. Glue spots may also be dissolved in this way.

If paintbrushes have become hard with paint, soak for an hour or more in turpentine, squeeze the bristles between the fingers until all the paint has been removed. After this treatment, rinse brushes in a fresh amount of turpentine.

To remove tarnish from silver, line a heavy large plastic vessel with a sheet of aluminum. To this, for every quart of very hot water add one teaspoon of salt and one teaspoon of soda. Place silver pieces in water. As the silver touches the bottom of vessel, which is lined with the aluminum, the tarnish will disappear. Now polish with silver polish.

To remove chewing gum from fabric, rub with ice and the gum will roll off and leave no mark.

Contributed by June White

To remove grease from soup, roll a paper towel and use one end to skim over soup surface. When the end becomes coated, cut off the used part and repeat.

Put an ice cube in cloth and agitate it just under the surface of the soup letting it collect the rising fat.

Contributed by Myrt McCorkle

To get smell off hands after cutting onions or cleaning fish, wet hands, sprinkle on some table salt, and rub the hands together. Rinse well and smell will be gone.

Contributed by Katie F. Ansley

Worcestershire sauce beautifully cleans and polishes un-lacquered brass. Apply with a damp cloth, wipe away any residue with another damp cloth, and dry. After you polish your brass, it makes you wonder about consuming this stuff.

Get rid of those ants with equal parts of vinegar and water sprayed or wiped on counters, cabinets, and floors--will keep ants away.

If you dampen your fingers slightly before removing eggs from the carton or refrigerator, you're less likely to drop one.

Sprinkle a small amount of salt into a pan before adding oil to help prevent splatters from frying meat. It also helps vegetables retain their color during stir-frying.

After cleaning outdoor garbage cans, toss in some dry laundry detergent. It will help repel flies and other insects.

To clear drain, pour equal amounts of soda, salt, vinegar (a half cup of each is plenty) down into the drain. Put stopper in, wait about 20 minutes, then pull out the stopper and pour in some hot water, wait a few seconds then pour in some cold water! Your drain will be clean as a whistle!

Contributed by Frances McNair McNaughton

This is a home remedy handed down from our Aunt Joyce Hinson who taught school in the Calvary School, now retired and lives in Marianna, Florida. She said, "Forget these modern drain cleaners, if you want to clear your drain do this!

To clean a cast iron skillet of a build-up of grease, soak in a mixture of 1 can Red Devil Lye and 5 gallons of water for 2 or 3 days. Remove and wash thoroughly in a mixture of baking soda and water. Dry completely. Grease inside and out with solid vegetable shortening. Heat for 1 or 2 hours in 300 degrees oven.

Contributed by Carolyn H. Chason

This was the method used by Sarah Washington.

Do not despair if you over-salt gravy. Stir in some instant mashed potatoes. You may need to add a little liquid, if too thick.

To ripen tomatoes, put them in a brown paper bag in a dark pantry, and they will ripen overnight.

Add raw rice to the saltshaker to keep the salt free flowing.

For flavoring hot tea, dissolve hard mint candy or old-fashioned lemon drops in your tea.

Place fresh mint in the bottom of a cup of hot chocolate for a refreshing taste.

Corning Ware can be cleaned by filling it with water and putting in two denture-cleaning tablets. Let stand for 30 to 40 minutes.

Contributed by Carolyn C. Brown

To clear a drain, drop in 3 Alka Seltzer tablets followed by a cup of vinegar. Wait a few minutes, and then run hot water.

So you don't have a thermometer, listen to the crickets! Count how many times they chirp within a 13-second interval. Add 40 to that number and you will have the approximate temperature.

If you cannot get the coffee filters apart, turn the stack inside out.

Contributed by Laura M. Brinkley

To remove ballpoint pen ink from fabrics, spray hairspray on the stain and blot it with a paper towel until ink has been absorbed.

Contributed by Claire C. Willett

Apply Vicks Vapor Rub to toe nails with fingers to cure fungus. If used at night, wear socks to protect sheets. This is an old remedy but was recently featured in a newspaper health column.

For thinning hair, mix 1 teaspoon ground sage and ¼ cup of water. Rub on scalp once or twice daily. (Earlier a "tea" was made by steeping sage in hot water and applying to scalp.)

Contributed by Sammie Harper

This remedy was shared by a friend who got it from her old nursemaid.

Guineas can count to 3, so always leave 3 eggs in the nest or they will find another place to lay. Guineas lay very rich eggs that are good cooked with rice.

When hoeing in your garden, if you haven't finished the job, be sure and lay your hoe down. Do not stand it up or you won't sleep good that night.

Plant flowers when the sign of the zodiac is of the virgin. You will have plenty of blooms. Do not plant peas or beans on this sign for they will bloom but not bear fruit.

If you must have an operation, the sign of zodiac should be in the knees (goat days), going down. You won't have nearly as many problems.

Contributed by Helen C. Bishop

These are from my in-laws, Marvin and Mag Bishop. Mr. Bishop was a grandson of pioneer Isaac Williams.

For strong fingernails: soak nails each night in a mixture of 3 parts lukewarm olive oil to 1 part freshly squeezed lemon juice. Put on cloth gloves and let the oil penetrate overnight.

Plant all root crops during the dark of the moon.

Corn should be planted when the moon is full.

Prune roses around February 14.

Plant Irish potatoes on February 14.

Contributed by Brian Chason

To make a flower arrangement with pleasing proportions, measure the height and width of the container; take the larger of the numbers, and multiply it by 1½. Cut your tallest flower stem this length and proceed with making your design. Our mother, who is a Master Flower Show Judge, taught us this, but emphasized that this was not a requirement (however, it does work!).

Contributed by Celeste C. Tyler and Claire C. Willett

342

Words We Live By

You will have bad luck if you:

Sweep house after sundown or take out ashes after sundown;
Cut out garment (dress, blouse, pants, or other items) on Friday;
Start a new job on Friday.

A friend in need is a friend indeed.
Honesty is the first step to greatness.
A man's word is his bond.

An old maid's party is like an early morning rain; it doesn't last long.

A bird in the hand is worth two in the bush.

Give some folks an inch and they'll take a mile.
Waste not, want not.
Use it up, wear it out, make it do, or do without.

An idle mind is the devil's workshop.
Better late than never.
Accept the things we cannot change.

If you lay with dogs, you're gonna get fleas.
It's not what you make, it's what you do with what you make.

**If you always do what you've always done,
you'll always get what you always got.**

You have to live today like tomorrow will never come.
Find a need and fill it.

Oh, what a tangled web we weave when first we practice to deceive.

Never buy anything from someone on the street who's out of breath.

Timing is everything.

Diplomacy is to do and say, the nastiest thing in the nicest way.

If you don't stand for something, you will fall for anything.

You can run, but you can't hide.

Don't quit till the hearse pulls up.

Never be too impressed by your own self-importance,
you are probably the only one that feels that way.

Water finds its own level.

If it ain't broke, don't fix it.

Don't wash, iron, or sew on New Year's Day
or some family member will die that year.

If a person acts as though he/she had no raising--he acts like the buzzards
(vultures) laid him and the sun hatched him or acts like Adam's off-ox.

If a person does a sorry cleaning job--he gave it a lick and a promise.

If you're not feeling up to par--I'm not good for buzzard bait.

If you make an unwise decision--
If you make your bed, you'll have to lie in it.

Get busy--Make yourself useful as well as ornamental.

I'm mad as a wet hen. I'm mad as a hornet.

If you're short of anything--
You don't have enough to say grace over.

Underweight or poor--He's poor as Job's turkey.

Red sky at night, sailor's delight.
Red sky at morning, sailor takes warning.

Dark sky in northwest, a sign of cold weather.

If it's too tight—Tight as Dick's hat band.

344

To dream of the dead is a sign of rain.

Willful waste makes woeful want.

He's got the world by the tail with a downhill pull.

Over excited--Running around like a chicken with his head chopped off.

That doesn't cut the mustard

I didn't just fall off a turnip truck.

I'm a workhorse not a show pony.

You can lead a horse to water, but you cannot make him drink.

A stitch in time saves nine.

You can take a hog, dress him up, give him a good bath, put a ribbon around his neck, turn him loose, and he will go straight back to his wallowing mud hole.

You can put a saddle on a donkey,
but he will not be a horse.
He will always be a donkey.

Spare the rod and spoil the child.

Train up a child in the way he should go,
and when he is old, he will not depart from it.

You can take the girl out of the country,
but you cannot take the country out of the girl.

You can put perfume on a pig,
but he will always be a pig and smell like a hog.

Caught pig always squeals (getting caught—person hollers, they did no wrong).

Run the chick over the pot (keep boiling soup for more people—add more water)

A watched pot never boils.

**You know it is going to get cold
when a dog sleeps with its rear end toward stove.**

Kicked dog always hollers (yelps).

> *We may live without poetry, music, and art*
> *We may live without conscience and live without heart;*
> *We may live without friends; we may live without a book;*
> *But civilized man cannot live without cooks.*

We laid out with the dry calves last night.

> If caught whistling in the house--
> **Whistling woman and a crowing hen
> neither comes to no good end.**

My Grandmother did not believe in sewing on Sunday and would tell us that if you sew on Sunday, you'll pull the stitches out on Monday with your toenails.

"Wake up! The Red Coats are coming!" This is what my mother would tell me when it was time for me to get out of bed and get ready to go to school. When asked why she said this, her reply was that her mother had said that when she was growing up—it was a family thing. (Is that a clue that I should be in the DAR?)

When there was a black cloud in the southwestern part of the sky, my dad would often say, "It's going to rain; it is dark in Peter's Mud Hole".

When we would see a 'low lying' fog, my parents would tell me that the rabbits were cooking supper.

Many times, I have heard people say, when asked if they would be at a certain place at a certain time, "If God's willing and the creek doesn't rise".

Contributions by Pat Bell, Esther Carter, Carolyn Herring Chason, Yvonne Childs, Catherine Lacy, Gwen Maloy, Winifred Maxwell, Cathy W. Moore, Nancy Nichols, Reba Perkins, Celeste C. Tyler, Mrs. W. J. Van Landingham, June White.

Those Were the Days . . .

Walker House

This large, comfortable home was built around 1900 for Dr. and Mrs. W. A. Walker. There was not a local sawmill that could saw timbers that were long enough, but a mill in Dothan, Alabama, agreed to do this and deliver them by mules and wagons to Cairo for two dollars a thousand feet.

Early Childhood in Cairo

All of the grandchildren of William Barnabus (Billy) Brown (1863-1929) and Claudia Catherine (Claude) Maxwell Brown (1872-1942) were familiar with and fond of the grand old two-story house "Billy" Brown built in southeast Cairo about 1912. The house still stands at the corner of Sixth Avenue and Fifth Street, S.E. (Tallahassee Highway). My earliest memories--as a small boy in the late 1930s and early 1940s--of the old house are of the big black wash pot (for clothes) out back by the garage. The family laundry was hand-washed until a washing machine was acquired. The well was attached to the back porch, our main source of water until city water was extended to the area.

The kitchen and dining areas of the W. B. Brown house, of course, were the focus of many family activities. Grandmother Brown (Claude) raised five children (a sixth died young) and cooked, sewed, and knitted for them and various boarders for many years. I remember in that kitchen the big cast-iron stove on which Grandmother and her daughters cooked so many delicious meals. Beef, pork, and poultry were standard fare for many meals, accompanied by vegetables raised in the family garden.

The aromas of Grandmother Brown's busy kitchen seem still fresh in my memory; in addition to the meat and vegetables, there were usually fruit pies or cakes, and last but not least, hot dinner rolls that melted in your mouth. One of my most prized possessions is the 28 by 15 inch wooden bread dough tray that Grandfather Brown hand-carved for his young wife over 100 years ago. She made hundreds of loaves of bread, biscuits, and rolls using that tray and my mouth waters as I write about it. Various visiting grandchildren or cousins would often vie for the privilege of "licking the bowl" of any special sweet treat being prepared by the busy cooks of the household.

Many of the recipes described in this cookbook no doubt were prepared using cast-iron stoves and bread dough trays much like Grandmother Brown's, long since replaced by modern utensils and appliances. However, I doubt that modern aromas and tastes are superior to those that resulted from "old-fashioned" equipment in the kitchen of the W. B. Brown home.

Thomas William Brown (born 1936), son of the late Perry Glenn and Aleyne W. Brown

The Grady Hotel

Back in the early thirties, the Grady Hotel was in its prime--the only place of its kind in the area. When I was a small child, my mother worked there for a short time while my father looked for work in Florida. This was Mother's first job; she liked the hotel business and helping people. When the hotel came up for sale in the early forties, my parents and a partner bought it, and we moved from Florida back to Cairo as owners of the hotel.

Both of my parents, Marvin and Laleah Walden, were Grady County natives, so we were moving home. My sister, Frances, and I had never lived in a hotel, so it "took some getting used to."

The hotel was not in the best condition, but with some repairs and decorating, it became a comfortable home and a place for people passing through to spend a night. The hotel was three stories high with a stucco finish. There were thirty-two rooms and most of the time they were occupied. The first pay phone I ever saw was in the hall for anyone to use.

If someone came in and had no money for a room, Mom always had a room for them with clean beds, towel, and bath. If you needed a meal, there was always something in her kitchen. There was a restaurant in the hotel, which was known as "The Grady Coffee Shop", which later was leased out, but it remained "The Grady Coffee Shop" until it was torn down.

One memory I have is of a young doctor who came to practice in Cairo. He stayed in the hotel until his family could join him. The doctor had no car and my father took him on his house calls. He had only one white shirt and a tie. After my mother had washed that white shirt to pieces, my father bought him a new shirt and gave him the keys to our car. That doctor never forgot my family and went on to become a great doctor in the county. Later when my father became ill with cancer, the wonderful doctor visited every single day until Dad passed away.

There were all types of people who stayed in the hotel--teachers, people down on their luck, ministers, and movie and stage stars such as Roy Acuff and Kit Carson.

The front porch had arches, and there were rockers where people could sit and rest. Ferns hung in every arch and there were flowers in the planters.

Mary Ellen Schafer

Songs of Yesteryears

When my mother, Zelda Sanders Hiers, and her sisters, Ruby S. Faircloth, and Lillian S. Durham, were very young--six to nine years of age-- an elderly lady, Mrs. Maggie Byrd (who was blind) taught them these songs. Unless one lived during those years, I doubt anyone has ever heard them. I thought it would be interesting to share them.

"THE LONELY GRAVEYARD"

I was walking one day in a lonely graveyard
When a voice from the tomb seemed to say...
I once lived as you live, walked and talked as you talk,
But from earth I was soon called away.
Oh, those tombs, lonely tombs, seem to say in a soft gentle tone.
Oh, how sweet is the rest in a beautiful heavenly home.
Every voice from the tomb seemed to whisper and say,
Living man you must soon follow me.
And I thought as I looked on those cold marble tombs,
What a dark lonely place that must be.
Oh, those tombs, lonely tombs, seem to say in a soft gentle tone.
Oh, how sweet is the rest in a beautiful heavenly home.
Then I came to the place where my Mother was laid,
And in silence I stood by her tomb...
And a sweet gentle voice seemed to whisper and say,
I am safe with my Savior at home.
Oh, those tombs, lonely tombs, seem to say in a soft gentle tone.
Oh, how sweet is the rest in a beautiful heavenly home.

"MY MOTHER WAS A LADY"

Two drummers they were seated, in a grand hotel one day.
While dining they were chatting in a jokers sort of way.
There came a pretty waitress to bring a tray of food,
They spoke to her familiarly in a manner that was rude.
At first she did not notice or make the least reply,
But one remark they made to her brought tear drops to her eyes.
She turned on her tormentors; her cheeks were blushing red,
Approaching as a picture, this is what she said.
"My Mother was a lady and yours I would allow

And you may have a sister who needs protection now.
I've come to this great city to find my brother dear.
You wouldn't dare insult me so if brother Jack were here."
The two sat there in silence, their heads hung down in shame.
Forgive me miss, we meant no harm; please tell me what's your name.
She told them and he cried aloud, I know your brother too.
We've been friends for many, many years, and he often speaks of you.
Come go with me when I go back, and if you'll only wed,
I'll take you to him as my bride for I love you since you said,
"My Mother was a lady, and yours I would allow,
and you may have a sister who needs protection now.
I've come to this great city to find my brother dear.
You wouldn't dare insult me so if brother Jack were here."

Yvonne Childs

Seventy Years Ago In Cairo

I was a five-year-old boy in Cairo, Georgia, in the early 1930s. Looking back, that was one of the best times of my life. The adults worried about recovery from the depression and all I had to worry about was the ice-wagon making home deliveries in my neighborhood. To my knowledge, no one in town had an automatic ice cube-making refrigerator. Most people owned an icebox, which looked like a refrigerator except that it had a compartment on top where you could insert a block of ice.

In downtown Cairo, they had this huge icehouse or refrigeration plant. They dispensed ice all over town to their customers on mule-drawn wagons. Each wagon was loaded with very large blocks of ice covered with a tarp. As soon as the wagon arrived in front of a house, the driver would jump off the wagon, go to the rear, pull up the tarp, and chop out a two-foot chunk for the customer's icebox. The chopping operation left a lot of small ice chips lying around on the wagon floor.

This is where a few friends and I came in. We would meet the wagon about five blocks from our house. The whole time we kept those loose ice chips off the wagon floor. On a hot day, nothing ever tasted as good as those ice-cold watermelons that my father picked up at the icehouse on a hot summer's day.

Ralph Sanders

Trouble Light

On a Saturday night, my father was underneath a farmer's car working on a mechanical problem. He had his trouble light focused on the trouble spot. When he finished his job and got out to talk to the man, the customer declared himself pleased with the service, but said he wished to pay his bill and buy the light. Dad said that he didn't realize the farmer had electricity on his place. The man agreed that he did not but told my father to just tie a knot in the cord to hold the electricity in and he would use the light until the electricity in the cord was used up.

John W. Walker

Stores Closing

Many farmers came to town on Saturdays on a combination business and social trip. They would visit with friends and then wait until almost time to go home to conduct their business. The stores and shops stayed open until 11:00 P.M. on Saturdays, but when the whistle was blown at the light plant, businesses had to close.

Since my father had a garage (and in the mid 1930s the Chrysler dealership) and my mother was the bookkeeper, I was allowed to play on the streets with my buddies until closing time. It was safe enough, but my parents had no idea of the mischief that Ralph Mixon and I got into!

John W. Walker

Fantastics

W. Powell Jones told of being on Dr. Walker's front porch on Christmas Day when the "Fantastics" came riding down the street. These young men were dressed up in their finery, screaming and yelling. They came in groups of three or four, on horseback, wearing masks and gay colored clothes, shooting pistols in the air while hollering like mad. They rode down the main streets of town and then away. This occurred when Powell Jones was a young boy and although he never found out the purpose, he never forgot that day!

From files of Powell Jones, submitted by Rebecca R. Cline

Cows and Pigs Uptown

As young lads, W. Powell Jones and his cousin, Leon Powell, went all around Cairo clearing the streets of stray cows and impounding the pigs and cows. The nickels and dimes they made were spent for candy at Muggridge's General Store. There were few stores and all were on the main street, with a few trees and hitching posts for horses. The street was unpaved, but had occasional walks across to ward off the mud.

From files of Powell Jones, submitted by Rebecca R. Cline

Milk Route

I grew up in the town of Cairo where it was not uncommon for families to own one or two cows. An uncle owned a large pasture (on what is now the south side of Martin Luther King Boulevard across from the Post Office) and our cows "spent the days" there and were brought home in the evenings to our barnyard.

Each morning, I got up early to milk those two cows and bottle the milk. There was more milk than our family could use; therefore, I had a milk route and sold milk for 10 cents a quart. That was how I made my spending money!

John W. Walker

Scrub Board

I remember when we had hogs on the farm. We would get a big croaker-sack and sew a strap on top to go around your shoulders and go pick sacks of corn. We would put the shucks in a wooden scrub board that had holes in it to scrub the floors. The ears of corn were shelled and boiled in a big pot in the yard for the hogs to eat. Boiled hominy corn, made with lye, was sometimes made for the family to eat. The children loved to help with the fires!

Margaret Courtney (1912 - 2003)

Yard Brooms

I remember going into the pastures, wooded areas, and around ponds to break down gallberry bushes, then going to the nearest wire fence and beating off most of the leaves and carrying them to Mom. She would bunch them together and tie a wire around the top of the bunch about 1½ feet from the bottom. That was the best kind of broom for a country yard that had no grass on it.

Margaret Courtney (1912 - 2003)

Making Butter

The making of butter began with putting raw whole milk into a bowl and allowing it to sit several hours so that the cream rose to the top. The cream was put into a separate bowl and each day more was skimmed from the day's milk and added until there was enough to churn into butter. For best results, the churn was filled no more than half-full.

A crock churn had a wooden dasher, which was raised up as far as it would go and pushed down in a regular smooth motion; however, some people used a plain glass jar, which would be shaken back and forth until butter formed. The Dazey was a different kind of churn; it had a glass container and a screw on top with a paddle attached. A handle turned this rotating paddle in a steady motion of a revolution per second or so. Later one was made with an electric motor.

Once the process began, the churning continued until a mass of butter gathered in the milk. This mass was then removed from the buttermilk and put into a bowl with a small amount of cold water where it was "worked". The working consisted of kneading the butter, pouring off the

milky water and repeating until the water was clear. A teaspoon of salt was added for each pound of butter and mixed in thoroughly. Then the butter was molded, wrapped, and stored in a cool place. Many pounds of butter were traded by housewives to a grocer in exchange for items not grown on the farm, perhaps, sugar, flour, Jell-O, or Post Toasties.

Carolyn Chason

Coffee Beans

I remember buying green coffee beans. We would bake them in the oven until brown. Then we would pour them into a can. Each day we would grind enough for a pot of coffee and boil it.

Margaret Courtney (1912-2003)

Can-Rollers

I remember when kids did not have a lot of toys to play with. We had to make the most of our toys with what we had. Lots of times we would let the boys make us can-rollers. They would take a syrup can or big coffee can and fill it full of sand or dirt. A hole would be made in each end for wire to go through. The wire handle would be long enough to pull the can-roller. Each child would have his own can-roller and have races.

Catherine Lacy

Broom Straw

I remember when we needed a new broom for the house to sweep floors, our mother would go to the pasture where farmers did not plant, and ring off the tall broom straw, and carry it home. You could bundle up a good handful and tie a string around it--close to the bottom and round and round until it was tight, so it would stay together. Those were the best sweeping brooms! We still have one in our house now.

STRAW BROOM

Margaret Courtney (1912-2003) & Catherine Lacy

Sears, Roebuck and Co. Catalog

Our family received Sears, Roebuck catalogs and ordered merchandise from them to be delivered to our house by mail. The new "wish books" were eagerly looked over to see the latest items and styles, but the old ones were treasured by us children. On rainy days my brother, Billy, and I would spend hours cutting out the models for paper dolls and choosing outfits. However, I do not recall ever actually playing "paper dolls!"

Carolyn H. Chason

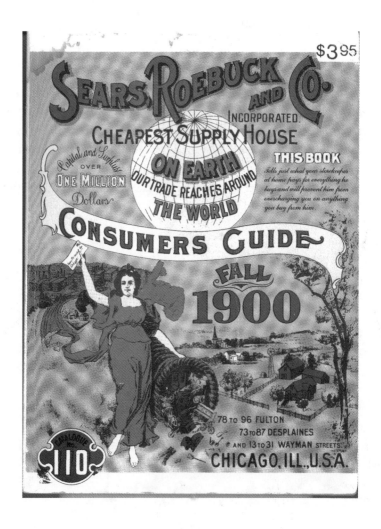

Feed Sack Clothes

During the middle to late forties when I was growing up, my grandmother and mother raised chickens. When the feed man came, Mother and Grandmother would go to the truck and select the sacks of feed with the prettiest prints. After the feed was emptied, the sacks were washed and the strings were unraveled, then my mother would make our dresses from the fabric. To add her special touch, my mother would purchase solid material and insert it into the patterns she used to make our dresses. The solids would reflect the main color of the print in the feed sacks.

One Sunday at Pine Level Baptist Church, I wore my new dress made of a pink printed feed sack with pink broadcloth inserts. For some reason my Sunday School teacher commented on my feed sack dress. I responded very quickly, "It is not feed sack; it is hen linen." I think my mother, Esther Harrison Carter, taught me that name for feed sacks or maybe it was my grandmother, Sarah Palmer Harrison Phelps.

My mother-in-law, Nellie Harrell, tells another story about feed sacks. She lived in town and the way of getting feed sacks was different. She and some friends (one was Lettie Smith) would go to different places in the country where feed was purchased and would buy the emptied sacks for 25 cents each. Each sack was about one yard of material. Some places they went were to Reno (Lottie Jo Strickland Reagan), a dairy farmer (A. M. Prince), and the Pascals. Mrs. Harrell made dresses for her daughter, Betty Sue, dresses for herself, and shirts and pajamas for the boys, Robert and Raymond.

Annette C. Harrell

Movie Theater

On Friday and Saturday afternoons, the manager of the movie theater would play music that was amplified from a speaker on top of the building. We could hear it really good for three or four blocks away and naturally, wanted to go to the movies that night. This was during the 1940s in a small town in Decatur County.

Betty W. Harrison

Salt Fish

Every fall we made a trip to the coast in wagons with several other families. It would take a couple of days to go and come home again. Our horses were slow and the roads like pig trails. We would carry old syrup barrels or homemade boxes. We would buy gutted fish with roe and pack them in the containers, alternating a layer of fish, then one of salt, then another layer of fish, etc. We would store these in the smoke house when we got home. The day before we wanted to cook fish, we would take out enough and soak them in a dishpan of water all night. Next morning, I would scale the fish and put them in some fresh water until I was ready to meal, fry, and serve them.

Margaret Courtney (1912-2003)

My Grandma

Honey Hough was Mary Knight Hough, wife of William Frank Hough, and grandmother of local residents Bannie Hough Barber, Hazel Hough Strickland Creel, Mary Hough Darsey, and Jean Hough. She taught her grandchildren to call her "Honey."

Honey came to Grady County from Yatesville, Georgia, around 1931 when her son's (Arthur Hough) wife, Cleo, died of "milk leg" (phlebitis) after giving birth to twins, Martha and Mody.

Honey raised Martha and Mody on Smith Road, east of Sholar's old store. From there, Honey walked to Cairo every day to work in Kramer's Department Store as a seamstress altering clothing for customers. Since it was dark when she left home to go to work, Mody and Martha, and sometimes Bannie, walked with her and carried the lamp to the main road. Then they'd go back and get ready for school--everyday.

Honey also worked for Ladd Maxwell's family gathering eggs and feeding chickens. She'd get paid in eggs plus a little money.

Jean Hough

Rolling Stores

Ahh memories! They're rich, and they serve as the foundation for our continuing, sometimes inexplicable, but awakening our longing to return to simpler times. One of the highlights of my early childhood was the weekly appearance of the rolling store. Back then, a trip into Cairo on Saturday afternoon supplied Mama with the staple items she needed for feeding and clothing our family. She didn't buy much because we raised nearly everything we needed to eat, and she was masterful in recycling clothing and crafting printed feed sacks into shirts for Earl and me, and dresses for Doris. Now and then, she'd forget something she needed, or an unexpected need would arise, which were occasions for hailing down the rolling store.

Mr. W.C. Rawlings made a weekly trip by our house with his rolling store and we children were quick to let Mama know it was coming. More often than not, she'd say, "I don't need anything today", and, disappointed, we'd wave him on by. But occasionally, she'd have us stop him; perhaps the kerosene was running out, she wanted a can of salmon, or a package of rick-rack braid for her sewing. On her way out to get what she needed, she'd say to us, "Yes, you can have two eggs to get you some penny candy." Mr. Rawlings would take eggs, even fryers and hens, in exchange for merchandise. After climbing onto the little stoop on the back of the truck, Doris' dilemma and mine, would begin. The exchange price of an egg would be about 2 or 3 cents and we'd have to choose between buying pieces of bubble gum, Mary-Janes, jawbreakers, peanut butter logs, or peppermint sticks. Mr. Rawlings was patient with us as we mentally calculated what was the best deal, getting the most out of the value of our egg. Invariably, we chose something different and argued later about sharing it.

I can still see that rolling store mounted on the back of a flat-bed truck, its assorted contents, and even smell the kerosene fumes that leaked from the tank on the rear. It makes me wonder if today's children would appreciate that nostalgic piece of Americana. I doubt it, not as we did.

Wayne R. Faircloth

Rolling Store Days

Living in the country had its drawbacks, but it also had many happy events. One of those events was the weekly arrival of the "Rolling Store". My memories of rolling stores were during the time my mother, sister, and I lived with my grandmother on Ridge Road in Grady County in the late 1940s and early 1950s. The Red Bullock Family ran the rolling store, on which Grandmother and Mother purchased many staple goods. I remember the excitement of my sister and my cousins, Voncile (Harrison) Davis and Dexter Harrison, on rolling store days. Some days we got an RC Cola and a Moon Pie and on special days, we got a Coca Cola and a bag of peanuts that we promptly poured into our Coke. Those were the days.

Annette C. Harrell

Party Line Telephones

When I was growing up in the 1930s and 1940s, our telephone was the oak box style that was attached to the wall in the hall, so that it could be heard all over the house when it rang. All families were on "party lines" (six or eight homes on one line). You had to listen carefully when it rang, for there were different combinations of rings assigned to each customer--we should only answer when we heard "one long and two shorts". Of course, anyone on the line could pick up the receiver and hear any conversation in progress. There was very little visiting and idle chatting on the Herrings' phone, for my parents always reminded me that someone else might really want to use their phone. In Cairo, there were telephone operators until the "dial system" was installed in 1952.

Carolyn H. Chason

Sitting Up With the Dead

Esther Harrison Carter, who is 90, remembers the practice of neighbors and friends "sitting up" with a body, usually at the home of the deceased. At that time (prior to embalming), the body was usually kept out only one day; the "sitting up" took place that night and the funeral was held the following day. Sometimes a homemade wooden casket was used and sometimes the deceased was laid out on a "cooling board". Esther remembers a neighbor being laid out in an open hallway where it was cooler.

Often, young people sat with the deceased and after several hours, talking and visiting (some said "carrying on") took place. She recalls a daughter of the deceased asking once whether the young folks had any "respect for the dead". Usually breakfast was served to those present on the morning after a "sitting up".

Since there were almost no florists, Esther's mother, Sarah Palmer Harrison Phelps, gathered flowers from her yard and, with needle and thread, tacked them to cardboard backing to make a wreath for the bereaved family. Many times, she did it on her own and sometimes her wreaths were requested.

As late as the 1960s, many families continued to carry bodies home prior to funeral services. Friends and neighbors kept on with the "sitting up" tradition, as well as preparing and carrying food for those present.

As told by Esther Harrison Carter to Annette Harrell

Making Caskets

I remember my father, Sam Lavar, building wood caskets for $24.50 each. He could build anything anyone needed. He helped build Capel Baptist Church.

Gwynette Cliett

Going Fishing On Sunday

My father-in-law, Roy Perkins, was a great fisherman. The story is told of him leaving, towing his boat on a Sunday morning to go to the Gulf. He passed the open doors of the Methodist Church and was seen by Brother Williams from his pulpit. On Monday, Brother Williams saw Roy and told him, "Next Sunday, you preach and I'll go fishing." Both gentlemen were well known in the community as "characters." Roy Perkins served Grady County as a State Representative for one term.

Susan Y. Perkins

Southern Family Life

Although I now live in Grady County, I grew up in Western North Carolina where it took much work just to provide food for the long, cold winters. Without electricity, food was preserved differently; each house, no matter how modest, had a basement or root cellar. Some had a springhouse where milk and milk products were kept and cold water was available from the spring.

Many products were dried, such as snap beans ("leather britches"), corn, peaches, apples, and okra. Pickling was popular and offered welcome additions to dried beans and white potatoes.

All family members participated in food preparation; many times I churned butter at the springhouse. Families looked out for each other and a neighbor in need received help from the rest. Survival meant pulling together.

We younger children did not enjoy the butchering, which gave us our meat supply. Some was canned, some dried, and some packed down in salt. As I remember all this, I believe I could survive without all the creature comforts we enjoy these days.

We had home schooling before it became a catchword; the teacher lived with us part of the time and taught us music as well as regular subjects. She was a beloved friend besides being our instructor.

At two different Christmas seasons, my daughter and I made tree decorations using many of the natural things I had known as a child: cornhusk dolls, cornhusk garlands, and cones of various kinds. My mother was talented as well as resourceful and taught me well. She could make great playhouses in the woods and neat things to play with. My dad had a sawmill and a small dairy and delivered milk to Asheville.

My daughter really enjoyed summers spent with her grandma where she heard the stories directly. My mother died at age 97 after living through many lifestyle changes.

Hazel Logue

School Lunch Memories

I remember carrying my lunch to school in a syrup pail that had a lid. I would pour syrup from a small bottle on the lid and sop my biscuit.

Gwynette Cliett

Sunup to Sundown . . .

BattynHester

Wilder House

Built around 1895, the Ali U., Sr. and Elizabeth Shiver Wilder family made their home at this residence after a move from a smaller house on the farm. They wished to be near the road so they exchanged homes with family to raise their seven children (4 girls and 3 boys—one of the girls was born in the home in 1896) in the house that is now the residence of Mrs. A.U. (Sammie Sasser) Wilder, Jr.

The "ARAB" Farms

In the fall of 1933, the Federal Emergency Relief Administration was established in Grady County to aid the desperate citizens who were in the midst of the terrible depression. During the next two years there was work relief (creation of jobs), direct relief, distribution of thousands of pounds of surplus commodities, distribution of field stuff, and a canning plant established for the preserving of beef (car loads of cattle were shipped in from other drought stricken areas). Other projects included drainage (for the prevention of malaria), rodent eradication, renovation of the court house, construction of two basketball "shells", community sanitation, construction of pit-privies, improvement of five school buildings and grounds, three new school construction projects, farm re-employment projects, and a rehabilitation program.

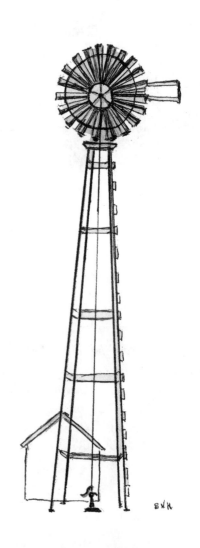

The Federal Rehabilitation plan was to enable farmers to pay a small amount of rent for a small farm that had a house, barn, fencing, windmill, and other items, which were necessary to begin farming. At some time, they would be allowed to make small payments and become owners of the farm. These "Rehab" farms became known, locally, as "Arab" farms--which was just a play on words!

The Wolf Creek Rehab Farms were located between Cairo and Whigham and involved fifty families.

The Cairo Messenger reported that Grady County's FERA Farm Rehabilitation project, one of four in Georgia and one of very few of its kind in the nation, had such significant results that it won national recognition. The Wolf

Creek Farms were developed along the lines of necessity and natural tendencies and, in this respect, were unique, since the projects elsewhere were said to be developed according to preconceived plans. The local project was self-sustaining in every respect.

Some of the families received vouchers for clothing and food, until they were able to "get on their feet". The government had purchased these lands from several different owners; a Mr. Tippett was one name mentioned.

Some of the timber was cut (to help pay for the project) and the stumps were left in the ground. Mr. Perry Merritt tells of using dynamite to blow up the stumps and then picking up the roots to have more land for cultivating. Even today, families who originally participated in the project own some of these farms.

Carolyn Chason

Sharecropping

While reminiscing with Ira Godwin, I asked about the rules of sharecropping since lots of families did this for a living when we were growing up (his father owned his farm and I wanted his views).

In the late 1800s and through the 1930s, unless you were lucky enough to own your own farm, families would sharecrop with a landowner. Most everyone was poor and this was, basically, the only way to have food and a place to live, if you wished to farm.

The landowner furnished the house and wood for stove and fireplaces. (The sharecropper cut his own wood.) Many owners had several houses, often called 'shanties' after they were old and run down. Timber was cut from the farm and houses were built from the rough lumber. Usually, there was an entry room with a fireplace that was used as a bedroom and family room, one other bedroom, and the kitchen; sometimes there was a little shed room on the end of the porch. Several children slept in one bed. There was an open well from which to draw water and an outhouse. The yards were swept clean, no grass. A mother was always proud of her yard and she kept it as clean as her house.

In sharecropping, the owner would furnish the land and the sharecropper the labor. (It was thought by some that this was a reason for large families; you had your own labor force.) The owner also furnished the tools, equipment, and mules.

The owner and sharecropper would each pay half of the expenses; however, the owner paid the taxes. At the end of the year, there would be an accounting of costs and sales. The sharecropper and his family moved often, sometimes every year, always looking for "greener pastures".

On some large farms there were commissaries where you could buy necessary items such as corn meal, flour, meat, salt, and sugar. This bill was deducted from the sharecropper's part at the end of the year.

In the early 1900s and before, oxen were used for most of the work: farming, pulling trees, pulling up stumps, hauling, and whatever was needed to be done. Alex Aldridge told me that his father looked after the oxen and mules on the Mize farm in the Spence community. He looked after their food, stables, welfare, and gear; he had a full time job doing that. The farm was a 21-horse farm, which meant it took at least 21 mules to farm his acreage. Kelso Cooper was born on this farm, where his father was the overseer who looked after the farm and sharecroppers. My family was sharecroppers, later owning their own land. Mr. Aldridge said the roads were three lanes: two for the buggy wheels and one for the mule. There was a lot of timber at that time and the Carter Tram Railroad, which went from Meigs to Spence, spurred off to haul lumber and produce from the farms.

When tractors came on the scene, the sharecropper furnished the tractor and gas and the owner the land, fertilizer, and seed.

When more than one family sharecropped with an owner, all farmers swapped labor by helping each other. This meant that you worked every day except Sunday. Sunday work was never done.

By the 1950s, most farmers had their own land, rented, or worked for a wage and sharecropping was no longer a common thing.

These were not "the good old days".

Latrelle Roland Gilliard

The Grady Electric Membership Corporation

Prior to May 1938, life in rural South Georgia was filled with darkness, hard backbreaking work, and chores that had to be done without the convenience and help of electricity. There were no electric lights, no water pumps to pump running water, no refrigeration, or freezers to keep the food, no electric heating or cooling systems.

The ceaseless cycle of labor for the farm family began hours before dawn and lasted way past sunset every day. The washing, ironing, cooking, canning, sewing, planting, plowing, and picking had to be done by the same methods that had been used by their parents and grandparents.

As a result of President Franklin D. Roosevelt receiving his first electric bill for his cottage at Warm Springs, Georgia, he determined his cost was eighteen cents per kilowatt hour (about four times as much as he paid in Hyde Park, New York). Hence, a study was conducted on the subject of getting electricity to the farms and feasible charges for electric current.

In 1935, there was a countywide meeting at the courthouse in Cairo. A large delegation of farmers met with County Agent L. H. Nelson to determine the necessary steps required to get electricity into the rural areas of Grady County. Many questions were asked concerning the wiring of homes and the cost of power. It was decided that an average member would use approximately $3.50 worth of power per month. The school districts would be canvassed for prospective members. A steering committee of fifty-one men from Grady and surrounding counties was named to make this dream project become a reality. (Mitchell County later decided to form their own organization.)

For the next several months, meetings were held often to turn in sign-up sheets and assist in the campaign. On January 7, 1937, a meeting of all signers was called and at that time, 438 members had signed up. A nominating committee selected ten men from which five were elected by ballot to serve as a temporary Board of Directors, with E. P. McClain selected as the engineer and S. P. Cain as the attorney.

J. H. Collins, B.M. Lee, G. E. Langley, T. E. Taylor, and W. G. Bullock, with J. H. Collins as president, were elected to serve as the first permanent Board of Directors. This board filed a petition to incorporate under the name of "Grady County Electric Membership Corporation".

The first charter was granted on September 27, 1937, and at a meeting in October, Noah Stanfill was hired to be the first manager of the newly founded cooperative. The first allotment of funds was received on October 15, 1937, for seventy-five thousand dollars; this would finance construction of the first seventy-five miles of line to serve 167 members. These lines were energized in May 1938, and Grady County EMC was in business. The first annual meeting was held on December 4, 1938.

Times were tough in the beginning for the co-op, but it was able to meet all payments required by the REA. The Grady County EMC continued to grow. In 1951, the merchants under the guidance of the local Chamber of Commerce in Cairo, started the first "REA Appreciation Day". This feature of the co-op history gained prestige and prominence throughout the United States. Schools were closed to allow the entire family to attend. There was a parade with beauty queens, floats, bands, and dignitaries riding in convertibles. Men of national prominence were guest speakers at the meeting of the co-op. Large crowds attended and the Grady County EMC was recognized as the only EMC in the nation to ever have a majority of its membership in attendance for an annual meeting.

Four managers have guided the cooperative through its sixty-six years of existence. Noah Stanfill served from September 1937 until June 1948. On August 1, 1948, Adrian V. Rosser was hired and he piloted the co-op with loyal and dedicated service until his retirement in December 1976. M.T. Shiver, who was the assistant manager, became the manager beginning in January 1977 and faithfully served until his retirement in December 1991. Thomas A. Rosser became manager in January 1992 and continues to serve in that position.

At the 55th annual meeting conducted on October 15, 1993, the membership elected to delete the word "County" in Grady County EMC and change the name to Grady Electric Membership Corporation.

Presented at February 2003 Grady County Historical Society meeting by Wayne Windham and Donnie Prince.

Tobacco

A major cash crop of this area was tobacco. The two main varieties grown here were flue-cured and shade. The flue tobacco was grown in an open field while the shade tobacco was grown under a cheesecloth covering.

The cured flue tobacco was carried to a market (there was one in Cairo during the early days of our county) where the piles of tobacco were auctioned to buyers from large tobacco companies to be used in the making of cigarettes.

Shade tobacco was sold directly to packinghouses from which it was re-sold to cigar factories for use as the outside wrapper of cigars. Shade tobacco brought a much higher price than any other tobacco, but the risks and expenses were tremendous; each leaf had to be free of blemishes, thin, and a bright even color.

These crops were harvested in the summer and many school age children earned spending money working in tobacco.

Carolyn Chason

Flue-Cured Tobacco

When I was a child in the 1930s and 40s, tobacco was gathered (cropped) and brought to the tobacco barn on a sled pulled by a mule and then carried to a tobacco bench built around the outside of the barn. A bar was built about 4½ feet high so that a tobacco stick would fit between two boards, until it could be filled by stringing tobacco on the stick. Three

Flue-Cured Tobacco Barn

A flue tobacco barn that was used until the modern metal bulk barn was introduced to the area circa 1960.

leaves would be handed the stringer and she would loop twine around it in a way to make it stay on the stick. Boys would hang the tobacco sticks in the barn. After the curing process, the tobacco would be taken off the stick to get it ready for market. We always looked forward to the selling day at the market, for this was when you received the money for a year's work, paid your farming bills, and could buy something special, if you had any money left.

Latrelle Roland Gilliard

Shade Tobacco Barn

A shade tobacco barn near Calvary was the scene of much activity until the 1970s. The tobacco was brought in from the fields to be strung and the sticks placed on rafters for the curing process.

King Tobacco

I was told that Elvis was "King of Rock-n-Roll", but at my home "Tobacco was the King". My father, as did most of the other farmers in our community, grew tobacco for the outside wrapper of cigars. My father grew for the King Edward Tobacco Company located in Quincy, Florida. The Child Labor Law was not in existence in my home, we all worked. While my friends searched for a summer job, mine was a continuation of the previous years.

Once the tender young plants had been transplanted into the big cheesecloth covered shades they were dusted, using an airplane, at specified times. I used to love to stand in the yard and watch the plane. It seemed that the pilot would just glide across the top of the shade, not disturbing the cheesecloth at all. One time, in particular, I was watching and Mr. Rutten, the pilot, wrote my name in the sky with the tobacco dust.

When the tobacco was ready to pick, the big leaves were loaded onto barges and pulled to the barns. We had three and four-wheeled barges, the four-wheeled was the one that I named "Hector". My brother was pulling the four-wheeled barge one time and came around the curve at the pond; the barge, loaded with tobacco, came loose from the tractor. The loaded barge went straight into the shallow end of the pond. My father just said, "Son, get it out." The tobacco leaves got wet, but nothing was damaged except our spirits at the barn.

Annette M. Lodge

Syrup Making

One of my favorite times of the year was syrup-making time in the fall. I'd get off the school bus, have a quick glass of chocolate milk and head down the road to my grandparents' place. I could hear the deep thwock-thwock of the mill as it ground the sugar cane stalks. Grandmother had a huge kumquat tree in her yard and I'd stuff my jeans pockets with green ones (I only ate the skins) and run out to the syrup mill. Papa always greeted me with, "Hey there, pretty girl!" and I'd stand near the furnace door to warm up. I loved the smell of the pine lumber that the farmhands would shove in the furnace. Soon the sweet fragrance of the syrup cooking would draw me to the other end of the cooking shed. There, as the syrup ran from the huge vat, delicious foam would form. I'd get a strip of cane peeling and scoop it up, usually having to dodge the honeybees who knew a good thing, too. It was always a mystery to me how the olive green "skimmins" would go to one side of the vat to be scooped into a barrel and fed to hogs, and the sweet syrup flowed to the other side to be captured and sold to Roddenbery's. Another thing I liked to do was play on the "pummin" piles. After the cane was pushed through the grinding mill, the crushed canes would be loaded onto a sled drawn by a mule and dumped in the nearby field. Later as they dried out, they would be burned. I liked to sneak a ride on the empty sled back to the mill. A little girl named Mildred (now Mildred Tucker) whose parents worked on the farm would come play with me and we'd pretend all sorts of adventures. I always loved that time of year, the crisp fall air, tangerines ripening on Grandmother's trees, the bluest sky in the world, and the smell of pine burning and cane syrup cooking. The first year I went away to college, I remember calling home to ask if it was syrup-making time yet. It's too bad my own children never had the privilege of going to a syrup mill; it's a childhood memory I'll always keep.

Gloria Dollar Knight

Collard Seed

Collards were planted and allowed to "seed out". When the seed had matured and dried, the plants were pulled up and placed on a sheet. The plants were beaten with a stick to separate the seed from the pod. Then the seeds were bagged and sold to a dealer in town who shipped them world wide. Cairo was once known as "The Collard Seed Capital of the World".

Willard H. Chason

Hog Killin'

I'll swear, my daddy, Henry Faircloth, would kill hogs on the coldest day of the year! It was usually in January when the signs of the zodiac were in the legs and feet, "a practical custom", he said, that his ancestors had rigorously practiced. I could understand the practicality of the cold weather, but I never did "tune-in" to that zodiac stuff. Nevertheless, he carefully laid his plans accordingly, solicited neighbors to help, and by daylight on the chosen day, he had a roaring fire burning beneath our cast-iron syrup kettle, which he had filled with water and added a little pine rosin. The boiling water was for scalding the carcasses to remove the hair. This had to be done prior to hanging them by their rear legs on gambrel sticks spaced along a stout gallows pole for disembowelment, or, as we usually said, "gutting'em."

Everyone helping had an assigned task and worked together in assembly-line fashion, with each step in the process depending on a previous one. Part of the neighbors' reward for helping with the butchering was the sharing of the fresh meat and trimmings. And among those assembled, there would be someone who wanted nearly every anatomical part of the hog. Since Mama and Daddy were fastidious in their eating habits, they were glad for most items in the viscera, like the sweetbreads (pancreas), lights (lungs), melts (spleen), maw (stomach), chitt'lins (large intestine), kidneys, hearts, and brains from the heads to be claimed. They would hold on to some of the livers. After each had picked his or her chosen parts, very little was left over as offal.

By the end of the day, a stack of hams, shoulders, ribs, and sides for bacon would have been salted down for curing, but a few cuts like pork chops, tenderloin, and some backbone were left for eating fresh. Mama and Daddy insisted that a generous portion of the lean muscle tissue be ground into sausage. The fat tissue and skins, however, were rendered into lard and yielded those tasty, crunchy cracklings, which would be used in some of Mama's cornbread next summer.

It would take another day or two to get the sausage seasoned and stuffed, the heads and feet cleaned and cooked for making souse ("hogshead cheese"), and the smokehouse readied for smoking the meat. Everything had to be cleaned up promptly, for the wash pots would be needed for next Monday's laundering, and very likely a neighbor would be asking us to help them kill hogs next week. Maybe, it won't be as cold then!

Wayne R. Faircloth

Hog Killing

Years ago folks used what they called bear grass to hang meat in the smoke house. They would put it in hot coals to make it limber. Once it was limber, you could tie it in a knot.

Clifford Bell.

Milling the Corn

Enough corn was grown on the farms to supply food for the animals and family. Mature ears of corn were gathered and put in the crib with the ears still covered with shucks. When the cans of meal and grits got low in the pantry, the farmer would shuck the ears, shell them, and bag up the kernels to take to the mill. There were several water mills and gristmills in the county that would grind the corn into meal or grits. The miller took out a portion of each for his payment; this was called a toll.

Carolyn H. Chason

Water Powered Gristmill

Many gristmills were located on creeks and ponds.

Shelling Peanuts

I remember, before planting season, all the neighbors would get together and shell peanuts for planting the next crop. The children would sit on the floor in front of the fire in the fireplace and see which hulls the fire would burn the furtherest out on the hearth where the adults had thrown them. Sometimes when they would throw a handful , it would put out the fire and they would lose the game. "Pinder" shellings were social events as well as chores.

Margaret Courtney (1912-2003)

Watermelon Bursting Instead of Cutting

Mr. John Faulkner and his partner Mr. Charlie ?? had grown a fine crop of watermelons. They had harvested the first wagonload of melons and parked the wagon near the empty boxcars on the railroad awaiting loading the next day. The two gentlemen were so pleased with the load of beautiful melons that they decided to celebrate. They became intoxicated. In their befuddled state of mind, they decided to load the melons at night, went to the wagon, and one by one tossed the melons through the open doors of the boxcar to the ground on the other side of the car. All of the melons were busted and the two men had to face their neighbors' laughter the next day.

Opal F. Lewis

Pole Bean Industry

According to information from an article by Joe McNair (1908-1983), the first pole beans grown for market in Grady County were cultivated about 1923 by some of the following: Joe Higdon, Henry Reeves, L.R. Maxwell, and H.G. Maxwell. The beans were peddled in nearby towns until a market was established in Calvary around 1930. They were a fall crop until about 1936, when fall and spring crops became the norm.

Some early varieties of pole beans used were Brown Seed Kentucky, Improved Brown Seed Kentucky, Ideal, and Tennessee Wonder. As the industry evolved, brokers and buyers came to the area from Tennessee along with a Mr. Zeigler from nearby Ochlocknee. Some locals involved in the business were Frank Maxwell, Howard Strickland, J.D. Strickland, and R.L. Butler.

The first grower to really hit the market was J.M. Herring. In 1936 or 1937 he readied a tobacco shade for planting, but since it was getting so late in the season he decided to plant Kentucky beans there. With all the fertilizer he had put out for the shade tobacco, there was a bumper crop and the pole bean market in Calvary was off and running. Farmers in the area were looking for money crops and McNair remembered an early crop ready for market on April 12, 1937. Paul Butler and J.T. Mayfield had planted four acres of Kentucky Wonder beans around mid-February, when a late cold spell threatened them after they were up and growing. Mayfield's wife, Marjorie, and her sister, Mabel Van Landingham, suggested covering the beans with newspapers, but the field was too big for that. The crop withstood the cold. Even 28-degree weather did not harm the beans at other times. Farmers, such as Aaron and Hubert Logue and Grady Strickland from near Whigham, began planting early to try to bring the first beans of the season to market.

In 1960, the Kentucky 191 became the standard variety and remained so for ten years until researchers introduced the Dade pole bean, which withstood hot weather very well. Some years, fresh pole beans were available from May 1 until mid November. In 1974, McNair bought enough beans from one farmer to fill a forty-foot open trailer; the entire load was sold to one Texas customer.

From the small beginning of a few bushels in 1923 to mammoth operations in later years, pole beans brought big money into the local economy and caused Calvary to be called "Pole Bean Capital of the World".

Mr. McNair gave credit to Zera Gainey Maxwell, Holmes Maxwell, H.P. Strickland, J.D. Strickland, J.T. Stephens, Sue Maxwell, Paul Butler, J.T. Mayfield, and Charles Butler for helping him gather information for his article.

Presented at May 2003 Grady County Historical Society meeting by Carolyn J. Hopkins.

Early Use of Tractor

Grandpa Chason was always one of the first to buy new products and accept new ideas; anyway, he had purchased a tractor before 1920. After his oldest son, Arthur, married, Grandpa told him to use that tractor. It was a very dry spring, but Arthur made a bumper crop (probably because the tractor allowed the seed to be planted deeper). However, the selling price was very low and he didn't make enough money to pay for the tractor fuel. The next year the mules were used and the tractor remained in the shed.

Willard H. Chason

No Fence Law

Until the late 1940s, livestock were allowed to roam and the farmers fenced their crops. Cows and hogs were branded or marked for identification (brands and marks could be registered at the county court house). Individual counties had elections to determine if the practice would continue in their county or whether the livestock would be fenced in or contained. Grady Countians voted to confine the livestock; this meant that pastures and pens would now be necessary.

When the law permitted animals to freely roam, the driver of a motor vehicle would, of necessity, be on a continuous lookout lest he injure an animal and be required to pay for damage. It was humorously said, "The highest priced cow was one that was crossed with a locomotive".

During the time that livestock could roam, most farmers had a "bell cow" that would lead the rest of the herd home at milking time. She actually wore a bell around her neck and when you called "co-ee", "qu-oit", or whatever, you'd hear the bell ringing and know the cows were on the way home.

Willard H. Chason

Turpentine was made by collecting gum from pine trees and distilling it. In January or February, the trees were hacked about 6 inches deep and tin or clay cups attached to the trees to catch the sap. These cups were emptied into barrels, which were scattered through the woods. The filled barrels were carried to the "still" where the process of distilling yielded oils or spirits of turpentine. Rosin was a by-product that also had commercial value.

There were, at least, five "stills" in the county: Harrell's Still (north of Whigham), Peebles' Still (northwest of Cairo), Prince's Still (Spence community), the still at Pumphrey (northeast of Reno), and Kemp's Still in Cairo (on 1st Avenue S.W. near the railroad where Campbell Soup was later located, then moved about 2 miles further west but still adjoining the railroad.)

Agriculture in Grady County

Grady County was once made up of many small farms, the average said to be a "two-horse" farm. This referred to 70 to 80 acres in cultivation (the amount of land a pair of mules could break up with a turning plow in one day). Present farms have become larger with modern equipment reducing the need for mules and much manual labor.

The term "diversified farming" is appropriate with vegetables, tobacco, pecans, corn, cotton, and peanuts being grown. Cattle and poultry were raised commercially as well. In the past, sugar cane was grown to make into syrup and tung trees were cultivated for their nuts, which were used in the paint industry.

Once upon a time Crine's, Joseph Campbell Company, W. H. Robinson Company, and W. B. Roddenbery Company played large roles in the local farming industry.

Carolyn Chason and Shirley Gale

Wilder Barns

Barns on the Wilder homeplace.

Travelin' . . .

Horse and Buggy

A common mode of transportation until the late 1920s was the horse and buggy. Great pride was taken in having a beautiful, well-groomed horse! Some larger families had a pair of horses to pull their surrey. Less affluent people would sometimes place boards across the sides of a wagon to make benches for their passengers.

Railroading in Grady County

The turn of the twentieth century was an exciting time for people of our area. Our agrarian economy was flourishing, with a farm product ready for market in every month of the year, making the area the "original diversified farming area of the southeast". The fertile soil and plentiful acreage were enticing families to relocate from less desirable areas (among those, the families of the Rockford, Alabama, exodus who relocated to the Whigham area).

The Atlantic and Gulf offered east-west access to the markets, via the Waycross "hub", and later became the Atlantic Coast Railroad. Passenger, freight, and mail service flourished for many years on this route with two trains each way on day and night schedules. The producers in the northern and southern parts of the county were hauling supplies and products by horse or mule drawn wagons to Havana, Tallahassee, and Pelham. A north-south route was needed.

The Pelham and Havana Railroad (P & H) was chartered in 1906 to build fifteen miles of track from Cairo to Calvary. The name of the railway indicates the intention to establish a through line from the Thomasville-to-Albany branch of the SF & W in Pelham to the GF & A in Havana. By 1910, the initial construction was completed, and the P & H owned two locomotives, two passenger cars, and a freight car. In 1914, the P & H extended four miles from Calvary to Darsey, Florida, and commenced the operation of two daily runs. In 1918, a final extension of five miles completed the connection with the GF & A at Havana.

Kelly-Clark Lumber Company had a large sawmill, employing about 200 workers, about two miles south of town on the old Ingleside Plantation. This site became the Gradyville station. The coming of the railroad was the beginning of Reno when a sidetrack was built about ten miles southwest of Cairo.

The P & H, known as the "Pore and Hungry" by locals, never extended from Cairo to Pelham, so its full worth was never realized. The P & H provided valuable product to market transportation as well as passenger service for the communities of Gradyville, Cranford, Reno, Calvary, Darsey, and at rural sidings along the way. The main "tonnage" consisted of logs and lumber; however, a tram spur, for logging purposes, extended from near Reno across the Ochlocknee River. The P & H was never a financial success and despite a powerful civic effort ("Push Hard") to keep it in operation, service ceased in 1924.

An unchartered (unless passenger was provided, no charter was required) railroad extended from Pelham through Spence. Also, the Boyd Lumber Company in Boydville had unchartered rail lines that extended southerly to Amsterdam and northerly to near the present location of Shiver School. Imagine the impact on Grady County if the Boyd Lumber Company line and the Pelham spur had extended the two or three miles necessary for connection, if the ten miles of rail from Pelham to Cairo had been built, and if all of those lines were chartered. Grady County would have been served from one end to the other by viable rail service. Spence would have been a rail head and on the heavily traveled Thomasville-to-Newton route. Capel, Boydville, and others would have been rail stops, trade centers, and towns rather than communities. Grady County would have been a center of transportation and commerce.

What kind of opportunity and legacy was lost with the demise of these lines? Since most major roads closely followed rail lines, it is safe to speculate that the Pelham-to-Havana route would have been a major, if not US route. A similar major route would have connected Pelham, the Whigham--Boydville area, and points to the south and west. Moreover, Grady County today would be a much more attractive destination for industry, whose lifeblood is no longer rail, but asphalt ribbons of throughways from factory to market.

Bill Bass, Sr.

The Log Train

Elmera Jane Lee (Mrs. Ellis Maxwell) was under five years old when the P & H log train passed near her parents' home (Arthur and Effie Rehberg Lee). Her father would hold her up to watch the train go by. She also remembers that mules were kept in a lot near their woods for pulling logs out to be loaded on the train. Then they were carried to Kelly-Clark Lumber Company at Gradyville (near present Ed Bell place).

Ellis Maxwell (now in his 89th year) remembers logs from his father's farm (John Emory Maxwell, Sr.) being loaded onto the train at the present Sofkee Road/Highway 111 junction where his Uncle Bud (Jesse Newton Maxwell, Jr.) lived.

As told to Shirley M. Gale

Recollections of Reno

During Reno's "heyday", Jesse Newton Maxwell, Sr. built a store by the P & H Railroad at the south end of the little village. It was built from trees sawed on his place and when the store closed, it was torn down and rebuilt as a shade tobacco barn at the farm of his son, John Emory Maxwell, Sr. That building was blown down by a storm several years back and was salvaged and used to build a storage barn at the John Emory Maxwell, Jr. place by Jesse Maxwell's great grandson, Arthur Reynolds Maxwell. How is that for recycling?

Shirley M. Gale

Party Time

Lois Maxwell (1906-1987) told of the P & H train stopping at her Uncle Bud's place when parties were in progress. The folks on the train would get off and spend time partying, then get back on and continue the trip!

As told to Carolyn H. Chason

Mud Balls and Train Engines

Harry Singletary (now 93 years old) remembers some local boys (himself not included!) throwing mud balls at the engine of a train as it went through the crossing near their homes. The fun turned sour when the mud went into the working parts and stalled the train.

As told to Shirley M. Gale

Nora's P & H Experience

Mrs. Nora Dalton Mitchell (1898-1987), daughter of William Bailey ("Mr. Billy") and Nancy Ann Clinard Dalton of Calvary, told the following story of an experience with the P & H Railroad.

"The P & H (often called the Poor and Hungry) connected Cairo and Havana and its route included Calvary my hometown. In 1919, I went to Norman College, Norman Park. I once got so homesick that I saved up the spending money my mother sent me and bought a train ticket home. My mother did not send a permission note to come home, so I FORGED one!! Well, after the P & H locomotive crossed the trestle about 2½ to 3 miles north of Calvary, the fuel and cargo cars fell through the trestle, leaving the passenger car on the other side of the creek. When the engineer got to Calvary, he discovered he had lost all the rest of his train, including his only passenger, so he backed up 2½ to 3 miles, loaded me and my luggage into the locomotive, and brought me to Calvary. I never wrote my own pass to come home again!"

Then she would say, "Be sure, your sins will find you out".

Frances Mitchell

Kelly-Clark Lumber/P & H Railroad

Born October 18, 1903, Leroy Hopkins, Sr. quit school in the sixth grade to work on the farm with his father. After working on the farm some number of years, he asked his father if he could hire a man to work in his place so that he could get a job with Kelly-Clark Lumber Company. His father agreed. Leroy got the job earning fifty cents per day. Out of this, he had to pay the salary of Tommy Jeter and the rent at the boarding house in Gradyville. He was sixteen or seventeen years old at this time.

Kelly-Clark Lumber Company built new railroad beds and maintained the P & H. Leroy was working when the P & H fell into the Ochlocknee River at the trestle where three men were killed. When the water in the river went down, Leroy helped lay the rails in order to back the train out.

Leroy and Ora Whitfield married in 1924 and moved to Gradyville. They went home on the weekends on a "hand cart" that was owned by the P & H Railroad.

Not very long after the train accident at the trestle, Leroy quit his job with Kelly-Clark and moved back to Reno to the farm.

Submitted by Carolyn J. Hopkins as told by Tom Hopkins

Excursions

Aunt Estelle (Herring) told of going on excursions to Lanark via the P & H Railroad after returning home from serving as a Red Cross nurse in France during WW I. The train left Cairo about daylight, picking up other passengers along the way. (At Havana, it joined with the GF & A.) Passengers would have most of the day at the beach resort, where the hotel provided meals, swimming, boating, and fishing. The train arrived back in Cairo before midnight.

These trips must have been real social highlights!

Carolyn H. Chason

The Hula

In the mid-1940s there was a passenger train called "The Hula" by the locals, since it shook from side to side, that stopped at the depot in The Village. Several times two or three girls and I rode the afternoon train to Bainbridge where we shopped or saw a movie and returned on a bus that went through Attapulgus at night. It didn't cross our minds that we might not be safe.

Betty Wade Harrison

Cairo's First Automobiles

The first automobiles in Cairo, were probably, owned by the medical doctors. I've been told that Dr. Oliver had the first car and Dr. Walker the next one. He had a white Buick with gears on the outside. Soon others were buying vehicles and learning to drive. When an automobile was purchased, the dealer would give one person in the family a driving lesson. The streets had to be shared with horses and buggies, mules and wagons, and other animals. Needless to say, there were many accidents!

1908 FORD Model T

Bus Service

In 1948, I began working with Modern Coach Trailways. The company slogan was "The Friendly Lines", and it was just that. We hauled chicken and cow feed and would even stop at families' houses that we were in close touch with (because of their age or infirmity) to get their grocery order from them. Then we would do their shopping while in Dothan or any other town on the route and deliver them on the return trip.

The buses were 25, 29, or 37 passenger capacity and powered by Chevrolet, Buick, or International engines. Thirty five to forty thousand miles was the life expectancy of an engine. The repair shops were so numerous that we were never more than 85 miles from one of them--most of them were closer than fifty miles apart.

Passengers could board the buses by standing by the road and flagging them down and could disembark by pulling the cord that created a buzz, alerting the driver to stop.

We hauled the mail, newspapers, and packaged freight. In the spring, we hauled lots of baby chicks. We would pick them up at one post office and deliver them to a bus station, so the owner would not have to travel to get them. We would also meet the mail trains, get bags of mail off the train, then deliver to the post office, mostly at night when the post office was closed.

As the buses got larger, air conditioning was added; then later, restrooms were added. This made it nicer for everyone, including the driver.

Now some of the larger buses will seat 65 passengers and it is common for a bus engine to operate five hundred thousand miles before it needs rebuilding or replacing. Therefore, bus repair shops are almost nonexistent.

There were four mergers with different companies during the 41½ years I drove for them. I logged almost 4 million miles in this period of time, traveling over a large area of the country (most of it was in the southeast). At the beginning of my career, fourteen buses served Cairo daily, but now there are only two. Even though I drove some of the same routes for a long period of time, each trip was different because different people were on the bus each trip.

Shirley Brown

Readin', 'Ritin', 'n 'Rithmetic . . .

Spring Hill School

This school was located six miles north of Whigham and was a typical school building circa 1900. This building burned around 1920.

School Days

Earl McCorkle started to Midway School in sixth grade, where he remained for two years. Because he hated school, his father, R. V. McCorkle, would allow him to stay out, but then he had to plow mules!

Once after being sent to school principal, Mr. Bowen, by his teacher, Mrs. Godwin, he was paddled and sent back to class. He told his friend, Wallace Miller, that, "One day I am going to buy the school and tear it down". At that time, there were seven classrooms, each with a wood-burning heater. An eight-foot fence surrounded the building. When Earl "graduated" from seventh grade, there were 25 students in the class and only four passed!

Years later, after he had started a family, he bought 45 acres of land from the Woolfolks and on the corner of it stood the old school. The deed to the school stated that when Midway School no longer existed, the land was to revert to the original owner. Since he had bought the property, the land was now his. An auction was held to sell the building, and the county declared a "no sell" because the highest bid was $1000 and Superintendent of Grady County Schools Lloyd Connell said $1100 was the minimum price. Earl and his father put in $550 each and closed the deal.

For years, the building was used to store fertilizer until Earl and his brother-in-law, Paul Eames, tore it down after Eames had bought R. V. McCorkle's share. Materials the two did not want, such as the tin from the roof, were sold to anyone who wanted it. Lumber was used to build Earl's home and brick from five chimneys were cleaned and used for the exterior.

The home of Earl and Myrt McCorkle stands just south of the old school location and the original school bell is located in their home. It had been taken down with the installation of an electric bell and had been stored under the stage where it was found during the demolition of the building. Some bricks still stand under an oak tree where spigots were located on the playground. Pine trees now sway where many children spent time at Midway School.

As told to Alice C. McCorkle

School Memories

Wallace Miller (1930-2003) started first grade at Midway when he was six years old. He walked to school each day and ate in a lunchroom operated by Mellie Miller and Dosie Morris. There was no charge for lunch.

Hands were washed under a pipe that had holes all along for several people washing at one time, while one person ran the hand pump. Each one brought a drinking utensil (jar, glass, or aluminum cup) and each was responsible for rinsing his cup and leaving it for the next time. Everyone knew his or her own cup!

There were blackboards in the classrooms, pencils could be bought for a penny each, and paper tablets were a nickel each. Seven silver bells (chocolate kisses) could be had for a penny. Because almost no one had money, the candy stayed there a long time.

At recess, the boys played baseball and basketball while the girls jumped rope and played hopscotch. Wallace remembered playing marbles with the principal's twin sons, Waldo and Wendell Bowen, and his friend, Earl McCorkle.

The boys' outhouse, which was a "three-holer", was located behind the school building in the edge of the woods. The dirt road beside the school wound all around and down to Tallahassee.

As told to Alice C. McCorkle

Outhouse

This structure was a common sight in the back yards of rural areas at least, until the late 1930s when electricity became a choice. It was an open-pit privy, but known as "The Johnny House", "The Necessary", "The Toilet", or "The Outhouse".

Schools

In the early days of Grady County, many small schools were near enough for students to walk to and from. After they advanced to upper levels, they often transferred to another larger school. Large families with several students in the same school allowed the older children to drive a buggy or wagon. If there was extra space, neighbors might be picked up. Arrangements would be made to pasture the horse or mule near the school until it was time to hitch up and go home. In his 1907 annual report, County School Superintendent, J. B. Wight reported forty white and twenty-three negro schools in Grady County, serving 3,667 pupils.

A survey done by the Georgia Department of Education in 1922 stated that there were too many small schools too close together. Of the ones listed in the survey only Calvary, Greenwood, Pleasant Hill, Sherwood, Sunnyside, and Walker had any semblance of a "library". The Cairo school building had burned and the operation was housed in temporary space. Only a picture of Whigham School was included with no statistics about organization or equipment.

Until the early thirties, many of the schools had only one or two rooms and most teachers taught more than one grade. Buildings were rather crude, but rooms had desks, potbellied stoves, blackboards, a dictionary, a few books, and a paddle.

Federal Relief programs provided some new buildings and allowed for consolidation. (These programs paid wages for construction workers.) Soon there were PTAs working with school trustees to improve the quality of education. Within the next few years, PTAs began making plans for each school to have a lunchroom, hoping to relieve students of having to bring lunches from home. Some carried their fried meat, biscuits, and small bottles of syrup in pails, while a few took light bread sandwiches in lunch boxes. The lunchrooms served good hot food, and pupils enjoyed new dishes, such as spaghetti.

Playgrounds around the schools were basically just open spaces. Some schools had seesaws, swings, and jump boards, and most classrooms had a large ball, softball, and bat, and a length of rope that was taken outside at recess for games. Students could jump rope, play dodge ball, softball, hopscotch (using colored glass for tokens), or Red Rover. When students were full of extra energy, teachers might suggest races, but most of the time pupils played as they wished. On rainy days, teachers led such inside games as Simon Says, Charades, Gossip, Musical Chairs, or have a spelling bee.

Betty N. Foster

Wayside Community Center

The Wayside Community Center was the former Wayside School, which was organized and constructed in the mid 1920s. Three neighboring schools had burned and Wayside was the new consolidated school for the area.

Elpino School

Elpino School had its beginning in 1889. My mother, Esther Carter, attended Elpino School in her 9th and 10th grades (1927-1929). She transferred to Elpino from New Home, which went through the 8th grade. Oak Grove, which she attended earlier, went through the 6th Grade. There was no 10th grade at Elpino; however, Mr. Jack Bowen, the principal, told anyone wanting to study 10th grade work he would teach it to them, but they would not receive credit. He also stated that the knowledge they acquired could not be taken from them, even though officially they received no credit. Since further education required traveling to Cairo, my mother officially only went through the 9th grade, but had 10th grade learning.

I began my schooling at Elpino in 1947. Mrs. Mary Bell was my first grade school teacher and I remember each of the eight teachers I had with love and respect. We were taught more than school subjects; we were taught to "love your neighbor as yourself," "to always tell the truth"—(one time I did this and ended up getting a "whipping" in the eighth grade); "to respect your elders", and "to play fair". I remember Mrs. Agnes Davis (my

6th grade teacher) inviting Reverend Jack Clarke (Pastor at Pine Level Baptist Church) to talk with us on the subject of Christ's Apostles versus Disciples.

One of my special memories of Elpino was playing basketball. Basketball between the country schools was quite competitive.

Another remembrance was attending chapel programs and watching movies in the auditorium. One special program was a "Tom Thumb Wedding". As a first grader, this ended my singing career when I was told you could hear me hollering "I Love You Truly" clear to the back of the bottom floor of the school. My first cousin, Voncile Harrison Davis, and I sang the song and we were bridesmaids in the wedding.

Other fond memories include the school library where I quickly developed my love for reading; potbellied stoves to warm by; May Day observance with beautiful colored streamers used to wrap the Maypole and King and Queen and their court; "shots" given by the county nurses with everyone trying to get to the back of the line; family suppers on stretched fence wire and Halloween Carnivals, outdoor toilets, and excitement of New Home eight graders coming to Elpino.

However, my most memorable event was our Eighth Grade Graduation. The school auditorium had been condemned and, much to my displeasure, the class decided not to have graduation services at a local church. The only alternative was to hold Graduation Services on the back porch of Elpino School. I think I am safe in saying we are the only "Eighth Grade Graduating Class" or perhaps the only graduating class to graduate on the back porch. I had one pleasant surprise though; my daddy, who was in the Western States at graduation time, had a watch sent to our Principal, M. M. Battley, to present to me at graduation. I still have the watch.

I was in the 8th grade at Elpino when "under God" was added to the Pledge of Allegiance to our American Flag (1954).

I believe, of my eight teachers at Elpino, three are still alive – Mrs. Mary Bell, my first grade teacher; Mrs. Agnes Davis, my sixth grade teacher; and Mr. M. M. Battley, my eighth grade teacher (who gave me my only paddling in school). Thank you, teachers, for caring enough to go the "second mile".

Annette Carter Harrell

The Health Department

Mrs. Lucille Reynolds, now ninety-six, was a nurse with the Grady County Health Department when it was over a store on Broad Street where the Old Citizen's Bank drive-thru is located. She was assigned to the area from the Mitchell County line to US 84 and from the Decatur County line to the Pelham highway. Mrs. Eleanor Prince was in charge of the eastern part of the county with Mrs. Mary Christopher over the Calvary and Reno areas. The nurses' specialty was visiting homes and weighing babies when neighbors told them of new arrivals in their neighborhood.

At the office, Louise White was clerk and Clarence Goodman was sanitarian. Everyone worked together as a family for twenty-something years. Nurses went out at 9:00 AM to visit homes or schools, going in twos and driving their personal cars.

Mrs. Reynolds remembers being called "the shot lady". Because typhoid fever had caused deaths, the nurses went to forty-three schools, to administer typhoid and smallpox inoculations. Needles were sharpened and boiled and ample rings of them, ready for use, were placed on three or four trays. After use, they were taken back to the office and made ready for the next time.

Once at a school inoculation clinic, a little boy became so upset about the upcoming shot that he ran into the woods and had to be hunted down and comforted.

Mrs. Reynolds retired from Grady County Health Department in May 1972. She could, without a doubt, tell many interesting stories. Thanks for your good work, Mrs. Reynolds!

Alice McCorkle

Cure for Measles

When I was a child in elementary school, I caught the measles. I remember lying on a bed beside the roaring fireplace at my grandparents' house (Marvin and Ruth Dollar) and being made to drink large quantities of ginger ale. This supposedly made the measles break out faster and thus I'd be well quicker. To this day, I cannot bear to drink ginger ale! I don't know which was worse, having to drink the ginger ale or missing my class train trip from Cairo to Thomasville.

Gloria Dollar Knight

GROVES TASTELESS CHILL TONIC PREPARED BY PARIS MEDICINE CO. ST. LOUIS.

2 FL. OZ.
PURE
castor oil
THE
FRANK
TEA & SPICE CO
CINTI.

Meetin' 'n Eatin' . . .

New Ochlocknee Baptist Church

The early records of the New Ochlocknee Baptist Church were destroyed, but there is a reference to it in the Baptist Church Records of 1849 at the First Baptist Church in Thomasville, Georgia. The church was organized and held meetings in a small house near the Ochlocknee River. The present church building, near the crossroads at Beachton, was built in 1862, thus the name "New Ochlocknee Baptist Church". The educational building was added in 1955. The existing records of the church go back to 1910.

Sacred Harp Singing School

When I was a small girl (approximately ten years old), my mother wanted the family to go to the Scared Harp Singing School at Mizpah Primitive Baptist Church (Grady County). She had attended this same school as a young girl. No musical instruments were used in the "singing school". Our teacher, Mr. Tidwell, taught us to sing by the four-shaped notes – "Fa So La Me." The school lasted for one week, after which there was a program. We were divided into age groups and each group would sing. One of the songs that we sang was "Amazing Grace". Parents and friends always came for this special program and a good ole' fashioned time was had by all.

Esther Harrison Carter (90 years young at this writing)

Singing School

When I was a small child, my father engaged Professor Daniel Dees of Pine Level to teach a singing school at Spring Hill. The Professor taught the "Shaped Notes" method in the ten-day school. This consisted of "Do-Re-Mi-Fa-Sol-La-Ti-Do", both backwards and forward. (He also taught me, "A, B, C, D, E, F, and G".) Adults as well as children attended these sessions. This was the beginning of my love for gospel music.

Many Sunday afternoons, people in our community would gather at a home for a time of informal singing. Through the years, scheduled "Sings" have been held in different parts of our county, and there are State Singing Conventions held annually in fourteen states, even today.

Evelyn Gainous Hester

Macedonia Baptist Church

My grandmother, the late Grace Pelham Cooper (Mrs. Alton), lived in the Spence Community most of her life. When asked to tell of her church, this is what she said:

"My first memories of Macedonia Baptist Church are of going to Sunday School in the warm weather months of the year and the teacher giving us picture cards with short Bible stories on the back. Our class assembled in the Women's Amen Corner, which was to the right of the pulpit.

I remember the inside of the church, about 1916, as one large room that would seat 400 or more people. It was built high off the ground and had three rows of pews and two Amen Corners. The ceiling was high, probably twelve or fifteen feet. The church had two front doors, one on the left hand side and one at the back to the right of the pulpit. For lights, there were two or three kerosene lamps hanging in the center of the church and two or three reflector kerosene lamps on each side of the church. About the only times these lamps were used were during summer "Protracted" meetings. Some may remember our uncomfortable pews for we used them until twenty or twenty-five years ago. For heat, we used a potbellied stove. My memory is that the pipe was run out of one of the windows. We had a lot of trees on the grounds and the men and boys would gather fallen limbs. Some would bring light wood splinters from their homes to start the fires. This system was never satisfactory, I can remember how coats would be pulled closer, and the people shivered. The outside of the church was painted white, but the inside was unpainted, until the first remodeling was done.

A table about three or four feet square was before the pulpit just as ours is today. It was painted black and was used as a desk for the church clerk and for the Lord's Supper."

Donna Cooper Powell

Dinner on the Ground

Do you remember the all-day meetings and "dinner-on-the-ground" at country churches in times past? By the time, I was old enough to understand, the dinners were not spread, literally, on the ground as my

parents remembered. Instead, they were served on a long section of wire fencing, which had been horizontally positioned and stretched tautly between two or more trees. Fence posts topped with two-by-fours were spaced beneath the fencing to keep it from sagging.

The meetings were generally held in early to mid summer, after the farmers had finished "laying-by" their crops and before harvest time arrived. During that short cycle, one could pick most any weekend and find a meeting going on at churches such as Centennial, Pine Hill, Poplar Springs, Long Branch, or Spring Hill. The practice of holding meetings in the month of June was so common that they came to be called "June Meetings." Even today, the expression can still be heard in referring to the Annual Meetings being held at churches such as Tired Creek, Mizpah, and Piedmont, who are among a few yet to adhere to the practice.

The church affiliation, whether it was Methodist, Missionary Baptists, Primitive Baptists, or Holiness didn't matter that much. It was the sumptuous meal that was the real "drawing card". Not only were the affairs a homecoming for friends and relatives, they were get-acquainted socials for total strangers, and then there were the freeloaders, which Mama sometimes called the "buzzard" crowd. And, it may have been in post depression times, but the bounty of the alfresco dinner gave no hint of hard times. The table would be laden with brimming bowls of fresh vegetables, platters of fried chicken and other various meats, potato salad, and, Oh My!, the assortment of cakes, pies, and custards. For us children, who sat beneath the table to eat, we could not resist begging for some exotic fare--like banana or pineapple sandwiches made with "light" bread and slathered with plenty of store-bought mayonnaise, which always showed up among the standard items.

The sweltering heat, the annoying gnats and flies, and even the threat of a sudden downpour were not deterrents to the festive dinners. Who could ever forget those gastronomical feasts?

Wayne R. Faircloth

Potpourri . . .

Cairo First United Methodist Church

In 1873, the first building, a white one-room structure with arched windows, was erected. This was adequate until 1902 when this new larger brick sanctuary was dedicated. Soon a frame building was erected on the west side for Sunday School classes and an Epworth League Hall. The present structure was dedicated in 1927.

War Memories

December the seventh, nineteen hundred and forty-one ... I remember where I was on that day as so many other people do. My father, mother, two sisters, and I were on our way back from Tallahassee, Florida, when the news came in over the radio that the Japanese had bombed Pearl Harbor. I had been hearing and reading about the war in Europe, but it had never occurred to me that the United States could be bombed.

Growing up we had heard our father and mother talk about the First World War (in which my Father had served). It was the war that was to "end all wars" and that was what I believed. Daddy had taught us some of the songs that were sung during that war such as "Over There, over there, send the word, send the word that the Yanks are coming" and "It's a Long Way to Tipperary, it's a long way to go". We often sang these in the car as we went to Granddaddy's house in Calvary every Sunday afternoon. These songs made you think that war would be ended forever.

I was a senior at the old Cairo High School. My brother Bob was a senior at the University of Georgia and brother Bill was a sophomore at Emory University. Mary, Beth, and I always looked forward to the weekends and holidays when the boys came home. I was looking forward to the adventure of college the next year. The impact of some of the meaning of this terrible war came as some of my friends joined one branch of the service or another as soon as they graduated. Others went off to work or college, many joining or were called to duty within the year. This happened at a time when they should have been "going off" to start their adult lives.

I still have mental pictures of the days when my brothers told the family that they were going to do their part. Bob went to the Coast Guard and Bill to the Naval Air Corps. It was exciting, I was proud and I was sad. I really did not know all that this meant. I remember the times that we as a family went to the train station to send them off and the serious expression on my father's face as he talked with them as we waited for the train to come to take them away.

The summer of 1942 was a mixture of unfamiliar feelings: seeing family and friends come and go in their uniforms, talk of rationing of gas, sugar, and coffee, planting "victory gardens", looking for the mail, convoys on the highways, planes flying over head, hearing adults talking. Many citizens found ways in which they could "help the cause". I knew there was more happening than I understood.

There was a tower built on Highway 93 on the right hand side going south. It was across the highway from where the new Cairo High School is now. People were asked to volunteer to man the tower to observe all air traffic and report what we saw. Some of my friends and I volunteered and with a little training and a chart of all the planes of the time, we would be on watch and report any we saw. We also had practice "blackouts" and they were very seriously followed. This brought to mind that the war could come right here in Cairo, Georgia.

It was always different at home and in the town from that time on. Everyone went about doing what they needed to do or had to do, but there was a feeling and attitude that I really do not have words for, nor can I explain. On looking back, I know some of the effects this Second World War had on my family, my friends, our town, our world, and me. Everyone has a story, those who were having to do the fighting, those who served at home, and those who waited. As time passes, I realize some of the effects it had on me that I did not realize before. But these are personal. The effects of this war-- that was not supposed to be--on our country have changed us as a people and as a nation.

Mabel Van Landingham Kral

World War II

Anyone whose age is sixty or less will not remember the World War II days of commodity rationing, but a growing number of us "senior" citizens, to use a term that is politically correct, proudly recall those times. It was probably the single period in American history when the nation was most solidly unified, not only politically, but also socially and culturally. Patriotism was passionately high. There was not a family anywhere who was not gladly sacrificing and doing what they could in support of their sons, daughters, or close relatives who were in combat, in either the European or Pacific theaters of the War. Everyone was engaged in the War effort in some way, ranging from collecting scrap metal, rolling and preparing surgical dressings, knitting scarves and sweaters for the Red Cross to distribute to GI's, contributing to saving-stamp and defense-bond drives, donating blood, joining the Georgia Guard for home defense, to taking part in blackout or air-raid drills. Even popular music rallied around the War effort, with Kate Smith's stirring rendition of Irving Berlin's nationalistic anthem, "God Bless America," topping the Hit Parade charts month after month. Newspapers boldly printed slogans urging men beyond mandatory draft to either "Go to War, Go to Work, or Go to Jail!", for example.

A major part of the War effort was adjusting to doing without some of the things to which we had become accustomed. Among the earliest items rationed were gasoline, tires, and inner tubes, but shortly thereafter shoes and refined, granulated sugar were added to the list. Rationing stamps became hot items and were as valuable as money. Many items that were not rationed were available only in short supply, like flour, coffee, and woolen clothes. People did not complain too much about these inconveniences, for just a little over a decade earlier they had survived similar deprivations caused by the Great Depression. In addition, as before, people learned to "make-do" with what they had.

Saccharin, a calorie-free, artificial sweetener some 500 times sweeter than cane sugar, had been developed for diabetic use, but market was superseded by its demand to sweeten tea and coffee when sugar became scarce. After folks learned to adjust the amount to use, many preferred it to cane syrup or honey as a beverage sweetener. Hobson Blackman of Wight & Browne's Rexall Drug Store once quipped, "We've sold more saccharin tablets during the War than we've sold medicine pills". After the War, though, folks resumed the use of sugar. Pure saccharin is yet available, and is now sold in grocery stores, but its demand is pitifully low. However, millions of diabetics and diet conscious folks still use a bit of it every time they open a packet of Sweet 'N Low.

Wayne R. Faircloth

Precious Sugar

One December during World War II, our family had no sugar and no ration stamps to buy any. (Mother had substituted syrup in some of the recipes so that we would have some holiday sweet treats.) When getting out the Christmas china, mother discovered that two sugar bowls had sugar in them. You cannot imagine how happy we were!

Ann Merritt Robertson

Remembrances of Mule Days

Early in 1973, President Leon Bryant led the Calvary Lions Club in their planning for a Mule Day to be held in the fall. They would have a mule parade consisting of wagons and mule-drawn farm implements (with Lions serving on the "scoop committee"), bands, a greasy pig contest, chicken throwing, diving mules, fish fry, fishing contest, and a barn and street dance. Over 5,000 people attended Mule Day. Lions President Dan Jones, who drove one of the wagons in the parade said, "I just couldn't believe the number of people lining the streets." There were black mules, brown mules, and white mules, big and small mules. E. D. Hopkins' mule was selected as the "prettiest". Lt. Governor Lester Maddox, Congressman Dawson Mathis, and former Governor Marvin Griffin made speeches praising the community. The plowing contest, between Robert Ray of the Georgia Agriculture Department and Jim Lee of the Florida Department of Agriculture was judged "a draw".

1978...The sixth annual Mule Day attracted a "throng" of 40,000. Faded overalls and T-shirts were the uniforms for the Cairo High School and Washington Middle School bands for the parade. They wanted to fit-in with the spirit of the day. Fred Larkin displayed the prettiest mule in the parade. Ross Langley entered the ugliest mule. The best pair of mules owned by Tom Williams was a matched pair of black horse mules hitched to a plantation-hunting wagon. First place in the parade went to a covered wagon entry by Eddie Griffin. The prize for the most unusual parade entry went to Donald Dalton, who entered a mule and plow complete with windshield, windshield wipers, and windshield washer, a fan, television and CB and conventional radios. Two area beauty queens also were dressed for the occasion. Joyce Dalton, Miss Grady County, rode atop a bale of hay in the back of a wagon while Swine

Time Princess, Sandra Kelley, was seated in the rumble seat of a Model A Ford.

1983… "There was a bunch of people at Mule Day" estimated at 63,000. On NBC's Friday edition of the "Today Show", Willard Scott, the weather announcer, donned his "Mule Day" hat, noted that the mule was the most misunderstood animal in the world, and invited all his listeners to visit Calvary on Saturday. Trophies were awarded for the "Prettiest Mule", the "Ugliest Mule", the "Best Pair of Mules", and the "Most Stubborn Mule". In other contests, Nathan Hatcher won the trophy given for catching the smallest fish and Tommy Gaines won the plowing competition. The tobacco-spitting contest was won with a distance of 18 feet 9 inches.

1988… A mule owned by Roy Lambert was judged the "prettiest" in the parade by a panel of judges consisting of Cuy Harrell, Jr., Pat Perkins, Sen. Harold Ragan, Peggy Chapman, and Henry Wynn. Other prize winners were: "best old car", a Model A Ford won by Milford Barver, "best all around entry", a two-mule ice wagon entered by Bobby White, "most unique entry", a red mule drawn four wheel wagon owned by Ricky Davis, and "most original entry", a John Deere wagon entered by Bowers Pump Service. Thirty-two mules were entered in the Mule Show. Dan Bullock riding "Jane" won both the cob race and the barrel race. "JJ" owned by Rickey Davis was judged the "best overall" mule in the show. Groups of singers and dancers entertained the throng of visitors. The "slingshot turkey shoot" proved as popular as the tractor pull, the clown act and the pony rides.

1993…The Lions Club considered canceling Mule Day because of the rainy weather, but decided to proceed as planned, "come rain or shine." Parade Chairman Wayne Windham reported that Wiley Smith, Jr. of Tennessee declared, "Hell yeah, we're gonna have a parade. It may have just one entry--me--but I drove 500 miles to get here and we're gonna have a parade." Mule Day Chairman Charles Butler said that the crowd was off some, but the club was pleased at the size of it. Most activities were held as planned and those attending did not seem to mind the 'seas of mud'.

Charles McNaughton

Grady County Work Camp

The Grady County Work Camp was located between what is now Highway 111 South and Washington Middle School. The prisoners (sometimes called "chain gang members") worked the roads. Corn and other food crops were grown on the "County Farm", which was located at the present day airport site. This food was used at the work camp.

Leland Harrison

Poor Farm

The county owned a "Poor Farm" on which there were several buildings for the homeless to live. Garden plots were available for the people to grow food crops. There was a cemetery on the southeastern edge of the property and even today, the unmarked gravesites are visible.

At this time, there was not a Department of Family and Children Service and paupers who needed assistance had to apply to the county for a pension. After their case was reviewed--and if approved--, they were lucky to receive three dollars a month.

The Poor Farm was located just north of town on the Pelham road. It was still there in the 1930s.

Leland Harrison

Blowing Cave

About one-fourth mile west of the Hawthorn Trail in north Grady County, there is a small hole in the ground called "Blowing Cave". The wind alternately blows out and sucks in from this hole. If a handkerchief is placed over the opening, one minute it will be up in the air, the next it will disappear into the ground.

Pine Park Suburbs

In 1881 William Rodgers surveyed a section of property in Land Lot 90 owned by B. A. Alderman. Mr. Alderman planned to have the property divided into lots to sell to people for house building sites. Thus the first suburb in Grady County was formed. The name of the community was "Leb" but in 1901, Mr. Alderman had the name changed to "Pine Park".

Opal F. Lewis

Pine Park Community Center

This structure was built as a Universalist Church circa 1900. A circuit rider preacher of North Carolina served the congregation. In the early 1940s it was purchased from the church headquarters to be used as the Triple G 4-H Center. Later it became known as the Pine Park Community Center.

Pope's Museum

Laura Atkinson Pope (1873-1953) "built" her first statue in 1907 for display in the family store near the Meigs and Ochlocknee roads. Mrs. Pope married J. F. Forester, after the death of her first husband and continued her work.

After World War I, she honored the veterans with statues of soldiers, General Pershing, Red Cross Nurses, and Gold Star Mothers; she also did various paintings. Her home and gardens were opened as a museum with visitors welcomed to see over two hundred statues and murals.

Mrs. Pope-Forester was widely acclaimed as a folk artist with her story and work featured in some national magazines and papers.

The home is no longer a museum and is not open to the public.

Carolyn Chason

The Chero-Cola bottling plant was in business in Cairo for several years in the 1920s. It was located east of Broad Street near the railroad. The "soft drink" was a favorite of the people here. An early slogan was "There's None So Good".

J.B. Wight House

*The Wight home was built circa 1907 by one of the area's leading citizens...a minister,
educator, business man, and nursery founder. This house burned and another house
now stands on the site.*

Index . . .

*A view of Broad Street in Cairo, Georgia,
under a canopy of Christmas lights.*

Index

413

D

Desserts... 285

A Dash...A Pinch...A Smidgen...
Grady County Historical Society
P.O. Box 586
Cairo, GA 39828

Please send _____ copy(ies) of **A Dash...A Pinch...A Smidgen...** at $24.95 per copy plus $5.00 postage and handling per book. Please add $1.75 sales tax per book if shipped to a Georgia address.

Name_____

Addresss_____

City_____State_____Zip_____

Make checks payable to Grady County Historical Society.

- -

A Dash...A Pinch...A Smidgen...
Grady County Historical Society
P.O. Box 586
Cairo, GA 39828

Please send _____ copy(ies) of **A Dash...A Pinch...A Smidgen...** at $24.95 per copy plus $5.00 postage and handling per book. Please add $1.75 sales tax per book if shipped to a Georgia address.

Name_____

Addresss_____

City_____State_____Zip_____

Make checks payable to Grady County Historical Society.